Jan Hendrik Hessels

Gutenberg: Was He the Inventor of Printing?

An Historical Investigation Embodying a Criticism of Dr. van der Linde's...

Jan Hendrik Hessels

Gutenberg: Was He the Inventor of Printing?
An Historical Investigation Embodying a Criticism of Dr. van der Linde's...

ISBN/EAN: 9783337041731

Printed in Europe, USA, Canada, Australia, Japan

Cover: Foto ©ninafisch / pixelio.de

More available books at **www.hansebooks.com**

ENBER

Was ... Inventor of P...

AN

H...RICAL INVESTIGA...

EMBODYING

A CRITIC... DR. VAN DER LINDE'S "...

BY

...IESSE...

LONDON:
BERNARD QUARITCH,
15 PICCADILLY.
, 1882.

WYMAN AND SONS, PRINTERS,
GREAT QUEEN STREET, LINCOLN'S-INN FIELDS,
LONDON, W.C.

TO

HENRY BRADSHAW,

IN TESTIMONY OF

MY HIGH ADMIRATION OF

HIS SINGULARLY PROFOUND, EXACT, AND ORIGINAL

Knowledge of Bibliography

AND KINDRED SUBJECTS,

AND

AS A MARK OF MY GRATITUDE

FOR THE GENEROUS INSTRUCTION

TO WHICH I HAVE BEEN SO LARGELY INDEBTED

FOR MANY YEARS.

PREFACE.

THE present work was originally intended to be merely a "review" of Dr. Van der Linde's "Gutenberg." When, in 1879, the editor of the *Printing Times and Lithographer* asked me to write such a review for that periodical, I readily undertook to do so, in the idea that Dr. Van der Linde had as ably handled the Gutenberg, as he had the Haarlem Coster question, and that, consequently, my task would be easy.

The Gutenberg question was comparatively new to me; it had scarcely any attractions for me, and my time was very much occupied by other work. But I hoped, that when I had read Dr. Van der Linde's 800 pages, professing to be based on documents, I should have obtained all the information I wanted, and should, at the same time, be able to lay before the English public such particulars with regard to this subject as might reasonably be desired.

I regret to say that Dr. Van der Linde's work proved to be quite insufficient to satisfy such a modest demand. We owe him, indeed, great thanks for having brought many things together which are worth reading. But it is clear that Dr. Van der Linde intended, in the first place, to write a book on Dr. Van der Linde himself, and that Gutenberg occupies a secondary place in his work.

In his "Haarlem Legend" Dr. Van der Linde complains that people often write books on the principle of "taking three books and making a fourth of it." It is singular that his own "Gutenberg" is compiled entirely on this principle, the only difference being that he has taken a greater number of books. I cannot believe that Dr. Van der Linde left his study, at any time, for even half a minute, for the purpose of research (*see* also p. 99).

I feel scarcely inclined to blame him for this shortcoming. Had I myself been able to realise beforehand the time, the trouble, and the expense that this Gutenberg-study would cost me, I should have abandoned the subject at the outset. The question is surrounded on every side by endless difficulties: little points, which by themselves seem to have no importance whatever, proved, on examination, to be real and substantial links in the chain of inquiry, which had to be mastered before anything further could be attempted, and they very often could only be mastered in far, out-of-the-way places, or from books which very few would think of consulting nowadays. I soon found that to quote from any author without verification was out of the question, least of all from Dr. Van der Linde. Apart from the reading of books and documents at home, I was compelled to go twice to Paris to consult books which are only to be found there in the National Library. I spent seven weeks in Germany, exploring the Libraries and Archives of Strassburg, Heidelberg, Darmstadt, Mentz, Frankfurt, Höchst on the Nidder (a private library, *see* p. 86), Würzburg, Brunswick, Wolfenbüttel, Hannover, and Hamburg.

That Dr. Van der Linde did not feel disposed for such labour is not surprising. But it is matter for amazement that his book, which I have found wanting in every particular regarding the main question, should have been written in such a tone of authority and decision, and with such remarkable intolerance of everything that Dr. Van der Linde does not approve. His vehemence in speaking of his opponents' mistakes, or errors of judgment, is never agreeable; but when we consider that he has fallen into as many mistakes as any of his predecessors and *imagined* a great deal more than any one of them, and yet had far better opportunities for obtaining trustworthy information, his vehemence becomes a phenomenon which I leave to others to explain.

Pages 1 to 33 of the present book have already appeared in the *Printing Times and Lithographer*, in the numbers for February, March, April, and May, 1880, and it was intended to insert the whole essay in this periodical. But my work began to be so frequently interrupted on account of the inquiries I had to make, and it increased so much, that it was not considered advisable to continue the articles in that periodical. The portions already published were at once printed off at the time in book-form, and re-appear, therefore, unaltered.

The title of my work asks: Was Gutenberg the inventor of printing? I regret that, after all my labour, I have not found anything which enables me to answer this question either with yes or no. Of the three principal documents one is lost entirely (*see* pp. 185, 186); the other two are only preserved in transcripts (*see* pp. 101, 121). In ordinary cases, transcripts may be safely relied upon, but —considering all the extraordinary forgeries and frauds perpetrated on this subject—caution is more than ever necessary. But, even if we accept the transcripts, and base ourselves on what we have, I can only see that these documents point to Gutenberg as a *printer*, but not as an *inventor* of printing, and—that is the main question. The Incunabula, which are usually ascribed to Gutenberg, tell us nothing about him, and, what is still more remarkable, they may with the utmost facility be ascribed to other printers, and have actually been ascribed to others.

On p. 189 I have stated the result of my inquiry as far as I feel at liberty to formulate it myself. This formulation is not based on speculations, but is legitimately deduced from facts explained in my work. If any one can point out errors in my inquiry, my formulation of its result must, of course, be erroneous also.

No one will be more ready than myself to accept new discoveries which may lead to a different result. I have, no doubt, fallen into mistakes (some I have already been able to discover myself, *see* the list of *corrigenda*); but I can honestly say that I have not been influenced by enthusiasm for one side or prejudice against another,—my only aim has been to arrive at the truth. Had I been able to pronounce in favour of Gutenberg's claim, or to bestow unqualified praise on Dr. Van der Linde's work, nothing would have been more agreeable to me.

But, though I must leave the main question of my book unanswered, I may yet claim, by the removal of old errors on the one hand, and the discovery of new facts on the other, to have narrowed considerably the issue with which we shall have to deal in the future. In the first place, the theory of a continuance of Gutenberg's printing-office till far into the 16th century through the *Fratres communis vitæ* of Marienthal and Friedrich Heumann of Mentz, can no longer be maintained (*see* pp. 130, 140, 141), unless all my researches prove to be wrong. *Secondly*, the discovery of the fraud in the "Prognostication," preserved at Darmstadt (*see* p. 111 sq.), has enabled me to remove at once seven books from the List of works usually ascribed to Gutenberg. *Thirdly*, the discovery of one of the initials of the 30-line Indulgence of 1454, in an Indulgence of 1489 printed by Peter Schoeffer, coupled with other circumstances (*see* pp. 166, 171) has enabled me to remove from this List also the 42-line Bible, and the other works in the same type, and to ascribe them to Schoeffer. Lastly, I have devoted a considerable portion of my work to the productions of the Bechtermunczes of Eltville, in order to see what truth there could be in the statement of certain authors regarding a continuance of Gutenberg's printing-office through them. Here again I had to leave the point at issue just as it stood for want of material necessary for a decision; but I have been able to describe with great care the four editions of the *Vocabularius Ex quo* issued from the Eltville press, and to describe a fifth work (*see* p. 179 sq.) produced at the same press, of which hitherto the printer had remained unknown. Of this latter work a photograph accompanies my book.

In short, I believe I may claim to have

shown, as far as possible, what are *facts* and what is *fiction* with regard to Gutenberg, and thereby to have made an historical and bibliographical treatment of the subject possible.

All that I have found could have been found, and ought to have been found, by Germans; and I have no doubt that more will be found, whenever the private and public libraries of Germany come to be properly explored. The Germans themselves have hitherto done very little more than talk about Gutenberg (*see* also p. 114). If every library could have its 15th-century books catalogued by competent persons on the system inaugurated by the late Mr. Holtrop in his "Catalogus librorum saec. xv° impressorum in Bibl. regia Hagana," published in 1856, and by Mr. Bradshaw in his publications (*see* p. 3), whom Mr. Sinker followed in his "Catalogue of the 15th-century printed books in the Library of Trinity College, Cambridge," published in 1876, our knowledge of these books would soon be on another footing.*

* When we mention books which have advanced our knowledge of xv[th]-century printing, we must not forget two very important works, which have not been matched any-

It will, perhaps, be thought that I have been too diffuse in treating of some of the documents; e.g. that of 1455, which occupies the pages 63–102. But it should not be forgotten that when I prepared myself for reviewing Dr. Van der Linde's work, I found him, to my astonishment, refer, in regard to this document, to a mere *title* (*see* his p. li, No. 376, at the end of his work), prefixed in 1712 to a *transcript* made in that year by Von Glauburg, from a *transcript*, which was asserted to have been made, in 1600, by Joh. Friedr. Faust von Aschaffenburg, from an original of which I could find no trace. When I further saw Dr. Van der Linde state that this Von Glauburg

where; namely, Mr. Holtrop's *Monuments typographiques des Pays-Bas*, and Mr. William Blades' *Life of Caxton*. The latter's work is unrivalled for its minute and thorough analysis and examination of Caxton's several types.

The "*Annales de la Typographie Néerlandaise au xve siècle*" (1874, 1878) by Mr. Campbell, the Librarian of the Hague, embody the Incunabula of the Low-Countries arranged in an Alphabetical order, which had been formerly described by Mr. Holtrop, arranged under towns and printers.

In 1880 the Authorities of the St. Gallen Chapter-Library published a Catalogue of their Incunabula, arranged like the "Annales" of Mr. Campbell.

(who himself said that he copied from a *transcript*) had also supplied Köhler with an authentic (!) copy, I felt bound to make inquiries (*see* p. 63, note). The process was a long one, and the result could, perhaps, have been given in a single page, but seeing the state of confusion in which Wetter and Dr. Van der Linde were with regard to this document (*see* p. 93), I thought it better to publish my article just as I had written it down while making the researches. Future authors on Gutenberg will be able to condense all I have said into a few lines. But we shall now know at least that they cannot speak again of an *original*, unless they have actually found one themselves.

I have avoided all direct reference to the tradition of a Haarlem Invention of Printing, because, having no opportunities at present to make researches in this direction, I feel bound to abide by the results which Dr. Van der Linde made known in 1870. I have never made any thorough examination of the Haarlem question, but such inquiries as I have made have led me to believe that the Haarlem claim cannot be maintained. At the appearance of Dr. Van der Linde's *Haarlem Legend* in 1870,

I was so struck by its excellency that I translated the work into English. Now, that I have made a thorough examination of his work on Gutenberg, and have found this book so singularly unreliable, I should wish to go over the ground by which he reached his results with respect to the Haarlem question. Dr. Van der Linde appears to be most easily led away by what he *reads*, if only it coincides with his views.* He believes, for instance, in

---

* I am, moreover, afraid that Dr. Van der Linde has not sufficiently realised the importance, in studies of this kind, of being able to read the contractions so common in mediæval writing and even in early printing. In the verses "Scema tabernaculi &c.," which appeared for the first time in the Institutiones Justiniani of 1468, and are said to have originated with Joh. Fons, the chief corrector in Schoeffer's office, Dr. Van der Linde (p. 287) prints, in line 13, *repetire*, a word which never existed. The edition itself has rep̄ire, which is, of course, rep*er*ire. Dr. Van der Linde's quotation has, in this instance, all the appearance of having been copied from the original, and as his book contains other misreadings of contractions (I remember at least two more examples: *see* his p. 290, line 6 from foot, *ita* for *iam;* line 4 from foot, *quoque modo* for *quoquomodo*), it seems not unreasonable to assume that his rep*et*ire is not a misprint. This deficiency on his part, and the fact that he is unacquainted with the dating of mediæval documents (*see* my pp. 12, 13), suggest the two questions: whether Dr. Van der Linde gives his documents correctly, and

everything that Madden (in his *Lettres d'un Bibliographe*, Paris, 1868–75) has written; e.g. on p. 260 he informs us that Madden has "strikingly shown" that in the first printing-offices an anagnostes (reader, lector) dictated to several compositors at the same time, and that consequently often three editions of the same work appeared at one and the same time.

It would lead me too far out of my way to discuss this point here. Suffice it to say that I have examined M. Madden's arguments, with the incunabula before me, and found them breaking down at the first touch. Guided by such "showings," however, Dr. Van der Linde seems quite ready to write anything; *see* his p. 454, where he suggests that the editions of the Donatus, which are, on good grounds, presumed to be Dutch productions, were perhaps printed in the convent at Weidenbach where Madden professes to have discovered a 15th-century printing-establishment. It is surprising that Dr. Van der Linde makes these

---

whether in his researches he does not *miss* certain points which would present that which he gives us in a different light?

suggestions without verifying any of Madden's points, and notwithstanding that he had expressed (on p. 99) his gratification at M. Campbell's proceedings in placing these incunabula at "Utrecht"?

In the Bibliographical descriptions of documents and incunabula, care has been taken to represent as exactly as possible the signs of contraction or peculiar types of the originals. Some of these types, however, were manufactured for the occasion, and it is possible that some of them may have become deranged in the process of printing. In some cases the contractions of the originals have been expanded by italics.

I have given no photographs of any book or document (except a page of an Eltville book, the type of which has hitherto remained entirely unnoticed), because Mr. Bradshaw has already several photographs made of works published by the primitive German Presses for the purpose of bringing out at some future time an atlas of such plates.

In the course of my researches in the British Museum, in the Paris National Library, and in Germany, I met everywhere great readiness to assist me. Especially I have to thank M.

Thierry, of the Paris National Library; the Darmstadt Archivists, Dr. Freiherr Schenk zu Schweinsberg and Dr. Wyss; Dr. Böckel, the Secretary of the Mentz Library; Dr. Grotefend, the Archivist of Frankfurt, and Dr. Ernst Kelchner, of the Frankfurt Town Library; Professor Dr. Otto von Heinemann, the Wolfenbüttel Librarian; Dr. Isler, the Librarian, and Herr Haack, the Custos, of the Hamburg Town Library; the Burgomasters of Hamburg (Dr. Kirchenpauer) and Frankfurt (Dr. Heusenstamm) granted me special facilities for research, which the ordinary rules of their Libraries did not allow to strangers; Herr Senator Culemann, at Hannover, gave me for two days unrestricted access to his treasures, among which a collection of Letters of Indulgence is certainly most remarkable. The only place where I met with strange incivility and an absolute refusal, was the Roman Catholic Seminary at Mentz, though I had an introduction to the authorities from the well-known Professor Schneider, Prebendary of the *Dom-Kirche* of Mentz. I cannot help thinking that this treatment was owing to some misunderstanding.

Professor Paul Meyer has kindly verified for

me, on three or four occasions, certain points in the Paris Library, and assisted me in other ways. Professor Dr. Karl von Halm, the Librarian of the Munich Library, has greatly facilitated my work by kindly forwarding to me the *Vocabularius Ex quo* of 1477 (*see* p. 149), and the *Thomas de Aquino, Summa,* of 35 lines (*see* p. 180). Of the latter work he allowed me to give a photograph of one of its pages.

Though my task has been difficult and wearisome, it was considerably lightened by the kind and generous interest which Mr. HENRY BRADSHAW, the Cambridge University Librarian, has taken in the progress of the work. His patience, his intimate knowledge of the subject, and his keen judgment, often helped me out of difficulties when I was perplexed by the intricacies of the subject. He has spent many hours in considering, weighing, and correcting certain portions of my work. I have often had occasion to mention him, but I am indebted to him for more than I have pointed out. In fact, Mr. Bradshaw has so freely communicated to me his views on many important matters, and I have so freely made use of all his suggestions, that my only fear is lest the publication of this work should lead him to think that he may dispense with the publication of a work of his own, for which he has been preparing a long time. This circumstance I should regret, for I must have left unsaid a great many things, and I feel sure that what I have said could have been brought out by him in a far better way.

J. H. HESSELS.

CAMBRIDGE,
April 12, 1882.

CONTENTS.

CORRIGENDA, ADDENDA, &c.

Page 41, right hand column, line 30, read *dangerous*, instead of *nice*.

,, 43, ,, ,, ,, ,, 6, read *quantity of pears* instead of *deal of beer*.

,, 46, ,, ,, ,, ,, 38, *at the reunion of the furriers* is wrong, as the German *under den Kürsenern* is the name of some locality (like Unter den Linden in Berlin).

,, 49, ,, ,, ,, ,, 13, read *baskets of pears* instead of *flasks of beer*.

[The above four corrections were pointed out by Dr. Wyss, one of the Archivists of Darmstadt, in a review of Dr. Van der Linde's work, published by him, in 1880, in *Quartalblätter des hist. Vereins für Hessen*, p. 16, when my translation of the Law-suit of 1439 (in which I had followed other authors, where I could not decide for myself) had already been printed.]

,, 9, line 19: "Mayence about 1400–1410 &c." These dates are, of course, quoted from Dr. Van der Linde. Dr. Wyss (l. c. p. 11) points out that, as in 1430 Gutenberg appears as a member of a political party, his birth must be placed earlier than "the end of the first decennium of the 15th century." Dr. Heffner in the *Archiv des hist. Vereins von Unterfranken*, xiv. 1. 168 sqq., speaks of Gutenberg as having been born in 1397.

,, 11, lines 16, 26, and 34, read 17 instead of 16.

,, 17. The contemporary Narrative, to which I refer as published by Bodmann, is regarded by Dr. Wyss (l. c. p. 22), as another forgery of this curious Prof. Bodmann. I gladly accept his opinion in the matter; but the question really arises: is there anything in this subject that we can trust? This Gutenberg-experience should cure us all from the weakness of *copying!* In the beginning of my work I have done it occasionally in unimportant matters where verification was *impossible*, and nearly each time fallen into the trap.

Page 49, right hand column, line 19, for the six words *to pay on St. Henry's day,* we must, probably, read *to repay* only. Dr. Grotefend, the Archivist of Frankfurt, told me last year that he did not think there was a date in the German text; he would read *zu* instead of *an;* cf. further Lexer's Lexicon, ii. 524, sub v. *rückes.*

„ 54, right hand column, line 13 from foot: But when the pilgrimage &c.—Dr. Wyss (l. c. p. 12) points out that this reference to a putting off of the Pilgrimage is rather surprising, as there can be no question of such a putting off, the pilgrimage having taken place in the year in which it was to have taken place. A septennial turnus was customary, and in a document of 1445 it is distinctly said that the last pilgrimage had been that of 1440, and that the next would be that of 1447; other documents speak of a pilgrimage of 1391; therefore there would be a series of 1391, 98, 1405, 12, 19, 26, 33, 40, 47 etc.—Perhaps Wencker or Schoepflin have been asleep here.

„ 58, line 4 from foot, read *Schmidt* instead of *Schmid.*

„ 59, line 1: it is 3 ft. &c. All this is not said by Dr. Van der Linde, but quoted by him from K. Klein's article (in Mainzer Wochenblatt, 1856, No. 45 sq.) on the so-called discovery of the Press.

„ 60, lines 26, 39, 45 read *Schmidt,* instead of *Schmid.*

„ 71, line 16 from foot, for *fidelino bis,* read *fideli nobis.*

„ 102, line 6, read *than,* instead of *that.*

„ 114, line 18, for 18 *Jan.,* read: (*am dorns tag sant Antonientag,* i.e. on Thursday, St. Anthony's day, i.e.) 17 Jan.

„ 119, line 5 from foot, for *Friday after Febr.* 24, 1468, read *Friday after Febr.* 25, *i.e. Febr.* 26, 1468. In the original draft of my work I had copied the dates of all the documents from Dr. Van der Linde's work. Finding afterwards that nearly all his dates were wrong, I verified them gradually before the sheets went to press. I have already pointed out some of his errors (see p. 12); but unfortunately the pages, where the two last dates occur, went to press without my remembering that I had not verified them. I now beg the reader to rectify them. The last document (Homery's bond of 1468) is dated *uff frytag nach Sant Mathys dag,* i.e. *on the Friday after St. Matthias day.* The Matthias day is, in common years, the 24th of Febr., but in the year 1468, which was a leap-year, it fell on the 25th, and as this was a Thursday, the Friday following it was, therefore, the 26th.

„ p. 131: Fratres communis vitae of Marienthal. Petzholdt's *Neuer Anzeiger,* April, 1882, contains an interesting article on the Marienthal Press, by Dr. Falk, the Catholic Pastor of Mombach, near Mentz, of which, a few days ago, he kindly sent me a copy, with a facsimile of the *two* real Marienthal types, and another of two types which Dr.

Falk ascribes also to the Fratres (and which he calls, therefore, types 3 and 4) on account of certain portions of the Marienthal Breviary of 1474, being mixed with portions of a Breviary printed in these types (3 and 4), preserved in the Library at Giessen. I am unable to investigate this matter just now, and can only remark here that Breviaries are sometimes made up of sheets or leaves belonging to different editions, and that I have reason to believe that Dr. Falk's types 3 and 4 are *not* Marienthal types, but belong to some Cologne printer.

Page 152, Dr. Wyss (l. c. p. 24) informs us that, in the Archives at Marburg, there is a copy of the Indulgence of Paulinus Chappe of 1454, which was issued at Erffurd. As nearly a third part (of the left hand side) has been torn off, the month and day of the month cannot be given. As Dr. Wyss says that the copy agrees with the facsimile given by Bernard I, pl. v No. 3, I presume that it is a copy of the 31-line Indulgence, and probably belongs to the issue *c*.

,, 153, line 7 (number 3). Dr. Wyss (l. c. p. 24) speaks of this copy as being in the Baronial Riedesel Archives at Eisenbach. As he gives no further information, it remains uncertain to which of the several issues this copy belongs.

,, p. 170, number 5. A facsimile of this Donatus may be seen in Fischer's Typogr. Seltenh. pt. 1; cf. ib. p. 53, and pt. 3 p. 23.

Sotheby (*Principia Typogr.* ii. 175) mentions *another edition* of 33 lines, in the same 42-line Bible type, of which the two remaining leaves are preserved in the Bodleian Library at Oxford. They had successively belonged to Dr. Kloss (see the Catalogue of his Library, sold by Messrs. Sotheby, May 7, 1835, No. 1287), and the Bishop (Butler) of Lichfield.

When I visited Paris in the summer of 1881 I took no notice of this Donatus nor of the edition mentioned on p. 171, because at that time I had no intention of inserting in this work a List of the so-called Gutenberg Incunabula; hence these two works are mentioned without any description.

GUTENBERG:

WAS HE THE INVENTOR OF PRINTING?*

DR. VAN DER LINDE, the latest author on the Invention of Printing, is a Hollander by birth, but a German by bias and inclination. He is a scholar of great erudition, and has been before the literary English public during the last eight years. He has always been a lover of books and equally fond of writing them. In 1864, a large portion of his enormous library, the catalogue of which occupied nearly 400 octavo pages, was sold at Brussels. We have from his hand treatises on the orthoepy of the English language—the orthography of the Dutch Dictionary (in German)—Bibliography of Haarlem—of David Joris—of Balthazar Bekker—of Benedictus Spinoza—several works on Chess—also the History and Literature of Chess, 2 vols. 8vo. (in German)—studies on Theology, Bibliography, &c. &c.

No one can be surprised that a Hollander of such varied literary attainments should have his attention drawn to what we may call the vexed question of the invention of Printing. Our readers are aware that a controversy has been carried on between several towns, not always very temperately, almost ever since the first spread of the art, as

* Gutenberg, Geschichte und Erdichtung aus den Quellen nachgewiesen, von Dr. A. van der Linde. 8vo. Stuttgart. 1878.

to which of them could claim the honour of the invention. Even now the issue can scarcely be said to be narrowed to the two well-known towns, Haarlem and Mentz.

Dr. Van der Linde was born at Haarlem, and wrote a Bibliography of Haarlem. He prepared himself for the study of the question of the Invention of Printing by conversations with the late Mr. Holtrop, Librarian of the Royal Library at the Hague. These conversations led to his researches in the Archives of Haarlem, which in their turn produced his work on the Haarlem Legend, published in Dutch in 1870, and afterwards translated into English (London: Blades. 1870), French, and German.

Dr. Van der Linde's pen is sharp and venomous. His "*Haarlem Legend*" is written in language as bitter as wormwood, and that of his present book is no less strong. Woe be to those who dissent from his views. Whether his antagonists are men of importance or not known at all, he attacks them all with the same relentless severity. His large views and cosmopolitan spirit induce him to ridicule, on all occasions, a country of such small proportions as Holland. That his countrymen ever claimed the honour of the invention of printing is to him not an error of judgment but a capital offence. That the Dutch never worshipped him for his vituperative language—that they did not at once, at the appearance of his "Haarlem Legend," destroy the statue erected to Laurens Janszoon Coster, the supposed inventor of printing—is to him the worst of all crimes they could perpetrate.

Dr. Van der Linde's merits, with regard to the history of the invention of printing, are great. The cobwebs of the Haarlem tradition were laid bare, and torn asunder by him with a masterly hand. But in every line he writes on the subject he displays a hatred and contempt for the country of his birth and his countrymen, which seem to me as misplaced as his indignation would seem to be unnecessary. That Dr. Van der Linde does not love Holland and the Hollanders is, perhaps, owing to bad treatment he has received from their hands. But who could expect the Dutch to fondle and caress the author of the Haarlem Legend and of the book before us? That he loves Germany and the Germans is a purely personal affair and a matter of taste, with which science has nothing to do.

In all that Dr. Van der Linde has written on the subject he has shown great talents, but in his antipathy against the Dutch he has overlooked one great point in the controversy. Bibliography, even in the widest acceptation of the word, is a field in which the labourers are few. These labourers can, necessarily, be only librarians and private collectors, or persons within easy reach of a library. The study of the early-printed books, on which the question of the invention of printing turns exclusively, is only a branch, though it be a very important branch, of bibliography, and the study of these books was not so easy in former years, when the volumes found in the large collections now concentrated in various towns and private houses were more or less scattered all over Europe, and that while travelling was not so easy as at present. Even in our time they are dispersed all over the globe, and access to them is difficult. Some of the great public repositories of these treasures—the British Museum, the Bodleian Library at Oxford, the Cambridge University Library, the Hague Royal Library, the Paris Library, &c., are open to every one. In a great many other towns we find at present collections which will enable any one to get at least some insight into the mystery of the incunabula. But even now, who would say that, for instance, in the British Museum the study of the early-printed books is easy? Or who would say that it is easy in the Paris Library, where there is not even a catalogue? In fact, with all the impediments in one's way, it is much easier to account for the rather superficial knowledge prevailing in this department of research than for the profound knowledge of incunabula which we meet with in Mr. Bradshaw. His intimacy with early-printed books was acquired by years of patient study. The results of this study are only a few pages published in 1870 (A classified index of the fifteenth-century books in the collection of the late M. J. de Meyer) and 1871 (List of the founts of type and woodcut devices used by printers in Holland in the fifteenth century), but these few pages have done more good for the study of the early-printed books than all the ponderous volumes under which the question of the invention of printing is buried. They have furnished us with an almost infallible guide for describing and classifying incunabula, and a guide which henceforth no cataloguer of these books can afford to discard. But Mr. Bradshaw's devotion to, and patience for, this study are exceptional. Very few men can afford to spend their time on a subject which requires almost more time and labour than any other, and, in a pecuniary sense, is the least remunerative of all. Very few men have time and inclination to acquire that intimate knowledge of manuscripts, of books, and of history which has enabled Mr. Bradshaw to arrive at his results.

Dr. Van der Linde ought to have considered all the disadvantages under which the study of the invention of printing and the incunabula is prosecuted, and that the misdeeds he so freely and harshly imputes to all those who have written on the Haarlem claims really arise from nothing but ignorance and are the result of difficulties in the way of this study. Dr. Van der Linde himself, with all his knowledge, training, and zeal has not been able to avoid the rocks on which so many of his predecessors have stranded. His book is deficient in arrangement. The information on certain important documents is very defective and scattered through his work, so as to make it almost impossible to collect it. He copies from others without saying who they are, so that it is not always easy to discover his sources. I shall feel bound, moreover, to point out some singular errors into which he has fallen, which, if he had detected them in others, would have made him wroth indeed. I am not the apologist of any author who has written on this most troublesome and complicated question, but I shall have to show that with respect to this subject at least Dr. Van der Linde lives in a glasshouse, and should not throw stones.

If what I have to say can induce Dr. Van der Linde to moderate his tone, and to dissociate the question from personal matters, I shall consider myself amply repaid for all the labour I have spent in endeavouring to supplement the shortcomings of himself and others who have written on this subject.

Curiously enough, in the preface to his book, Dr. Van der Linde asks the reader to have patience with *his* errors of *orthography*, for, he says, "man errs as long as he occupies himself with bibliography and orthography." Surely such a request seems strange in a man who treats every one as a knave who commits the most insignificant error in writing on Koster or the Haarlem question. But let us turn to his book.

Dr. Van der Linde has happily divided his work into two parts—*History* and *Fiction.* I shall occupy myself exclusively with what he himself considers to be the historical part. The task of perusing the legendary part may be left to those who have time and inclination for reading not always pleasant or profitable. Even the historical part of Dr. Van der Linde's book is interspersed with hard language, which we do not agree with him to have been necessary.

The author commences with an explanation of the difference between xylography and typography, *i.e.*, *printing from wooden blocks* and *printing with movable cast types*, and it will, perhaps, not be superfluous to follow him to some extent. The art of printing, *i.e.*, the art of impressing by means of certain forms and colours, figures, pictures, letters, words, lines, whole pages, &c., on other objects, existed long before the fifteenth century. Wuttke, in his "History of Writing" (Leipzig: 1872), remarks that, in Ninive, centuries before our era, the strokes of cuneated letters were impressed without any difficulty in soft clay, by means of a graver; that the Babylonians cut the same characters in relief on wooden blocks, in order to impress them by these means in wet clay. In China, the art of *printing books* was invented much earlier than in Europe; the earliest printed work known—the books of Kungtse—is said to have been prepared between 890 and 925. It is well known that the Mongols, when they conquered China in the thirteenth century, adopted Buddhism and learned Chinese writing and block-printing. Afterwards they overran the East of Europe, and remained there for nearly two centuries. Though we have no documents to prove that the Mongols introduced block-printing into Europe, it is certain that about 1400, *xylography* became known all over Germany, as far as Flanders. At the same time, we begin to hear of linen-paper, stuff-printing, &c.

Engraving, which may be said to be inseparably connected with printing, was practised from time immemorial, but the idea of multiplying representations from one engraved plate or block was wanting to the ancients. As late as the second half of the fourteenth century, every book, including school and prayer books, were written by hand; all figures, even playing-cards and images of saints, were drawn with the pen or painted with a brush. One of the picture-books of the Middle Ages, the *Biblia Pauperum*, is well known. It contains the life of Christ; and we have MSS. of this work as early as circ. 1300 (cf. Camesina, *Die Darstellungen der* Biblia Pauperum, Wien: 1863, in which is described a MS., of the beginning of the fourteenth century, preserved in the Chapter Library of St. Florian, on the Enns in Austria; *and* Laib und Schwarz, Biblia Pauperum, Zürich: 1867, in which is described another MS. of about 1300, preserved at Constanz). A remodelling and development of this work is the *Speculum humanæ salvationis.*

In the fifteenth century these and other picture-books were multiplied by means of wood-engraving and a mode of printing technically called (anopisthographic) *block-printing* or *Xylography.* At first the pictures alone were printed by this process, and the text afterwards added in manuscript; as time went on, text and pictures were printed simultaneously. A goodly quantity of single leaves produced in this manner, either without any text, or with short in-, super- and sub-scriptions, have been found from time to time, especially in the bindings of early-printed books. Some of these leaves have dates which raise them to the rank of historical documents. We may mention *the Brussels Mary-engraving* of 1418 (though doubts have been expressed as to whether the date has not been tampered with); *the St. Christopher* of 1423, in Lord Spencer's Library and the National Library at Paris; *the St. Bernardinus* of 1454, a so-called *Schrot-blatt* or dotted print, &c. &c.

Of dated block-books, *i.e.* works of more than one xylographic leaf, we have *an illustrated alphabet*, of 1464—of which a perfect copy is at Basle, an imperfect copy in the British Museum; a *Biblia Pauperum* (in German), printed at Nördlingen, in 1470; the *Defensorium* of 1470 and 1471; the *Entkrist* of 1472; the *Ars moriendi* of 1473 and 1504, &c. &c.

Books, exclusively consisting of texts, without any pictures, either were but seldom made, or have been lost, owing to their possessing but little attraction. We know, among such, the *Alexander Gallus, Doctrinale*, 1446; *Donatus de octo partibus orationis*, Ulm, 1475, &c.

Printing with wooden blocks was, however, not the only mode in use in the fifteenth century; pictures were also engraved in metal. We have a leaf of a cycle of engraved pictures of the passion (formerly in the possession of M. Renouvier at Montpellier) of 1446; a copper Mary-engraving of the Master P with the date 1451 (but see Willshire, Ancient Prints, I. 49, 288); a Last Supper-engraving, preserved in the British Museum, dated 1457, &c. &c.

The number both of *dated* and *undated* leaves and block-books is at present considerable. It is not my plan either to enumerate them or to enter into the details of the various processes of engraving or printing. The latter have been treated in so many books that I may fairly suppose the reader to be acquainted with them, or at least with the books treating on these subjects.

One great desideratum still exists, namely, a list or catalogue of all the *prints* or engravings and *block-books* which have been discovered to this day, and have been the subject of such elaborate discussions and treatises. Messrs. Berjeau (Cat. illustré des livres xylogr., Lond., 1865) and Weigel (Verzeichn. der xylogr. Bücher des xv. Jahrh., Leipz., 1856; Weigel and Zestermann, Die Anfänge der Druckerkunst in Bild und Schrift, 2 vols., Leipz., 1866) have done much towards the compilation of such a list, but we are still very far from having a catalogue of all there are. To give an idea of the vast quantity of single prints, which have been discovered from time to time, we need only say that the rich *Collectio Weigeliana*, described in the last-named work, contained about 100 early copper engravings, more than 150 wood engravings, about 80 so-called *Schrot-blätter* (dotted prints), 5 woodcuts in metal frames (one of 1468), 10 prints on stuff (silk, tick, linen), 5 prints on paste, and 60 metal engravings.

The sculptors (*pyldsnytzer, beeldesniders*), engravers (*plaet-snyders*), printers (either *briefdruckern*—from *breve*, i. e. *scriptum*—and *druckern*, printers, or *prentern*, printers), briefmalern (*i. e.* painters of briefs), &c., &c., constituted everywhere separate guilds. There existed one at Nördlingen, 1428; at Ulm, 1441; at Antwerp, 1442; at Bruges, 1451. As *briefdrucker* we know Jan the prenter at Antwerp, 1417; Wilhelm Kegel at Nördlingen, 1428; Henne Cruse of Mainz, at Frankfurt, 1440, &c. The xylographers regarded themselves as printers, and the expressions used in their art were afterwards transferred to typography. A xylographic Bauernkalender is said to be "printed at

Regensburg;" Dinckmut says, under his xylographic Donatus: "Per Cunradum dinckmut Vlmensis oppidi Civem impressus." From the diary of the abbat Jean Le Robert we know that in 1446 he bought a Doctrinale, which was *jeté en moule* (*i. e.* mechanically printed from a wooden block or other instrument, on vellum; I copy Dr. Van der Linde), and in the privilege which the Paris printers obtained in 1474, from Louis XI., it is said that they obtained it "pour l'exercise de leur ars et mestiers de faire livres de plusieurs manières d'escriptures *en mosle* et autrement." Philippe de Comines wrote in his "Mémoires," under the year 1498, of Heronyme (Savonarola), that he had all his sermons *fait mettre en moule*, which in the edition of Petitot, is altered to "il les a fait imprimer."

Dr. Van der Linde lays stress on the point, that not printing, the *ars impressoria*, was waiting to be invented, but *typography*, i. e. the multiplication of writing by means of cast (individual, movable, metal) types or letters. Typography is the art of printing, but the art of printing was not yet typography. In the new art, printing was also the end and the result, but the means to obtain this end were quite different. Not the movability of the elements (letters) of the writing to be printed, but the art of forming the types, was *the* invention. The simple movability or individuality of the types, he says, is not sufficient; their body has to be of the utmost geometrical precision, which can only be obtained by a correct manufacture of the *patrices* and *matrices*, which are really the essence of the invention of typography. The cutting and casting of metal types, and the printing of single leaves or books, constitute the original typography, the terminology of which is perfectly plain. Not only is it called *ars imprimendi*, *ars impressoria* (1457), but also *ars caracterizandi* (from *caragma*, a character, letter). Gutenberg (I copy Dr. Van der Linde) is called (1468)* *protocaragmaticus.* On account of the great signification of the cutting of the letters (*i. e.* punches) the printer Jenson in Venice calls himself (1471) even a cutter of books "librorum exsculptorem." Sensenschmied says, in 1475, that the Codex Justiniani is cut (insculptus); also that he has cut (sculpsit) the work of Lombardus on the Psalter. Husner, of Strassburg, says of the

* Dr. Van der Linde writes 1466 on p. 16, but this is plainly an error for 1468.

Speculum Durandi (1473) that it was printed *exsculptis ære litteris,* and of the Praeceptorium Nideri (1476) that it is printed *litteris exsculptis artificiali certe conatu ex ære.* The goldsmith and printer Cennini, of Florence, says, in 1471, that he printed the "Legenda della mirabile Vergine beata Chaterina de Siena" *expressis ante Calybe characteribus et deinde fusis literis.* Jenson says equally plainly of the Breviarium August. (1485) that it was printed *litteris divine sculptis ac conflatis,* and Schoeffer lays stress on the casting of the types; the Grammatica vetus rhytmica (1466) says: *At Moguntia sum fusus in urbe libellus.*

At this point I approach the substance of Dr. Van der Linde's book, namely *the life of John Gutenberg.* It was natural that the author, having satisfied the literary world that the history of a Dutch invention, and Dutch inventor, of printing, is a fiction, should wish to write the history of "Johann (or Henne) Gänsfleisch zu Gutenberg, born at Mayence about 1400–1410, the son of the patrician Frilo Gänsfleisch and Else zu Gutenberg."

I have considered it necessary to examine this portion of Dr. Van der Linde's work carefully: 1st, because it is the main portion of the big tome before me; 2nd, because the rest of the book cannot interest any one very much if that portion prove disappointing.

It will clear the reader's view, as far as the writer of the present essay is concerned, when I say at the outset that the perusal of Dr. Van der Linde's book, however learned it may be, has grievously disappointed me. I took it up in the hope that this enormous work (700 pages, large 8vo) would remove all earthly doubts as to the inventor of printing, but what I looked for in the book I have not found, and I have found what I certainly did not expect to find. To cut the matter short, in the case of Gutenberg—that is to say of Gutenberg as inventor of printing—far more forgeries have been perpetrated than in that of the Haarlem inventor. To satisfy myself I had to make independent researches, and to supplement Dr. Van der Linde to a considerable extent. The title of my essay indicates the result of my inquiry. However irksome it may be, I shall have to enumerate all the documents which at any time have served to make up Gutenberg's biography, and to trace their history.

I approach this task with considerable diffidence. The documents I have to deal with are by no means pleasant reading, even if they were written in the most easy language. But this is not the case with the German of the fifteenth century. Besides, their history is most complicated, and in tracing it I had to consult an enormous mass of books which it was difficult to find, and, when found, most laborious to go through. Sometimes it took me several hours, sometimes whole days to trace certain statements backwards to their origin And even now I have stuck at certain points where I could not go further.

Moreover, I cannot conceal from myself that it is not a light matter to criticise the work of a man gifted with such brilliant talents and such an unfortunate readiness for abuse as is Dr. Van der Linde. The mere fact that I cannot agree with him will expose me at once to his bitter attacks, and the most insignificant slip on my part may cause him to denounce me as a dishonest man.

For all these reasons I have hesitated and still hesitate to come forward as Dr. Van der Linde's criticiser. When I see, however, that Dr. Van der Linde, on pp. 42, 81, 152, tells his readers three times over that a certain Donatus bears the manuscript notice Heydersheym 1451, without qualifying this statement; when I see that Dr. Van der Linde accepts the enthusiastic utterances of Madden and De Vinne as gospel truths; and more especially when I see that Dr. Van der Linde, with singular credulity and confidence, accepts *discoveries* without verifying them, and on the strength of such discoveries sets up systems,—I then feel my courage revive, and I may hope to say something sensible, without falling into too many errors myself.

I shall treat of the documents relating to Gutenberg in chronological order. I shall number them consecutively, adding, to those which Dr. Van der Linde has republished, the number they bear in his work between parentheses. I shall explain their contents as far as I think it necessary and desirable. I shall state, wherever I can, how, when, where, and by whom they were discovered, and where and when they were published. I shall not, in the first instance, give any opinion on them myself, but quote from other writers as much as is wanted for my purpose. After having treated of all the documents, then I shall venture to say what I think of them myself. Those years which are of special importance will be found printed in a more distinctive type.

1. A letter dated 24 March, 1424, written from Strassburg by *Henne Genszfleisch genannt Sorgenloch* to his sister Berthe, a nun in the Convent of St. Clara (Reichenklara) at Mentz.

This document was published *for the first time* by Oberlin (Essai d'Annal. de la vie de Gutenberg, 1801, p. 3). In the following year Fischer (Essai sur les Mon. typ. p. 23) published it in the German of the original, adding Oberlin's translation. In 1830 it was declared by Schaab (Erfind. der Buchdruckerkunst, i., pp. 29, 32–43) *to be one of Prof. Bodmann's forgeries.* See also Van der Linde, p. 19.

It will not be superfluous to narrate briefly the reasons which induced Schaab to pronounce this judgment on this document and on document No. 16. He says—

We must take it for granted that they originated with Bodmann, as he lived for twenty years after their publication and never repudiated the discovery ascribed to him. Prof. Bodmann left nothing, among his many papers which passed through my hands, about this discovery, nor did he say a word about it in his writings. Prof. Fischer alone gives us an explanation. Of document 1 he says (Essai sur les Mon. typ. 23) that his colleague Bodmann discovered it in the Archives of Mentz, without mentioning the particular Archive in which he had found it, and even without trying to see and examine himself this *autograph* of Gutenberg. Of document 16 Prof. Fischer says (Typogr. Seltenh., Lief. i. 42): "A document, existing in the Archives of the University, and written by Gutenberg himself in 1459, makes it clear that Johann Gutenberg, on midday of the brightest day of May, had not only printed several books, but had even the best intentions of going on with printing, and I give herewith a correct copy which I have obtained from citizen Prof. Bodmann, the superintendent of the Archive." Prof. Oberlin, who published document 1 for the first time, merely says that Bodmann discovered it and document 16. It is certain that Oberlin and Bodmann corresponded together, as several letters of the former are found among Bodmann's papers. And Fischer only tells us that Bodmann discovered it in the Archives of Mentz; that it is preserved in the Archives of the University, but that he only obtained a copy from Bodmann.—Schaab then gives no less than nineteen reasons for declaring against the two documents: (1) He did not find anything about these documents among the papers which Bodmann's widow had placed into his hands; (2) nor was anything found by Prof. Lehne, who made an inventory of Bodmann's literary property left for the grand-ducal Government; (3) nor was anything regarding these documents found in a packet on which Bodmann himself had written *Genszfleisch'sche Urkunden;* (4) nor did Schaab, after a search of eight days, find anything in the Archives of the University; (5) nor anything about them in a MS. which Bodmann's son had given to Schaab, and in which his father (Bodmann) had made several annotations; (6) Fischer never said that he saw the letter of 1424, and of the document of 1459 he only obtained a copy from Bodmann; (7) the engraver Johann Lindenschmitt, a friend of Bodmann, who engraved the family-seals of the Gensfleisch on copper, which Fischer added to his first impression of the 1459 document, declares openly that he had seen neither the documents nor the seals, but engraved them after a drawing which Fischer had handed to him; (8) had Bodmann possessed this document, it would have been found, after his death, among his collection or in the University-Archives; (9) Bodmann was so versed in the documental language of the Middle Ages, that he was able to imitate every kind of writing of all ages, and to prepare documents of all kinds. Of this capacity he constantly and everywhere boasted. He could draw the most perfect seals with the utmost facility, and he left behind several thousands of them, among them those of Gensfleisch with the pilgrim, in all shapes; (10) Prof. Bodmann probably considered it, as was his wont, a good joke, or an innocent thing, to assist, with his inventive imagination, his colleagues Fischer and Oberlin,—who worked in 1800-1802 at a history of Gutenberg's invention and hunted everywhere for Donatus fragments and remains of Gutenberg—and to fill up the gaps in Gutenberg's life from 1420–30, and from 1455–1460; (11) no Gutenberg incunabula were found in the library of the Reichenklaren-convent at its dissolution in 1781; (12) because the 1459 document speaks of the brothers Henne Genszfleisch von Sulgeloch genannt Gudinberg and Friele Genszfleisch. Why, asks Schaab, does the latter not call himself also von Sulgeloch? Why is Henne alone called von Gudinberg, and not Friele also, who called himself von Gudenberg elsewhere? (18) no Bertha, no Hebele are found among the nuns entered in the Necrology of the St. Clara convent, preserved in the Mentz town library, though it contains the names of Gutenberg nuns of the Gensfleisch branch, &c. &c.

Schaab's other reasons amount to this: the wag Bodmann had been napping; being under the impression that the name of Sorgenloch belonged to our Henne Genszfleisch (*i. e.* H. G. genant Gutenberg), he forged the two documents 1 and 16, which are contradictory to the others.

Fischer wrote in 1851 from Moscow, where he resided, to Aug. Bernard, that he had never been able to obtain any communication of the document (No. 1) itself (cf. Bernard, Origine de l'imprimerie, i. p. 118).

2 (II). A contract, dated (Feria Secunda ante Anthonii, i. e.) Monday, Jan. 16,* 1430, with Else zu Gudenberg,

* In this and some other dates of the documents, I differ from Dr. Van der Linde, who seems either to have regarded them as of no importance, or to be unacquainted with Mediæval dating of documents. Nor are other authors more accurate. The date of this document is explained by Dr. Van der Linde to be June 11; Schaab (i. 45) has June 13; Bernard (Origine de l'imprimerie, i. 118) has

Gutenberg's mother, regarding the money which Friele Gensfleisch had to pay her. In this document, which was found in an account-book of the town of Mentz, is mentioned *Henne*, son of the blessed *Friele Gensefleische*.

It was published *for the first time*, in 1741, by Köhler, *Ehren-Rettung*, p. 81, No. 14 (Aus dem Schuldbuch der Stadt Mayntz, p. 3). Schaab, Erfind. der Buchdruckerk. i. (45), 53, tells us that the original of this MS. was preserved in the family archives of the Zum Jungens at Frankfurt, and at the extinction of this family came into the collection of Mr. Von Glauburg, where it still is, and whence a copy, also of document 5, was sent to Prof. Köhler at Göttingen. Dr. Van der Linde adds, that *Elschin zu Gutenberg* appears moreover in a document of July 25, 1425, and of 1457 (Schaab, Gesch. der Erfindung der Buchdruckerkunst, ii. 284, 286), and he asks whether *Henne Gudenberg*, 1392 (Schaab, No. 41), might have been her father?

3 (1). A document dated (*off den Dienstage nehst kommen ist der Suntag da man sang in der Kirchen* letare Jherusalem, i. e. Tuesday next the Sunday on which the Church sings Letare Jherusalem, i. e.) Tuesday, March 28,* 1430, relating the reconciliation, effected through the intervention of the Archbishop Conrad [III.] of Mentz, between the town of Mentz and a number of expatriated citizens. In it we find mentioned *Henchin zu Gudenberg* as "nit inlendig," *i.e.*, as "not being in Mentz."

This document was published for *the first time* in 1727 by Geo. Chr. Joannis in chapter xii. (p. 460) of his work: *Scriptorum historiæ Moguntinensi cum maxime inservientium tomus novus*, fol., Francof. ad M. The 12th chapter itself is headed: G. C. J[oannis] *De patriciorum veterum Moguntinensium familiis, discrimine, iuribus, contentionibus, fatis*

June 12. But Mr. Bradshaw tells me that the ordinary St. Anthony (the abbat, not the modern St. A. of Padua, the Franciscan Saint), who is honoured on Jan. 17, must have been meant in the date. *Feria Secunda* is Monday, the *second day of the week*. As Jan. 17 fell on a Tuesday in 1430, Feria 2da ante Anthonii must mean Monday Jan. 16.

* Dr. Van der Linde has 18 March; Schaab (ii. 222) 18 March; Bernard (i. 118) 26 March. But the Sunday on which the Church sang Lætare J. is the Fourth Sunday in Lent. As Easter fell on April 16 in 1430, the Fourth Sunday in Lent, being three Sundays earlier, will be March 26. The Tuesday following this is, therefore, Tuesday March 28.

commentariolum. In the table of contents Joannis says of this Commentariolum "*e duobus libellis manu exaratis, nondumque editis, superioribus annis a me confectum, et brevibus quibusdam adnotatiunculis nunc illustratum.*"* In the introduction to the chapter itself Joannis says (p. 451): "*Obtigere mihi ante hos octo annos duo libelli, sermone uernaculo confecti, iique manu scripti. Alter agebat de* funesto *illo,* Dietherum Isenburgium *inter et* Adolfum *Nassouium, de Archiepiscopatu Moguntino infestis animis et armis desertantes,* dissidio : *alter* de statu civitatis Moguntinensis ante et post intestinos *illos* motus, *ad universam illius perniciem, ut eventus docuit, gliscentes; ab anno scilicet MCCC ad annum usque sæculi sequentis xxx. Uterque, præsertim posterior, loco non uno* de Patriciorum ueterum Moguntinensium *simul agebat* familiis discrimine *itidem eorum,* iuribus, contentionibus ac fatis; *strictim quidem et in compendio; satis tamen plane, præcipuisque rerum capitibus in medium allatis. Inde consilium cepi, omnem de hoc argumento narrationem exinde excerpere, excerptam in commentariolum quoddam conferre, et tum ueste latina donare, tum nonnullis ad rem facientibus, quæ mihi aliunde bona sors obiiciebat, augere iuxta illustrareque. Quod etiam, quantum per alia licuit negotia, horis subseciuis factum.*"† The first Patrician family mentioned by Joannis is called *Zum Jungen;* Latine, *de Iuueni.* A Peter *de* Iuueni, Peter dictus Iuuenis civis *Moguntinus,* is mentioned in documents of the years 1297 and 1300, and regarding him Joannis refers to Chronicon Santalbanense, lib. i. sect. ii. p. 767.—

* *i.e.* "Compiled by me in past years from two unpublished manuscripts and illustrated with short notes."

† "Eight years ago I found two manuscripts, written in our vernacular. The one treated of the calamitous dissension between Diether of Isenburg and Adolf of Nassau, disputing with hostile feelings and arms about the Mentz Archiepiscopate; the other of the condition of the town of Mentz before and after these domèstic broils which culminated, as the event has shown, in its universal destruction —namely from the year 1300 to 1430. Both MSS., especially the latter, often treat of the ancient Patrician families of Mentz, of their distinctions, rights, disputes, and fate, briefly, it is true, but yet plainly, setting forth the chief points of the matters. Hence I resolved to excerpt from them the whole narrative of this subject, and to gather it into some short treatise, and not only to put it in a Latin dress, but to augment and illustrate it with several other relevant matters which I happened to find elsewhere. I have done this in my leisure hours as far as other occupations allowed it."

The sixth family is *Gelthus* zur *jungen Alen.* And Joannis adds: "Forte ex his *Adamus* ille *Gelthus* fuit, qui *Joanni Gensfleisch* hoc scripsit epitaphium": [the epitaph follows which A. Gelthus, a relative of Gutenberg, is supposed to have written in Wimpfeling's Oratio in memoriam Marsilii ab Inghen, Mainz, P. Friedberg, 1499, in which Joannes Gensfleisch is called *artis impressoriæ repertor*, and where it is said that *ossa ejus in ecclesia D. Francisci Moguntiæ feliciter cubant.* This latter assertion is incorrect, according to Bockenheimer, *Gutenberg's Grabstätte*, Mainz: 1876, 8vo.; and the same Bockenheimer asserts that the writer of the epitaph is not Gelthus, but Wimpfeling himself.]—The twenty-third family is *Gensfleisch* von *Sorgenloch.* In his notes we find Joannis stating that *Ioannes vero Gensfleisch, arte typographica diuino auspicio inuenta atque excogitata, æternum sibi peperit nomen. Is enim et Ioannes Gudenberg unus idemque est,* and in proof of this last assertion quotes the words which "Marcus Antonius a Kraft, olim e tabulis an. MCCCCXLI, viii. Kal. April. et an. MCCCCXLIII (sic), xv Kal. Decembr. confectis, ac ædis Thomanæ Argentoratensis libro Salico B f. 293[a] et f. 302[b] insertis, descripsit: Ioannes dictus Gensfleisch, alias nuncupatus Gutenberg, de Moguncia, Argentinæ commorans." He then quotes from "uetusto quodam Calendario, siue libro Ciuitatis Moguntinæ fœnebri olim f. 74," the items of which I speak below under document No. 5. Finally comes, as § 11 (on p. 460), the document of which we here treat.

This document was recollated and republished by J. D. Köhler, in his *Ehren-Rettung*, Leipzig, 1741, p. 67, Lit. Bb., who says that it was "copied from an old written *Volumine Actorum* between the Council and Community of Mayntz, from A. 1332–1445." Dr. Van der Linde (p. 513) explains that: "Allusion is made to a Codex of the Frankfurt Town Library, *Sagen von alten Dingen der verehrlichen Stadt Mentze,* 1581, and that [Köhler's] copy was made by Johann Ernst von Glauburg († 1733)." (Cf. Schaab, Erfind. der Buchdruckerkunst, i. p. 44, note 2, 53, 467.) It is to be remarked that the difference between the text of Joannis and that of Köhler is rather great.

The Frankfort MS. mentioned by Dr. Van der Linde seems to be identical with the *libellus de statu ciuitatis Moguntinensis*, referred to by Joannis.

It is to be observed that the compiler or writer of the MS. is not mentioned, nor is it stated whence the compiler got the document of 28th March, 1430. We know, however, that the Frankfort Library acquired the MS. in 1690, after the death of Joh. Maxim. zum Jungen (born at Frankfort, Sept. 11, 1596), who pretended to descend from Gutenberg (see Bockenheimer, Gutenberg's Grabstätte, Mainz, 1876, p. 5).

Consequently our date does not go further back than **1581**. Dr. Van der Linde gives us (on p. 520) a notice, which is written by the side of the document of which we treat. He says :—

"On the 28th of Oct., 1443, *Ort zum Jungen*, Senior, lets his house (*hof*) *zum Jungen* to Henne Gensfleisch Senior for three years [observe, for three years: the inventor was coming to erect a press at Mentz]. From these names and the Strassburg date appears the incorrectness of a notice in (this MS.) on fol. 56 verso: *Henchin zu Gudenberg*, ex familia *Gänsfleisch*, primus et verus ille typographicæ artis Inventor à domo habitationis (ut moris tunc temporis in Moguntia inter nobiles erat, neglecto gentis hæreditaris nomine à domo vel curia habitationis se denominare) *Zum Gudenberg* dicta denominatus [*Friele* and *Henne Gensfleisch zu Gutenberg* bear, on the contrary, the name of *both* their parents, as *e.g.* the Spanish Lopez y Mendez; Van der Linde], patreque *Frilone Gänsfleisch* natus. Obiit denique et apud majores sepultus Moguntiæ in Ecclesia D. Francisci [repetition of an error in the epitaph of Adam Gelthus 1499; Van der Linde] ao. Dm. MCCCCLXXVIII. [sic, Van der Linde; cf. Schaab, Erfind. der Buchdruckerkunst, i. 456, where Jacob von Sorgenloch is said to have died in 1478] ibidemque Insignia ejus gentilia sunt suspensa. Qui *Henne Gudenberg* ao. 1443 *Henne Gensfleisch* senior audiit et domum Zum Jungen ab Ortone zum Jungen eodem ao. in Moguntia locationis titulo pro x florensis [*sic*] aureis annui census possedit."

This notice is, according to some (cf. Schaab, i. 467), *an addition* of Johann Maximilian zum Jungen. Others thought it was written by Geo. Chr. Joannis, but we are now requested to believe that it was added by Joh. Ernst v. Glauburg, who, in 1728, caused researches to be made in the Franciscan Church at Mentz for Gutenberg's grave (cf. Van der Linde, p. 521; Bockenheimer, p. 5). But Von Glauburg could not say *ibidem insignia ejus gentilia sunt suspensa*, as he was unable to find Gutenberg's grave (see Köhler, Ehren-Rettung, 103, 104).

The other MS. mentioned by Joannis, is, no doubt, identical with the MS. which was partly published by Franz Jos. Bodmann (in Rheinisches Archiv für Geschichte und

Litteratur. Herausgegeben von N. Vogt und J. Weitzel, vols. 4 and 5, Mainz, 1811) under the heading :—

Complete narrative, compiled by a contemporary and eye-witness, of the hostility between the two archbishops, Diether v. Isenburg, and Adolf v. Nassau, concerning the possession of the Archbishopric of Mainz, and of the capture and subjugation of the town of Mainz, treacherously effected at that time by the latter.*

I do not think the MS. will be of much importance in the present inquiry; but as it is evidently a compilation of the same character and of the same period as the other MS. used by Joannis, and as its compiler constantly alludes to circumstances connected with early printing at Mentz, I will give in a few lines what I have found about it. Bodmann says of the manuscript :—

"The MS. from which I extract this narrative contains, except an enormous mass of documents, for the most part unpublished, concerning the late archbishopric of Mainz, also several historical essays which have been added at the end, e. gr. the war of K. Albert I. with the Archbishop Gerhard—the transactions between the Archbishops Heinrich and Gerlach—the diplomatic history of the dispute between the Archbishop Sifrid II., with the bishop Leopold of Worms—the transactions between K. Heinrich Raspo and the Archbishop Sifrid III. on the one hand, and the Roman King Conrad IV. on the other hand, with all the documents belonging thereto. The above collection of documents extends as far as the year 1416, and is written on vellum; it betrays a hand of the same period, and writer; on the other hand the additional historical treatises appear to emanate, according to the handwriting, from different compilers. They are written on paper with different watermarks; the first, third, and fourth are Latin, and are a copy of treatises contemporary with the events they relate; but the second seems to have been planned only in the 15th century; it is in German, and unusually detailed. After this follows, but in a different hand, the narrative which I here communicate. It is preceded by a detailed narrative of the first election of the Archbishop Diether, his differences and war with the Elector Friedrich von Pfalz, the celebrated battle of Seckenheim, and the reconciliation of both parties; everything from and with documents. We omit these here and commence with the narrative."

On p. 139, of vol. 4, we read :—

"Her Diether von Isenburg liesz auch ein offen brieff hin und widder

* Vollständige, von einem gleichzeitigen und Augenzeugen gefertigte Nachricht von der wegen dem Besize des Erzstifts Mainz zwischen den beiden Erzbischöffen Diether v. Isenburg und Adolf v. Nassau geführten Fehde, und der damals von lezterm verrätherischer Weise geschehenen Einnehmung und darauf erfolgten Unterjochung der Stadt Mainz.

anslagen, darinn er sich hoch beswert seiner absetzung halben, welche er alsz vnrechtmessig beclagt, erpeüt sic rechtensz, und einer appellacion, vnd seint *vil exemplar getruckt werden von dem ersten Buchtrucker zu Mentz Johan Gutenbergck*, des Inhaltsz wie volgt . . . ."

Bodmann adds in a note: "I possess a copy of this which is several feet (*Schuhe*) long and consists of sheets pasted together." The document referred to is the Manifest of Diether the Elector, of 4 April, 1462. Schaab also had a copy (Erfind. der Buchdruckerk. i. 417, 418) and says that the document was not printed by the first printer of Mentz, Johann Gutenbergck, but by Fust and Schoeffer. Schaab adds that there are many indications of the MS. having been written nearly 100 years after the events which it relates. E. gr. on p. 340 we read ". . . dasz wirthshusz zum Spigell, Fausten Husz . . . ." which shows (says Schaab, ii. 114) that the MS. is not contemporary, but written about the middle of the 16th century, as Johann Fust never called himself Faust, or was so called by others. And on p. 50 of vol. 5: "Die zum Mulbaum. *Ist jetz die Druckerey.*" The latter addition shows (Schaab, ii. 117) that the MS. is a whole century later than the event it records, and must have been written between 1550 and 1560, as it was not until 1552 that the printer, Franz Behm, settled in Mentz and in the Hof zum Maulbaum.

[Bernard (Origine de l'imprimerie, i. 118) says:—"It appears that Gutenberg made a journey to Mentz, in 1432, no doubt to make some arrangements about interests." He refers to Köhler's Ehren-rettung, p. 82, where the contract of May, 1434 (see below, document 5), must be the one which suggested this idea to Bernard.]

4 (III). An Act, dated (*Sonntag nach St. Gregorien tag des H. Pabsts*, i.e., Sunday after Pope St. Gregory's day, i.e.) March 14,* 1434, by which *Johann Gensefleisch der Junge*, genannt *Gutemberg*, at the request of the council of *Strassburg*, where he resided in the monastery of Arbogast,

* Dr. Van der Linde has March 12; but St. Gregory's day itself is March 12 A. The Sunday letter in 1434 was C, therefore the Sunday after St. Gregory's day must be March 14, 1434. Bernard (Orig. de l'imprimerie, i. 119), speaking of the date of this document, says that "it is very difficult to determine it, as there are two popes of the name of Gregory, and moreover two feasts for the first—Gregory the Great—namely 12 March and 3 September." But the day of Gregory's commemoration, March 12, is no doubt meant in the document.

released Niclause, the secretary of Mentz, and relinquished the money (310 Rhenish guilders) which the town owed him.

Schaab, Gesch. der Erfind. der Buchdruckerk. i. pp. 26, 30, tells us that this document was discovered about the middle of the 18th century by the learned professor and untiring antiquary Joh. Dan. Schoepflin, in a Register of contracts (ex libro contractuum) of the year 1434, preserved at Strassburg. He published it *for the first time* on p. 3 of his *Vindiciæ Typographiæ.* (*Documenta typographicarum originum ex Argentinensibus tabulariis et bibliothecis nunc primum edita*), 4to., Argentorati, 1760. Dr. Van der Linde remarks on this document that Gutenberg showed himself in it greater as a youthful knight than as a practical man of business.

5 (IV). A contract, dated (Dominica proxima post Urbani, i.e., the Sunday after St. Urban, i.e.) May 30,* 1434, with *Hengin Gudenberg,* son of the blessed Friele Gensfleisch, respecting 14 guilders, which were settled on his brother Friele residing at Eltvil.

This entry was published for the first time by Köhler, Ehren-Rettung (1741), p. 82, No. 16, from a MS. account-book of the town of Mentz (Aus der Stadt Mayntz Schuldbuch in MSSt., p. 32), the same volume which supplied Köhler with document No. 2 (q.v.). Joannis (Scriptt. rer. Mogunt. iii., 1727, p. 456) published however an entry to the same effect, in which it is said that Gudenberg obtained a new letter about this transaction, and had returned the old one. Cf. Schaab, Erfind. der Buchdruckerk. i. 45, 53.

6. A document setting forth an action brought in 1437 by *Anna Zu der Iserin Thüre* against Gutenberg for breach of promise, the end of which affair was not stated in the document. (Jo. Dan. Schoepflini Programma, quo typographiæ, A. 1440 inventæ, festum seculare indictum, Argentorati, A. 1740, Idibus Octobris;—this Program was republished (?) at Basle in 1741 (Commentatt. Hist. et crit. Jo. Dan. Schoepflini, p. 557); Mémoires de l'Académie des Inscriptions, xvii. 1740, p. 762 (766), Dissertat. sur l'origine de l'imprimerie, par M. Schepflin; Schoepflin,

* St. Urban is May 25 E; the Sunday following must be May 30, 1434.

Vindiciæ typogr., 1760, p. 17, cuius exitum *charta* non docet).

Dr. Van der Linde says (p. 34) that in 1740 Schoepflin [who himself tells us so on p. 13 of his Vindiciæ] received this document (*urkunde*) from the [Strassburg] Archivist Wencker [the same person from whom he received another document, see below, Nos. 7 and 11], and he adds:—

"It was surprising that he [Schoepflin] *did not* publish this document, whereas he printed all the rest *entirely*. When Meerman [Origines typogr., i. 168], after the publication of Schoepflin's *Vind. typ.*, asked for a copy, the latter replied on the 20th of February, 1761, that *no such document existed* (ejusmodi chartam non exstare) and that the information in question was merely contained in a marginal annotation (verum unice annotationem quandam)! But even the marginal annotation was not produced! This document, therefore, was *nothing*; consequently, I take an item, pretended to have been copied from a Helbelingzollbuch 'that *Ennel Gutenbergen* had given this tax' [cf. below document No. 11], to be a forgery which was meant to complete the nothing-saying marginal annotation, as it occurs *in another place*, without a year. At that time notes were not made in *such* a way, documents are not published in *such* a way, and we may not represent Gutenberg as married, either ecclesiastically or secularly, on the ground of such miserable acts."

It should not be forgotten that Dr. Van der Linde speaks here, not I; the words between [ ] *are mine, however.*

Schoepflin himself speaks of this breach of promise case on several occasions. First in the Program which he wrote and seems to have published in 1740 at the time of the tercentenary of the invention of printing. In his *Commentationes historicæ et criticæ*, published at Basle in 1741, this Program appears on p. 557, with the following heading: "*Programma, quo Typographiæ, A.* 1440 *inventæ, Festum seculare indictum, Argentorati, A.* 1740, *Idibus Octobris.*" Speaking of several towns celebrating in that year the tercentenary of the Invention of Printing, he says that these very towns serve the cause of Strassburg. They do so, however, unwittingly, as they are not aware that

"Gutenberg at the very time of the birth of Typography had been *supporting a family, during a series of years, at Strassburg;* had there applied himself to the invention and practise of several arts, and, for that purpose, had formed divers associations in our town, which he made, like a citizen, his abode for a long time . . . . *In the year* 1437 *he was accused before the Episcopal judge of Strassburg by a certain noble maid Anna, Zu der Eisernen Thüre, the last of her race, and afterwards married her.* In the years 1441 and 1442 he appears as a bail and surety in documents of the St. Thomas Chapter. For several years he pays the taxes imposed by the magistracy of our town, and during all the time that he resided at Strassburg, he was an adroit and sedulous investigator of wondrous things ; this we learn from the sentence pronounced by the Strassburg judges, in 1439, when a controversy had arisen between him and his associates to whom he had communicated his secrets. What forbids us to conjecture that the rudiments of the typographical art were among these very secrets ?" *

In the same year 1740 he sent a "Dissertation sur l'origine de l'Imprimerie" to the "Académie des Inscriptions," in which he says :—

"A few years afterwards [after 1434] Gutenberg had an intrigue with a noble lady, Anne Porte-de-fer, the last of her family, and as he, very probably, refused to carry out his promises, she caused him to be summoned before the Strassburg Magistracy in 1437. We do not find the judgment given on this occasion; but either in virtue of a sentence, or according to arrangement, the lady became his wife, and appears in this quality in our public registers where she is called Anne de Gutenberg. We still find Gutenberg established at Strassburg, and having children (!) in 1444. . . . The Archives of the city and those of the collegiate Church of St. Thomas at Strassburg contain many acts executed by Gutenberg during the years 1439, 1441, 1442. . . . The most remarkable is the first, by which he associates with three citizens of this city to work up several arts and marvellous secrets which approach the miraculous (these are the terms of the treaty written in German), without, however, specifying what these secrets consisted of. This same act reminds us of an anterior one, in virtue of which one of the associates had previously contracted an association with Gutenberg for the polishing of stones, which had been successful." †

* ". . . . Latet eas, Guttenbergium illis ipsis Typographiæ nascentis temporibus, per plurium annorum seriem Argentorati aluisse Familiam, variis artibus inveniendis tractandisque ibidem incubuisse, eique fini diversas in civitate nostra inivisse societates, adeoque diuturni temporis incolam, civis instar, cum animo commorandi fortunarum suarum sedem in ea fixisse constanter . . . . Ille A. 1437. apud Episcopalem Argentinensium Judicem, a nobili quadam Virgine Anna, Gentis suæ ultima, quæ a (Zu der Eisernen Thüre) *Ferrea Porta* nomen tulerat, accusatus est, eamque deinceps duxit uxorem. Ille Annis 1441. & 1442. Capitulo Thomano vadem & sponsorem solemnibus formulis se obtulit ; Ille per plures annos nova, quæ Magistratus, temporum necessitate coactus, imposuerat tributa solvit ; atque per totum illud temporis spatium, quo Argentorati versatus est, solers sedulusque rerum mirabilium fuit indagator ; Id quod sententia, cum A. 1439. inter eundem & socios, quos arcanorum suorum participes reddidit, controversia oriretur, a Judicibus Argentinensibus lata nos docet. Enimvero quid conjicere nos vetat, inter ipsa hæc arcana, typographicæ quoque Artis extitisse rudimenta . . . ." On p. 560 Schoepflin adds, in a note, that he owes the public documents to the liberality of the Councillor Wencker.

† "Peu d'années après, il eut une intrigue avec une Demoiselle

Schoepflin has never, as far as I know, said any more about the *children*, of which he speaks here. Meerman (Orig. typogr., 1765, i. 168) thought that Schoepflin was, in 1740, under the impression that Anna Gutenberg was Gutenberg's daughter, whereas, in 1760, he had come to the conclusion that she was his wife. But Meerman, in suggesting this explanation, overlooked the fact that even in 1740 Schoepflin refers to Anna G. as Gutenberg's wife, so that he could not speak of her at the same time as his daughter. The *children* were to be produced, I suppose, in another *document*.

The same Schoepflin says, in 1760 (on p. 13 of his Vindiciæ):—

"Jacobus Wencker, Custos of the [Strassburg] Archives, and afterwards public Councillor, informed me [in 1740], from the Archives of the [Strassburg] Court, that Gutenberg had married at Strassburg a noble Alsatian wife, had paid public taxes to the city, and had entered into an association with citizens in respect to a secret art." *

And (on p. 17 of his Vindiciæ):—

"Gutenberg had in 1437, before the ecclesiastical judge, a law-suit with Anna (Ennelin *zu der Iserin Thüre*), a noble maid, a Strassburg citizen, it seems on account of a marriage promised her, the end of

---

noble, *Anne Porte-de-fer*, dernière de sa famille; & sur ce que, vraisemblablement, il refusoit de remplir ses promesses, elle le fit citer à l'Officialité de Strasbourg en 1437. Nous ne trouvons point le jugement qui fut rendu sur cette instance : mais soit en vertu d'une sentence, soit par accommodement, la demoiselle devint sa femme, & paroît en cette qualité dans nos registres publics, où elle est appelée *Anne de Gutenberg*. Nous trouvons encore Gutenberg établi à Strasbourg, & ayant des enfans, en 1444. . . . . Les Archives de la ville, & celles de l'église collégiale de St. Thomas de Strasbourg, conservent plusieurs actes passés par Gutenberg, pendant les années 1439, 1441, 1442. . . . . Le plus remarquable est le premier, par lequel il s'associa trois bourgeois (nommés André Treize, Jean Riff & André Heilmann) de cette ville, pour *mettre en œuvre* plusieurs arts & *secrets merveilleux qui tiennent du prodige* (ce sont les termes du traité écrit en allemand) sans toutefois spécifier en quoi consistoient ces secrets. Ce même acte en rappelle un autre antérieur, en vertu duquel un de ces associés avoit contracté ci-devant avec Gutenberg une association pour la polissûre des pierres, qui avoit eu du succès."

* ". . . Gutenbergium Alsaticam Nobilem Argentorati duxisse uxorem, onera publica solvisse civitati, societatem circa artem occultam cum civibus inivisse, ex scrinio Curiæ me docuit Vir de re literaria præclare meritus, JACOBUS WENCKERUS, tabularii custos, dein Reip. Consul."

which was not stated in the document. But as [the Helbelingzollbuch] expressly states that Anna Gutenberg had paid the same tax as Gutenberg, I conjecture that she had become Gutenberg's wife." *

Finally in his "Alsatia illustrata" (Colmariæ, 1761, vol. ii. p. 346) Schoepflin says:—

"Gutenberg . . . having left his country, fixed the seat of his fortune at Strassburg, where he married an Alsatian wife (the last of a noble family, Ennelia [Anna] *zu der Isernen Thür*) and for ten years enjoyed the right of citizenship . . ." †

7 (V). Six entries in different parts of three several MS. registers of the city of Strassburg, containing all that is known of the Law-suit between *Jerge* (*Georg*) *Dritzehen* and *Johan von Mentze genant Gutenberg* in 1439.

First entry: the depositions of the 13 witnesses of *Jerge Dritzehen*: Barbel von Zabern; Ennel, the wife of Hanns Schultheiss; Hanns Sidenneger; Hannsz Schultheisz; Cunrad Sahspach; Wernher Smalriem; Mydehart Stocker; Peter Eckhart; Thoman Steinbach; Lorentz Beldeck; Reimbolt von Ehenheim; Hans Niger von Bischovissheim; Fridel von Seckingen.

Second entry: the depositions of the 3 witnesses of *Gutenberg* against Jörge Dritzehen: Anthonie Heilman; Hans Dünne; Midehart Stocker.

Third entry: Querimonia of Lorentz Beildeck.

Fourth entry: List of Gutenberg's witnesses against Jerge Dritzehen.

Fifth entry: List of Jerge Dritzehen's witnesses against Hans Gutenberg.

Sixth entry: Sentence of the Council, dated (Vigil. Lucie et Otilie Anno xxxix., i.e.) Dec. 12, (14)39.

The *first two entries* were written in a volume (A) which seems to have contained the entries of the actual depositions of witnesses in suits before the Council as the cases

* "Idem Gutenbergius a. 1437. coram Judice Ecclesiastico litem habuit cum *Anna* (*Ennelin zu der Iserin Thüre*), nobili virgine, cive Argentinensi, promissi, ut videtur, matrimonii causa; cuius exitum charta non docet. At idem Catastrum [the Helbelingzollbuch] Annam Gutenbergiam idem vectigal, Gutenbergio jam profecto, solventem, nominatim cum exprimat, Gutenbergii conjugem eam devenisse conjicimus."

† "Gutenbergius . . . relicta patria, fortunæ suæ sedem fixit Argentorati; ubi Alsaticam ducens uxorem (postremam gentis nobilis, Enneliam *zu der Isernen Thür*) per decennium jure incolatus gavisus est."

came forward. Schoepflin (*Vindiciæ typogr.*, p. 5, *Documenta*, Num. II.) calls it: *Protocollum Senatus Majoris*, and it bore on the outside the title: *Dicta* . . . . Testium magni consilij Anno Domini M°.CCCC°. Tricesimo nono.*

Leon De Laborde, who examined the entries about 1840, describes this volume (*Débuts de l'Imprimerie à Strasbourg*, p. 22), as

"consisting of two quires, each of 42 sheets or 84 leaves, in all 168 leaves; they were covered by a sheet of parchment which had become yellow and soiled, on the recto of which the above title was written. The paper, which had turned yellow and brown on the edge, bore perpendicular water-lines; in the greater portion of the leaves the water-mark was a pair of scales; the fourth leaf had a small ox-head; the last leaves a still smaller ox-head, the water-lines of these leaves being different; the size of the paper was 10 inches (*pouces*) and 9 lines in height and 9 inches in breadth. The first deposition of Dritzehen against Gutenberg (*first* entry) is found on the recto of the 107th leaf, with the heading: *Dis ist die Warheit*, &c., and continues on the recto and verso of the leaves 107–110, till it ends with the deposition of Fridel von Seckingen. The depositions of Gutenberg's witnesses against Jörge Dritzehen (*second* entry) occupy the two leaves 117 and 118, and terminate with that of Midehart Stocker."

The *third*, *fourth*, and *fifth* entries were written in a volume (B), which Schoepflin (*Vindiciæ typogr.*, p. 27, *Documenta*, Num. IV.) also calls: *Protocollum Senatus Majoris*, and which bore the title: *Queremonie & testes registrati Magni Consilii, Anno Dni M°.CCCC°.XXX nono.* Though De Laborde says nothing of this title, he tells us that

"this volume was also bound in parchment, and consisted of 24 sheets (= 48 leaves) of paper sewn together in a single quire (except an old addition of some leaves). There are 43 leaves written upon, and the 5 leaves 31-36 are left blank. The complaint of Lorenz Beildeck is on the recto of the 21st leaf. The first list of the witnesses [*i.e.* of Gutenberg's witnesses, with the heading, *Dis ist Gutenbergs Worheit*, &c.] occupies the lower half of the verso of leaf 38; the second list (which includes Lorentz, the servant of Gutenberg, and his wife), which bears a heading [*Dis ist Jerge Dritzehen Worheit*, &c.], fills the whole recto of the 44th leaf. Everything connected with the Law-suit is written in the volume by the same scribe, who, each time that he resumed his work, imparted a little more firmness to his hand; a circumstance which makes it appear as if several scribes had taken part in the work, whereas it is evident that it is that of a single one.

* In De Laborde's facsimile of this title there are some strokes of other letters visible immediately following *Dicta*, but I am unable to decipher them.—J. H. H.

It is, moreover, certain that it is the original redaction,—indeed, the original *minute* of the transaction,—because all the erasures and the additions written in the margin are in the same ink and in the same hand, and could not have been found in a copy, however clumsy this may have been."

From this description of a careful eye-witness we gather that the *Querimoniæ* and the lists of *Testes registrati* were written separately, the former in the earlier, the latter in the later portion of the volume.

The above two volumes, A and B, were, according to De Laborde :—

"Inclosed in a gray pasteboard case, which has the form of a box ; the back resembles that of a bound book, and on a printed title (*titre imprimé*), which dates, without any doubt, from Schoepflin's time, we find : *Documenta typographiæ Argentorati inventæ.*"

The *sixth* or last entry was written in a volume (C) which seems to have contained Decisions of the Strassburg Council. Schoepflin (*Vindiciæ typogr.*, p. 21, *Documenta*, Num. III.) calls it : *Protocollum contractuum*, i.e., a Register of Contracts. The entry is the sentence of the Strassburg Senate in the above Law-suit, and is dated : *Vigil. Lucie & Otilie* (i.e., 12 Dec.), *Anno xxxix.* (i.e. MCCCCXXXIX).

De Laborde omits all notice of *this* volume, though he professes to give the documents all from his own transcripts. And as I cannot find that any other author has attempted to describe this volume, we have no bibliographical description of this book as we have of the volumes A and B.

It is observable that while De Laborde prints the *Depositions* line for line, apparently as they were in the MS., he prints the *Querimonia* and the *Sentence* in the ordinary way. Again, whereas De Laborde gives facsimiles of eleven different passages from the volumes A and B, he gives none from vol. C. So that we have no evidence from this that De Laborde ever saw the Register C.

Schoepflin tells us in 1761 (p. 347 of vol. ii. of his *Alsatia illustrata*), that that part of the Acts, which contains the sentence of the Senate, had been *communicated* to him in 1740 by Jac. Wencker, Councillor and Chief of the Public Archives at Strassburg ; which, of course, refers to this vol. C. And on the same page he says that the depositions of the witnesses (therefore the Registers A and B) were found in 1745 by Jo. Henr. Barth (then Archivist) on the clearing out of the Record tower.* The two latter volumes are stated to have been preserved in the Town Library of Strassburg till 1870, when they are believed to have been destroyed during the bombardment of that city by the Germans. Vol. C may have shared the same fate, but it is nowhere explicitly mentioned. The three volumes seem all to have contained different kinds of documents. I have called the Registers A, B, C, but of course the entries interlace in point of time. The lists of witnesses to be brought forward would naturally be registered in B, before the trial began. The Querimonia in B refers to what happened after the complainant had given the evidence recorded in A. The decision would, of course, come last. It would be interesting to learn what has become of the rest of the series of Registers of which these two (or three) were selected and kept in the case described by De Laborde.

Schoepflin speaks already in 1740 of the Sentence of the Senate (vol. C). In the Program which he wrote in that year, on the occasion of the tercentenary of the Invention of Printing (of which I have already spoken under document No. 6, *q. v.*), he mentions the documents 4 and 6, and the documents of 1441 and 1442, adding:—

> "during all the time that he [Gutenberg] resided at Strassburg he was an adroit and sedulous investigator of wondrous things; this we learn from the sentence pronounced by the Strassburg judges, in 1439, when a controversy had arisen between him and his associates to whom he had communicated his secrets."

At the end of the Program, referring again to the documents, he says that he owed the public ones to the liberality of the Councillor Wencker (Publica amplissimi Viri Consularis Wenckeri liberalitati debemus).

In his Dissertation on the origin of printing, which he wrote also in 1740, and was inserted in vol. xvii. of the *Mémoires de l'Académie des Inscriptions* (see above, document 6), he says, speaking of the documents of 1439, 1441, 1442:—

> "The most remarkable is the first, by which he [Gutenberg] associates himself with three citizens (named Andres Drizehen, Hans

* "Partem actorum, quae sententias Senatus An. 1439 continet, ex Contractuum Protocollo mecum An. 1740 jam communicavit Jac. Wenckerus, Consularis, publico tum tabulario praefectus. At An. 1745

Riff, and Andres Heilmann) of this city to work up several arts and marvellous secrets, which approach the miraculous (these are the terms of the treaty written in German), without, however, specifying what those secrets consisted of. This same act reminds us of an anterior one, in virtue of which one of the associates had previously contracted an association with Gutenberg for the polishing of stones, which had been successful."

I do not find that Schoepflin, on this occasion, mentions Wencker.

In 1760, however, he does not make the same omission. On p. 12 of his Vindiciæ typographicæ, he says :—

"When in the 40th year of this century many German and Dutch towns celebrated the memory of the Invention of Printing, I considered it the proper occasion to investigate its origin more closely. I began to examine more carefully the public documents of all kinds, the commentaries and registers preserved in the Archives of our city, and hitherto neglected by my predecessors. In the course of time success responded to my investigation. That Joh. Gutenberg lived at Strassburg in 1441 and the following year is shown by two documents [Nos. 8 and 10] of the Church of St. Thomas which Scherzius had discovered in the Archives of that Chapter. Jacobus Wencker, the keeper of the Archives, has informed me [in 1740] (from the Archives of the Court) that the same Gutenberg had married at Strassburg a noble Alsatian, paid public taxes to the city, and established an association with citizens [of Strassburg] for the sake of a secret art. . . . I have explained this in an Academical Program [in 1740], and in the same year sent a dissertation to the Royal Academy of Inscriptions on this subject [see above]. Five years afterwards [*i.e.* in 1745] full light was thrown upon my investigation when the tower called the *Pfenningthurn* (where the Strassburg treasures were preserved) began to be destroyed. When I was inspecting again the Strassburg flag and standard, the wax tables, the charters provided with golden *bullæ*, and other antiquarian stores, several times seen already by me before, I at last entered into a room which was more rarely unlocked before, where I discovered in a long row the old protocols of the Senate, namely, small folio paper codices, marked with the years. Henricus Barthius, at that time the chief of the Archives, and myself, drew them forth from the darkness. We examined them, and I myself excerpted several. But when I took up the codex of the year 1439, I had hardly opened the MS. when I saw the name of Gutenberg. Looking further, I found a long series of witnesses who gave their testimonies regarding the Gutenbergian secret, most of which designated plainly the typographical art. The authentic codex, which is preserved in a sacred place, and in which the Acts of the Senate and the declarations of witnesses before the delegates of the Senate have been written, is of a venerable authority. In it are registered the witnesses produced in the law-suit brought

Jo. Henr. Barthius, custos Archivi, effata testium, qui in causa hac auditi sunt, reperit, cum Nummariæ turris destruendæ occasione veteres chartæ et codices in publica Curiæ scrinia transferrentur."

against Gutenberg when one of his associates had died and his heirs wished to be admitted to the secret, which really was nothing but the secret of typography."*

Dibdin visited Strassburg in 1818, and what he then *saw* appears plainly enough from what he *says* on p. 53 of vol. 3 of his "Bibliographical, Antiquarian, and Picturesque Tour in France and Germany," published in 1821:—

"However, of other MSS. you will I am sure give me credit for having examined the celebrated *depositions in the law-suit between Fust and Gutemberg*†—so intimately connected with the history of early printing, and so copiously treated upon by recent bibliographers (see the authorities quoted, and the subject itself handled, in the *Bibliographical*

* ". . . Quadragesimo autem hujus seculi anno secularem inventæ Typographiæ memoriam apud Germanos et Batavos multæ quum celebrassent civitates, originis ejus propius investigandæ mihi nata occasio.—Publica omnis generis Acta, Commentarios, Registra, quæ decessores neglexerant, in tabulario Civitatis tum curatius investigare incepi. Investigationi per temporum intervalla successus respondit. Joh. Gutenbergium, a. 1441. & sequenti civem Argentinæ vixisse, jam pridem Instrumenta duo me docuerant Thomana, quæ in scrinio Capituli detexerat SCHERZIUS, Antiquitatum Teutonicarum scrutator illustris. Eundem Gutenbergium Alsaticam Nobilem Argentorati duxisse uxorem, onera publica solvisse civitati, societatem circa artem occultam cum civibus inivisse, ex scrinio Curiæ me docuit Vir de re literaria præclare meritus, JACOBUS WENCKERUS, tabularii custos, dein Reip. Consul. . . . Academico hæc Programmate paucis exposui, cum ad secularem, Typographiæ inventæ, orationem, a literato juvene habendam, Academiæ cives invitarem. Eodem tempore Regiæ Inscriptionum Academiæ Dissertationem super hoc argumentum Lutetiam transmisi. . . . . At plenum denique investigationi meæ lumen post quinquennium accessit, quum Nummaria turris (lingua patria *Pfenningthurn*) cimeliorum Argentinensium custos . . . . superiore ex parte destrui cœpisset. Carrocium atque vexillum Argentinense, tabulas ceratas, diplomata, aureis bullis instructa, aliamque antiquitatis supellectilem, a me prius jam identidem visam, quum denuo inspicerem, in Cameram denique incidi, rarius ante reseratam, ubi vetera Protocolla Senatus, chartaceos nempe codices, formæ folii minoris, annis signatos, longa serie deprehendi. HENRICUS BARTHIUS, tabularii tum Præfectus, Vir amantissimus literarum, eos mecum ex tenebris protraxit. Excussimus singulos, nonnullos excerpsi. Cum autem ad Codicem a. 1439. pervenissem, vix evolvi volumen, quum Gutenbergii nomen in meos oculos incurrit. Inquirens ulterius longam testium seriem reperi, qui de Gutenbergiano arcano testimonia perhibent, quorum pleraque typographicam artem designarunt aperte. —Codex authenticus, loco sacro servatus, in quo publice perscripta sunt Acta Senatus, testiumque effata coram delegatis Senatus fideliter consignata, venerandæ auctoritatis est . . ."

† I copy Dibdin word for word; the italics are also his; he confounds, of course, the law-suit of 1455 with this.—J. H. H.

Decameron, vol. i. p. 316, &c.).—I own that I inspected these depositions (in the German language) with no ordinary curiosity. They are doubtless most precious ; yet I cannot help suspecting that the *character* or letter is *not* of the time ; namely, of 1440. It should rather seem to be of the sixteenth century. Perhaps at the commencement of it. These documents are written in a small folio volume, in one uniform hand—a kind of law-gothic—from beginning to end. The volume has the following title on the exterior ; "*Dicta Testium magni concilij Anno dni m°.cccc°. Tricesimo nono.*" The paper is strong and thick, and has a pair of scales for the water-mark. The younger Schweighæuser thinks my doubts about its age not well founded ; conceiving it to be a coeval document. But this does not affect its authenticity, as it may have been an accurate and attested copy—of an original which is now perished. Certainly the whole book has very much the air of a *copy :* and besides, would not the originals have been upon separate rolls of parchment ?"

It is evident from this quotation that Dibdin only saw volume A. Dr. Van der Linde, speaking (p. 514) of Dibdin's visit to Strassburg in 1818, says, with his usual amiability :—"Dibdin examined in 1818 the document with English stupidity."

Schaab (Geschichte der Erfindung der Buchdruckerkunst) also speaks of the law-suit. On p. 27 of his first volume he mentions the

"Declaration which Gutenberg made before the Great Council of Strassburg regarding the complaint of Georg Dritzehen, and his detailed defence, on which on the 12th of December, 1439, the sentence of this Council followed. In Schoepflin Vind. typogr., docum. No. 3."*

On p. 30 Schaab explains :—

"This important declaration of Gutenberg before the Great Council of Strassburg, and the still more important sentence of this Council, was discovered by Mr. Wencker, the Archivist of Strassburg, among the Protocols of Contracts of the year 1439." †

This, therefore, refers to the *Sentence of the Senate* (vol. C.), which is Schoepflin's docum. No. 3.

* "Die Erklärung Gutenbergs, welche er vor dem grossen Rath zu Strassburg auf die Klage des Georg Dritzehen gab, und seine ausführliche Vertheidigung enthält, worauf am 12. Dezember 1439 von diesem Rath das Urtheil erfolgte. In Schoepflin vind. typog. docum. No. 3."

† "Diese wichtige Erklärung Gutenbergs vor dem grossen Rath zu Strassburg und das noch wichtigere Urtheil dieses Raths hat Hr. Wencker, Archivist in Strassburg, unter den Protokollen der Kontrakten des Jahrs 1439 entdeckt."

On p. 43 Schaab mentions :—

(1). "The Protocol of the Great Council of Strassburg of the year 1439, on the hearing of 14 witnesses in the law-suit of Jörg Dritzehn, citizen of Strassburg, against Johann von Mentze genannt Gutenberg." (2). "Another Protocol, conducted before the same Great Council at Strassburg, on all complaints which came before it, and the names of the witnesses which were brought forward in these complaints. Among the first is that of Lorenz Beildeck, the servant of Gutenberg, against Georg Dritzehn, because the latter accused him of having given a false testimony in the cause of his master. Among the latter are those mentioned who had been heard in Gutenberg's and Dritzehn's cause." *

This, therefore, refers to the entries in the Registers A and B. Schaab refers here to Schoepflin's Documenta II., III., IV.; but this is a slight mistake, as Schoepflin's No. III. is the Sentence.

On p. 49 Schaab returns to the latter two acts, saying :—

"Schoepflin discovered these two important Acts at Strassburg in an old tower, called the *Pfennigthurm*, among the old Protocols of the Council, all bound in small folio, and marked according to the years, among those of the year 1439. At present [1830] they [*i.e.* these particular volumes A and B] are preserved in the Town Library at Strassburg. The circumstances of the discovery of these and all other Protocols of the Council of the once free city of Strassburg; the place where they were fonnd, and the fact that those of the year 1439, mixed up with those of former and later years, agree most minutely with the latter in their exterior and interior form, should have protected them against every, even the slightest, suspicion of falsification; but Dibdin, the otherwise so esteemed English bibliographer, intimated, on his tour through France and Germany in the year 1818, to the Librarian, Schweighäuser, who showed him these Protocols of the Council in the Town Library, some suspicion as to their genuineness. [Here follows the above quotation from Dibdin's Tour]. . . . Dibdin, who in his former writings had shown a conspicuous antipathy against Gutenberg, who even regarded the latter's 42-line Bible as a product of Fust and Schoeffer, who says himself that he does not understand a word of German, could not form a critical

* "Das Protokoll des grossen Raths zu Strassburg vom Jahr 1439, über die Abhörung von vierzehn Zeugen in dem Prozess des Jörg Dritzehn, Bürgers zu Strassburg, gegen Johann von Mentze genannt Gutenberg."——"Ein anderes Protokoll geführt von dem nemlichen grossen Rath zu Strassburg über alle Klagen, welche vor ihn gebracht und die Namen der Zeugen, die in diesen Klagsachen angegeben worden. Unter den ersten stehet die von Lorenz Beildeck, Bedienten von Gutenberg, gegen Georg Dritzehn, weil dieser ihn beschuldigt, ein falsches Zeugniss in der Sache seines Herrn gegeben zu haben, unter letztern sind jene namentlich genannt, die in Gutenbergs und Dritzehns Sache waren abgehört worden."

judgment on the originality of these precious Acts. His opinion that these Protocols might be a correct and attested copy from an original which can no longer be found, is based upon nothing, and has not even the appearance of probability; equally incorrect is his assertion that the original Acts would have been written on separate rolls of parchment. Had he been speaking of the depositions of witnesses of the 13th and even of the 14th century, he might have been right; at that time the use of parchment rolls was customary, of which the declarations of witnesses still bear the name in the German judicial practice; but these had fallen into disuse in the 15th century, when linen paper had been invented and its use had become general. At that period we find already in the whole of Germany Protocols of Councils and judicial Acts written on paper. The Librarian, Professor Schweighäuser, Jun., wrote to me [Schaab] about these two important sources on the 22nd April, 1836, as follows:—No. II.* is from a comparatively small folio volume, of which Schoepflin has correctly given the title; No. IV.† is from a much thinner volume, also correctly indicated by Schoepflin. These two volumes are in our Library, where I showed them to Dibdin. It is inconceivable how he could doubt their authenticity, as they bear all external and internal evidence of it most plainly. They are old volumes, entirely worn at the edges, bound in rough parchment, which has become brown-yellow, and repaired at the back with old parchment or strips of leather, in which many other unimportant matters are contained. Besides the complete uselessness of copying such things in the 16th century, the fact that in the volumes frequently whole or half pages have been crossed out, and others have been left blank, proves plainly that the documents are the original. . . . ."‡

---

* This is evidently a reference to Schoepflin's documenta, whose No. II. contains the *first* and *second* entries, or the depositions of the witnesses, and is therefore our Register A.

† Schoepflin's No. IV. contains the *third, fourth,* and *fifth* entries, and is therefore our Register B.

‡ "Schöpflin hat beide wichtige Aktenstücke zu Strassburg in einem alten Thurm, der Pfennigthurm genannt, unter den alten Rathsprotokollen, die alle in klein Folioformat gebunden und nach den Jahren gezeichnet waren, und zwar unter denen vom Jahr 1439 entdeckt (Schoepflin Vind. typ. 1760. 13, 14). Jetzt sind sie in der Stadtbibliothek zu Strassburg aufbewahrt. Die Umstände der Entdeckung dieser und aller andern Rathsprotokolle der einst freien Stadt Strassburg, der Ort, wo sie gefunden worden und dass die von dem Jahre 1439 unter denen der früheren und späteren Jahre vermischt gelegen, mit diesen in äusserer und innerer Form auf das genaueste übereinstimmen, hätten sie gegen jeden, auch den leisesten, Verdacht der Verfälschung sichern sollen; allein Dybdin, der sonst so achtbare englische Bibliograph, äusserte bei seiner Reise durch Frankreich und Deutschland im Jahr 1818 dem Hrn. Bibliothekar Schweighäuser, der ihm diese Rathsprotokolle auf der Stadtbibliothek vorlegte, einen Verdacht gegen ihre Aechtheit . . . . Dybdin, der in seinen früheren Schriften eine auffallende Abneigung gegen Gutenberg bewiesen, der sogar dessen 42 zeilige Bibel für ein Produkt von Fust und Schöffer

It is plain that we have here only a description of the volumes A and B.

About the year 1853 Aug. Bernard visited Strassburg, and on p. 121 of the first vol. of his work *De l'origine de l'Imprimerie* (Paris, 1853) he states:—

"the pieces of this Law-suit still exist in the original in the Library of Strassburg, where I had the pleasure of perusing them and verifying their authenticity." *

Therefore, Schoepflin (1740—1761), with all his verbosity on the *finding* of the Registers and other matters, does not say one word as to whether he ever saw with his own eyes the *Sentence of the Senate* (in vol. C.). Dibdin (1818—1821) does not even speak of it. Neither Schaab nor Schweighäuser (1826—1830) gives us the slightest hint

---

hielt, der selbst sagt, dass er nicht ein Wort deutsch verstehe, kann wohl kein kritisches Urtheil über die Originalität dieser kostbaren deutschen Aktenstücke fällen. Seine Meinung, diese Rathsprotokolle möchten eine richtige und beglaubte Abschrift von einem nicht mehr vorfindlichen Originale seyn, hat er durch nichts begründet und sie hat auch nicht den Schein der Wahrscheinlichkeit; eben so unrichtig ist seine Behauptung: die Originalverhöre seyen gewiss auf einzelne Pergamentrollen geschrieben gewesen. Wenn er von Zeugenverhören des 13. und selbst noch des 14. Jahrhunderts redete, so mögte er Recht haben, dort war allerdings der Gebrauch der pergamentenen Zeugenrotuln, von denen noch in der deutschen Gerichtspraxis die Erklärungen der Zeugen den Namen fortführen; allein diese waren im 15. Jahrhundert in Abgang gekommen, als das Leinenpapier erfunden, und sein Gebrauch allgemein geworden war. Jetzt trifft man schon in ganz Deutschland Rathsprotokolle und Gerichtsakten auf Papier geschrieben.——Prof. und Bibliothekar Schweighäuser der Jüngere zu Strassburg, schrieb mir über diese beide wichtige Quellen am 22. April 1826: "No. II. ist aus einem beträchtlichen klein Foliobande, dessen Titel Schöpflin richtig angegeben hat; No. IV. ist aus einem weit dünneren, gleichfalls von Schöpflin richtig bezeichneten. Diese beide Bände sind auf unserer Bibliothek, wo ich sie Dybdin gezeigt habe. Wie dieser an ihrer Authenticität zweifeln konnte, ist gar nicht zu begreifen, denn sie tragen alle äussere und innere Kennzeichen derselben aufs Augenscheinlichste an sich. Es sind alte am Rande ganz vergriffene, in rauhes, braungelb gewordnes Pergament gebundene und hinten mit altem Pergament oder Lederseiten nachgeflickte Hofeln, worin zugleich viele andere unwichtige Sachen enthalten sind. Was, ausser der gänzlichen Unnützheit, solche Dinge im 16. Jahrhundert abzuschreiben, augenscheinlich beweisst, dass es die Originalakten sind, ist, dass darin häufig ganze oder halbe Seiten ausgestrichen, andere aber weiss gelassen sind . . ."

* "Les pièces de ce procès, qui existent encore en original dans la bibliothèque de Strasbourg, où j'ai eu le plaisir de les parcourir et d'en constater l'authenticité . . ."

as to whether they had seen volume C, though the latter actually lived at Strassburg and described the volumes A and B. Bernard (1853) does not refer to vol. C. And as De Laborde (1840), who is so careful and minute about the volumes A and B, has not one word to say about the one containing this *Sentence*, it would seem that this document has *never yet been seen by any human being;* Wencker, the *discoverer*, of course excepted!!

Schoepflin published all the entries of the Law-suit in 1760 (fifteen years after the discovery of the depositions, and twenty after that of the Sentence), in his *Vindiciae Typographicae*, accompanied by a Latin translation. They were republished from his text, first by Meerman (*Origines typogr.*, Hagae Comit., 1765, ii. p. 58 sq.), who gave also Schoepflin's Latin version, with some modifications in some of the most material parts, and afterwards by Wetter (*Krit. Geschichte der Erfind. der Buchdruckerk. durch Joh. Gutenberg*, 8vo. Mainz, 1836, p. 56 sq.). De Laborde republished (*Débuts de l'imprimerie à Strasbourg*, Paris, 1840, 8vo.) the German text *from the original* (at least the first *two* entries), and added a French translation. English translations of the most material parts of the Law-suit may be found in Dr. Van der Linde's Haarlem Legend (Engl. translation, Lond., Blades, 1871); in W. Skeen's Early Typography (8vo. Colombo, 1872), and De Vinne's The Invention of Printing (8vo. Lond., 1877, p. 380). The German text was reproduced by Dr. Van der Linde, in his "Gutenberg" (p. vi. of the *Urkunden*). He does not state from whom he takes it, but as his text is arranged exactly like that of De Laborde, we must presume that he followed him, especially as he prints the latter part of Midehart Stocker's deposition in the same way as De Laborde, though this author printed it defectively, as appears from the facsimile which he traced with his own hand and added to his work.

A great many authors have commented upon the Law-suit, but even after all that has been said and done in the matter, I do not consider a *literal* and *unabridged* translation of the entries we have to be out of place. I give the original and my translation in parallel columns. I have followed De Laborde's text, and have only altered those words which deviate from his own facsimiles. As space does not allow printing the text line for line as De Laborde gives it (apparently from the MS.), the place where his lines break off has here been marked by ||. Schoepflin's readings are given in notes.

[*First* entry.]

Dis ist die worheit die Jerge dritzehen||[1] geleit[2] hat wider Johan[3] von Mentze|| genant gutenberg In præsentia Claus Duntzenheim und Claus zur Helten.

Item Barbel von Zabern die Koüffelerin hatt geseit das sü|| uff ein nacht allerleye mit Andres Dritzehen gerett habe und|| under andern Worten sprach sü zu ime wöllent nit dolme|| gon slaffen, do habe er ir geantwurt Ich musz disz vor machen,|| Also sprach dise gezugin, aber hülffe Gott was vertünt er grosz|| geltes es möchte dolme über x. guldin haben costet, Antwurt|| er ir wider und sprach du bist ein dörin, wenestu das es mich|| nuwent x. gl. gecostet habe, hörestdu, hettestu als vil als es|| mich über III[c]. bare guldin gecostet hett du hettest din leptage|| gnüg, und das es mich minder gecostet hatt dann v[c]. gl. das ist|| gar lützel one das es mich noch costen würt|| darumb ich min eigen und min erbe versetzt habe, Sprach|| dise gezugin aber zu ime: heiliges liden misselinge uch dann|| wie woltent ir dann tun, Antwurt er ir uns mag nit|| misselingen, ee ein jor usskommet so hant wir unser houbtgut wider|| und sind dann alle selig, Gott welle uns dann blogen.||

This is the truth which *Jerge Dritzehen* has deposed against *Johan von Mentze* named *Gutenberg.* In the presence of Claus Duntzenheim and Claus zur Helten.

Item, *Barbel von Zabern,* the trades-woman, has said that one night she talked about several things with *Andres Dritzehen,* and, among other words, she said to him: 'Will you not go and sleep?' but he replied: 'I must make this first.' Then this witness said: 'but, help [me] God, how much money do you spend; this must have cost you more than x guilders.' He answered again and said: 'thou art a fool, thinkst thou that it has cost me only x guilders? Look here, if thou hadst as much as it has cost me over 300 guilders ready money, thou wouldst have enough for thy life, and what it has cost me less than 500 guilders is very little, besides what it will still cost me; wherefore I have mortgaged my house and my ground.' Then this witness said to him: 'Holy passion, if you fail, what will you do?' He replied: 'we cannot fail; before a year is passed, we have our capital back and will all be happy, unless God wished to afflict us.'

[1] In this heading the first two lines are divided according to De Laborde's facs., the remainder is printed in the ordinary way, as De Laborde's facs. does not go further than *gutenberg,* and he does not divide the lines in his text.

[2] De Laborde prints *geseit,* but his facs. shows *geleit;* the latter word is also found in Schoepflin's text.

[3] De Laborde prints *Johann,* but

Item frouwe Ennel Hans Schulheissen fruwe des Holzmans hatt|| geseit das Lorentz Beildeck zu einer zit inn ir hus kommen sy|| zu Claus Dritzehen irem vetter und sprach zu ime, lieber Claus|| Dritzehen, min[1] Juncker Hanns Guttemberg hatt uch gebetten das[1]|| Andres xiij[2] selig hatt iiij stücke Inn einer pressen ligen do hatt[3]|| gutenberg[4] gebeten das ir die vsz der pressen nement vnd die von einander|| legent vff[5] das man nit gewissen kune was es sy[5] dann er hatt nit gerne das das Jemand sihet||

Dise gezugin hatt ouch geseit, Als sye by|| Andres Dritzehen jrem vetter gewesen|| sy do habe sü jme desselben wercks dick helffen|| machen tag und naht, Sie hatt ouch geseit|| das sü wol wisse das Andres Dritzehen jr vetter selig|| in den ziten sin pfennig gelt versetzt habe ob|| aber er das zü dem werck gebrucht habe wisse|| sü nit.||

his facs. shows *Johan*, which latter form is also found in Schoepflin's text.

[1] De Laborde prints *min — das* between ( ), and places a star after the word *das*, but does not explain what he means. Schoepflin, however, tells us that after the name Dritzehen, the following words are written in the original: *min Juncher Hanns Gutemberg hatt uch gebetten das*, but have been deleted.

[2] So in De Laborde's facs., *i.e.*, Dritzehen.

[3] Here follow apparently two letters according to De Laborde's facsimile, but they have been struck through, and I am unable to decipher them.

[4] The first word in the line is *uch*, but it is struck out, and *gutenberg* is added in the margin. See De Laborde's facsimile.

[5] vff—sy added in the margin.

Item Dame *Ennel*, the wife of Hans Schulheiss, wood-merchant, has said that *Lorentz Beildeck* at one time came into her house to *Claus Dritzehen*, her cousin, and said to him: 'dear Claus Dritzehen,[1] *the blessed Andres Dritzehen has four pieces*[2] *lying in a press; now, Gutenberg has requested that you will take them out of the press and separate them, the one from the other, that no one may know what it is, because he would not like that anybody saw it.*'

This witness has also said: 'When she was [staying] with *Andres Dritzehen*, her cousin, she often helped him to make the work by day and night.' She also said 'that she knew well that *Andres Dritzehen*, her blessed cousin, had, at one time, mortgaged his capital, but whether he used that for the work she did not know.'

[1] Here follow in the original the words "*min Juncher* (*Juncker*, De Laborde) *Hanns Gutemberg* (*Guttemberg*, De Laborde) *hatt uch gebetten das;*" *i.e.*, "my Juncker (Nobleman, esquire), Hanns Gutemberg has requested you," but the words seem to have been struck through.

[2] Schoepflin has *paginas*.

Item Hanns Sidenneger hat[1] geseit das jme|| Andres Dritzehen selig dick und vil geseit habe,|| das er gros gelt uff das egemelte werk[2] geleit|| habe . . . . .[3] und in vil costete und sprach|| damit zü diesem[4] gezugen er wuste nit wie|| er darinne tun sollte,[5] Also antwurte jme dieser[4]|| gezuge und sprach Andres bistu darin|| kommen so müstu je ouch darus kommen,|| Also sprach Andres aber zü disem|| gezugen er müste das sine versetzen, antwurt jm|| diser gezuge so versetze es und sage nyemand|| nutzit davon, das habe nu Andres geton|| ob aber der summa uf die zit vil oder lutzel gewesen sy|| wisse er nit.||

Item *Hanns Sidenneger* has said 'that the blessed *Andres Dritzehen* had told him over and over again that he had spent much money on the said work . . . . and that it cost him much, and, therefore, said to him (witness), he did not know how he should act in this matter.' Then this witness answered him and said: 'Andres, hast thou got into it, thou must get out of it also.' Then Andres said to this witness: 'he had to mortgage his property,' and this witness answered him: 'yes, mortgage it and tell nobody anything about it;' Andres has done this now, though he did not know whether the sum, at that time, had been large or small.

Item Hannss Schultheiss hat[1] geseit das Lorentz|| Beildeck zu einer zit heim inn sin huss kommen|| sy zü Claus Dritzehen als|| dieser[4] gezuge jn heim gefürt hette, Als Andres Dritzehen|| sin bruder selige von todes wegen abgangen was, und|| sprach da Lorentz Beildeck zu Claus Dritzehen, Andres|| Dritzehen uwer bruder selige hat iiij. stücke undenan inn|| einer pressen liegen,[6] da hatt uch Hanns Gutemberg gebetten|| das ir die daruss nement und uff die presse legent|| von einander so kann[7] man nit gesehen was das ist,|| Also gieng Claus Dritzehen und suchete die stücke do vant|| er nutzit, Diser gezuge hat ouch geseit das er vor|| guter zit von Andres Dritzehen gehört habe ee er von todes wegen|| abgangen sy das er sprach, das werck hette jn me dann|| III^c^ guldin costet.||

Item *Hanns Schultheiss* has said that *Lorentz Beildeck* at one time came to his house to *Claus Dritzehen*, when this witness had conducted him thither, when *Andres Dritzehen*, his blessed brother, had died, and then *Lorentz Beildeck* said to *Claus Dritzehen*: '*Andres Dritzehen*, your blessed brother, *has four pieces*[1] *lying underneath in a press*, and *Hanns Gutemberg* has requested you *that you should take them out of it and lay them separate on the press*, so that nobody can see what it is.' Therefore *Claus Dritzehen* went and searched for the pieces,[2] but found nothing. This witness has also said that he had heard, some time ago, from *Andres Dritzehen*, before he died, that he had said the work had cost him more than 300 guilders.

[1] hatt, Schoepflin.
[2] werck, Schoepflin.
[3] De Laborde places here five spots; Schoepflin's text runs on.
[4] dis-, Schoepflin.
[5] solte, Schoepflin.
[6] ligen, Schoepflin.
[7] kan, Schoepflin.

[1] Schoepflin has *paginas*.
[2] Schoepflin has *formas*.

Item Cunrad Sahspach hatt geseit das Andres Heilman|| zu einer zit zu jme komen sy inn Kremer gasse und sprach|| zu jme, lieber Cunrad als Andres Dritzehen|| abgangen ist da hastu die pressen gemaht[1] vnd weist|| vmb die sache do gang dohin vnd[2] nym die stücke|| vss der pressen vnd zerlege sü von einander so weis niemand[3]|| was es ist, da nu diser gezuge das tun wolte und|| also suchete das were uff Sanct|| Steffans[4]tag nehst vergangen do was das ding hinweg,|| Diser gezuge hatt ouch geseit das Andres Dritzehen selige|| zu einer zit gelt umb jn gelehenet habe das|| habe er zu dem werck gebruchet, Er hat[5] ouch|| geseit das Andres Dritzehen selige jme zu einer zit geseit habe|| und clagete er müste pfenning gelt versetzen, sprach diser|| gezuge das ist böse, doch bistu darin kommen, so mustu ouch|| darus, und also wisse er wol das er sin pfenning gelt|| versetzt habe.||

Item *Cunrad Sahspach* has said that *Andres Heilman* came to him at one time in the Kremer street and said to him: 'dear Conrad, as *Andres Dritzehen* has died and *thou hast made the press and knowst of the affair, so go thither and take the pieces*[1] *out of the press and take them the one from the other, then nobody knows what it is.*' Now, when this witness wished to do this and searched, which was on St. Stephen's day last, the thing was gone. This witness has also said 'that the blessed *Andres Dritzehen* had, at a certain time, borrowed money from him, which he used for the work.' He has also said 'that the blessed *Andres Dritzehen* had told him at one time and complained that he had to mortgage his income,' to which this witness replied: 'this is bad, but if thou hast got into it, thou must also get out of it;' and therefore he knew well that he had mortgaged his income.

Item Wernher Smalriem hatt geseit das er|| . . . . [6]|| by iij. oder vier koüffe geton|| habe, wen aber das anegienge wisse er nit, und under|| andern ist ein kouff gewesen by C. und XIII. guldin,|| an demselben gelt hant ir drye für LX. guldin|| versiglet, do hatt Andres Dritzehen selige XX. angehürt,[7]|| und uff ein zit vor dem zile sprach Andres Dritzehen zu|| disem gezugen er solte heim kom-

Item *Wernher Smalriem* has said that he . . . . had made about three or four purchases, but did not know whom it concerned; and among other things there was a purchase of 113 guilders, towards which money three of them had subscribed for 60 guilders, while the blessed *Andres Dritzehen* engaged for 20 guilders. And at a certain time, before the term, *Andres Dritzehen*

[1] So in Laborde's facsimile.

[2] There seems to be *er* after *vnd* in De Laborde's facsimile, but he does not give it in his text.

[3] Schoepflin and De Laborde print *nyemand*, but the latter's facsimile gives *niemand*.

[4] Steffanns, Schoepflin.

[5] hatt, Schoepflin.

[6] De Laborde prints here a line of spots, but does not say why; Schoepflin's text runs on.

[7] angebürt, Schoepflin.

[1] Schoepflin has *paginas*.

men und die XX. gl.|| nemen, Antwurt jme diser gezuge er solte jme das|| gelt zusamen bringen und insammeln das tett Andres,|| und also darnach kam Andres Dritzehen aber zu disem|| gezugen und sprach, das gelt wer by einander inn Herrn|| Anthonien Heilman hus da[1] solte er das holen, das|| tett diser gezuge und nam das gelt inn Herrn Anthonien|| hus, und das übrige[2] gelt das habe allewegen|| Fridel von Seckingen bezahlt.[3]||

said to this witness 'that he should come home and take the 20 guilders.' But this witness answered, 'he should bring the money together and collect for him,' which *Andres* did. But afterwards *Andres Dritzehen* came again to this witness and said: 'that the money was together in the house of Mr. *Anthonie Heilman*, where he could fetch it,' which this witness did, and took the money in Mr. Anthonie's house, and the rest of the money was certainly paid by *Fridel von Seckingen.*

Item Mydehart Stocker hat[4] geseit Als Andres|| Dritzehen selige uff Sanct Johannis tag zu Winachten[5]|| do man den Krutzgang tett sich nydergeleit habe|| und siech wart do lag er inn dis gezugen stuben|| an eim bette, Also kam nu diser gezuge zu|| jme und sprach, Andres wie got es,|| Antwurt er jme ich weis werlich mir ist gar tötlich|| und sprach damit, soll ich sterben so wolte ich das|| ich nye inn die geselleschafft kommen wer, sprach diser|| gezuge wie so, sprach er aber do weis ich wol das mine brüdere|| mit Gutemberg nyemer überkommen kunnent, || sprach diser gezuge, ist dann die gemeinschaft[6] nit|| verschrieben[7] oder sint keine lute da gewesen, sprach Andres|| ja es ist verschrieben,[7] do frogete jn diser gezuge wie|| die gemeinschafft zugangen wer, do seite er jme wie|| das Andres Heilmann,[8] Hanns Riffe, Gutemberg und er inn|| eine gemeinschafft kommen werent, darin hetten Andres|| Heilman und er jr je-

Item *Mydehart Stocker* has said: 'When the blessed *Andres Dritzehen*, on St. John's day at Christmas, when the procession took place, lay down and became ill, he was lying in the room of this witness on a bed. And this witness came to him and said: 'Andres, how are you?' to which he replied: 'I know I am mortally ill,' and also said: 'if I were to die I should wish never to have joined the partnership.' This witness asked, why. To which he replied: 'I know well that my brothers never can agree with *Gutemberg.*' Said this witness: 'has then the association not been written down, or have no persons been present?' Said Andres: 'yes, it has been written down.' Then this witness asked him, how the partnership had been made, to which he replied 'that *Andres Heilmann, Hanns Riffe, Gutemberg*, and himself had entered into partnership, to which, as he recollected, *Andres Heilman* and him-

[1] do, Schoepflin.
[2] überige, Schoepflin.
[3] bezalt, Schoepflin.
[4] hatt, Schoepflin.
[5] Winahten, Schoepflin.
[6] -schafft, Schoepflin.
[7] verschriben, Schoepflin.
[8] -man, Schoepflin.

glicher LXXX. guldin geleit, alz er behalten habe|| Also sü nu inn der gemeinschafft werent do werent|| Andres Heilman und er zu Gutemberg kommen zu[1] Sanct|| Arbogast do hette er nu ettliche Kunst vor jnen verborgen|| die er jnen nit verbunden was zu zeugen, darane hetten|| sü nu nit ein gevallen gehebt und hetten daruff|| die gemeinschafft abgeton und ein ander gemeinschafft|| mitteinander verfangen also das Andres Heilman und er jr jeglicher zu den ersten|| LXXX. guldin so vil geben und legen solte das es V^c guldin|| wurdent, das[2] sie auch gethan habe[2] und|| werent sü zwene ein man inn der gemeinschafft,|| und desglich soltent Gutemberg und Hanns Riffe|| jr jeglicher innsunders ouch als vil legen als die zwene,|| und daruff solte Gutemberg alle sine kunst die er kunde|| nit vor jnen verbergen, und darüber wer ein gemeinschafft|| brief gemaht worden, und wer das jr einre inn der|| gemeinschafft abgienge so soltent die übrigen[3] gemeinere desselben|| abgangen erben C. guldin harus geben, und das übrig[3]|| gelt und was inn die gemeinschafft gehorte solte dann under den andern|| gemeinern inn der gemeinschafft bliben. Diser Gezuge hatt ouch|| geseit das jme Andres Dritzehen selige zu der zit ouch|| geseit habe so wisse er ouch das von jme selbs wol, das|| er ettlich sin pfenning gelt versetzt[4] habe, ob aber das|| vil oder wenig oder obe er das zu dem werck gebruchet|| habe oder nit wisse er nit.||

In præsentia Diebolt Brant und [5] Rotgebe.||

self had each contributed 80 guilders.' And when they were in this partnership, *Andres Heilman* and himself came to *Gutemberg* at St. Arbogast, *where he had concealed several*[1] *arts*[1] *from them, which he was not obliged to show them.* This did not please them; whereupon they had broken up the partnership and replaced it by another to this effect, that *Andres Heilman* and himself should each add so much to the first 80 guilders that it would make 500 guilders, which they did, and they two were one man in the partnership.

And in the same way *Gutemberg* and *Hanns Riffe* should each contribute as much as the two, and then *Gutemberg* should *conceal*[2] *from them none of the arts he knew.*[2] Concerning this an association contract was made, and in case one of the partners died, then the others should pay 100 guilders to the heirs of the deceased, and the rest of the money and all that belonged to the association should remain in the partnership as the property of the other partners. This witness has also said that the blessed *Andres Dritzehen* had told him at that time 'that he knew very well from himself that he had often mortgaged his income,' though he did not know whether this was much or little, nor whether he had employed it for the work or not.

In the presence of Diebolt Brant and Rotgebe.

[1] Laborde prints *zu* without saying anything; Schoepflin prints between ( ) "supply *zu*."

[2] Schoepflin omits das—habe.

[3] überigen; überig, Schoepflin.

[4] versetzet, Schoepflin.

[5] Schoepflin adds: Jocop.

[1] Schoepflin translates: *nonnulla artis suæ arcana.*

[2] Schoepflin translates: *omnia artis suæ, quæ nosset, arcana communicaret.*

Herr Peter Eckhart lutpriester zu Sanct[1] Martin dixit|| das Andres Dritzehen selig in den Winahten virtagen noch||, jme schihte er solt sin Bihte hören, und da|| er zu jm kam und er gerne gebihte da|| fragete jn diser gezuge ob er yeman schuldig wer,| oder ob man jme schuldig wer, oder ob er utzit,| geben hette das solt er sagen, da sprach Andres er|| hette gemeinschafft mit etlichen, Andres Heilman | und andern, und da hette er wol II[c] guldin oder III[c] ussgeleit|| das er keinen pfenig hette, und seit ouch, das Andres Dritzehen dann zemol in den cleidern lege am bett.||

Mr. *Peter Eckhart*, parish priest at St. Martin, has said that the blessed *Dritzehen*, during the Christmas feastdays, sent to him to hear his confession, and when he came to him and he confessed freely, witness asked him 'whether he owed anybody anything, or whether any one was indebted to him, or whether he had given anything, he should say so;' whereupon *Andres* said, 'he had a partnership with several persons, *Andres Heilman* and others, and had laid out certainly 200 or 300 guilders, so that he had not a penny left;' and he also said that *Andres Dritzehen* at that time was lying in the bed in his clothes.

Thoman Steinbach het geseit das Hesse der underkouffer uff ein zit zu jm kam und,, frogte jn ob er keinen kouff wüste do man lutzel an verlure wann|| er wuste ettliche, und nante domit Johann Gutenberg, Andres|| Dritzehen und einen Heilman die bedörffte wol bar gelt,|| Also do kouffte diser gezug jnen xiiij. Lützelburger und wuste do-|| mit wol einen kouffman der sü wider kouffen wolt, und verkouffte sü ouch| widerumb und wurdent bi den XII½ guldin daran verlorn und ware[2] Fridel von Seckingen burge für sü und wart ouch in das|| kouffhus buch verschriben.||

Thoman Steinbach has said that *Hesse*, the retail-dealer, came to him at one time and asked him 'whether he knew of any purchase in which little could be lost;' as he knew several [persons], but mentioned among such *Johann Gutenberg*, *Andres Dritzehen*, and a [certain] *Heilmann*, who were likely to be in want of ready money. Then this witness bought for them 14 Lützelburger,[1] and knew a merchant who would buy them again, and he did sell them again, and 12½ guilders were lost by it; *Fridel von Seckingen* remained surety for them, and it was written down in the book of the sale-house.

Lorentz Beldeck het geseit das Johann Gutenberg jn zu einer zit|| geschickt het zu Claus Dritzehen, nach Andres sins bruders|| seligen dode und det Clausen Dritzehen sagen das er die presse|| die er hünder jm hett nieman oigete zoigete,[3] das ouch diser|| gezug det,

Lorentz Beildeck has said that *Johann Gutenberg* had sent him at one time to *Claus Dritzehen*, after the death of his blessed brother *Andres*, to tell *Claus Dritzehen that he should not show to any one the press which he had under his care;* which witness did. He

[1] Sant, Schoepflin.

[2] wart, Schoepflin.

[3] *oigete* and *zoigete* mean one and the same thing; one of the words is therefore superfluous.

[1] i.e. *Luxemburger*. I do not know what article is meant by this word.

und rette ouch me und sprach|| er solte sich bekumbern so vil und gon über die presse|| und die mit den zweyen würbelin uff dun so vielent die stucke|| von einander, dieselben stucke solt er dann in die presse|| oder uff die presse lege so kunde darnach nieman gesehen noch ut gemercken,|| und wenn jr leit uskeme so solt er zu Johann|| Gutenberg hinus komen[1] dann er het ettwas mit jn ze|| reden. Diser gezuge ist wol ze wissen das Johann Gutenberg Andres|| seligen nut ze dun sundern Andres Hans Gutenberg ze dun wer vnd|| jm sollichs ze zilen geben solt, in den zilen er ouch abging. Er het ouch|| geseit das er in nie keiner burse bi jme gewesen|| sig wann die burse nach den Winahten anging. Diser|| gezug het Andres Dritzehen seligen dick gesehen by Johann|| Gutenberg essen aber er gesach jn nie kein pfening geben.||

[Gutenberg] said, moreover, that he should take great care and *go to the press and open this by means of the two little buttons, whereby*[1] *the pieces would fall asunder.* He should, thereupon, *put those pieces in or on the press,*[1] *after which nobody could see or comprehend anything.* And if[2] he happened to go out[2] he was to come to *Johann Gutenberg*, who had something to talk about with him. This witness knew well that *Johann Gutenberg* owed nothing to the blessed *Andres*, but that *Andres* was indebted to *Gutenberg*, and was to pay him this debt by instalments, but died while he was paying it. He has also said that he had never been present at their reunion, since their reunions had taken place after Christmas. This witness had often seen the blessed *Andres Dritzehen* dine at *Johann Gutenberg's*, but he had never seen him give a penny.

Reimbolt von Ehenheim het geseit das er vor den Winahten|| unlang zu Andres kam un[2] frogte jn was er|| also mehte mit den nötlichen dingen domit er umging,|| Antwurt jm Andres selige Es hett jn me dann V^c guldin|| costet[3] doch so hoffte[4] er wann es us gefertiget wurde das|| sü gelt lösten ein güt notdurfft, do von er disem gezugen||

Reimbolt von Ehenheim has said that shortly before Christmas he came to *Andres* and asked him 'what he did with those nice things with which he was busy.' The blessed *Andres* answered him 'that it had cost him more than 500 guilders, but he hoped, when it should be ready, to gain a good quantity of money, with which he

[1] kumen, Schoepflin.
[2] und, Schoepflin.
[3] kostet, Schoepflin.
[4] hofftet, Schoepflin.

[1] Schoepflin has *ut paginae dilabantur in partes, easque partes vel intra vel supra prelum poneret.*

[2] Schoepflin translates: "utque justis solutis." De Laborde (Débuts de l'imprimerie à Strasbourg, p. 33) translates: "et quand il sortirait." Dr. Van der Linde (Haarlem Legend, the Hague, 1870, p. 25) translates: "en mogt hy uitgaan," *i.e.* in Engl., "and if he happened to go out." I have adopted this translation, but am unable to say whether it is correct. The German *ir* must mean *their;* but I do not know the meaning of *leit.*

und andern gelt geben möhte und ouch alles das leides ergetzet|| würde. Diser gezug het geseit das er jm des selben moles|| VIII. guldin lech wenn er gelt haben müst. So hett ouch dis|| gezugen kellerin Andres ettwie dick gelt geluhen, Andres|| kam ouch zu einer zit zu disem gezugen mit einem ring|| den schetzet er für XXX. guldin, den versatt er jm ze Ehenheim|| für V. güldin hünder die Juden. Diser gezug het ouch geseit|| das im wol wissen sig das er im herbst II. halb omen|| gesottens wins in zweyen vesseln gemaht het do schanckte|| er Johann Gutenberg+ Omen und den andern[1] halben omen|| schenckte er Midehart und schenckte ouch Gutenberg|| etwie uil biren, Andres bat ouch disen gezugen zu einer|| zit da[2] er jm II. halb fuder wins kouffte, das ouch diser gezug|| dett, und von denselben II. halben fudern hand[3] Andres|| Dritzehn und Andres Heilman Hans Gutenberg|| das eine halb fuder gemein geschenckt.||

should pay this witness and others and see all his sufferings rewarded.' This witness has said that on that occasion he lent him 8 guilders, as he was in want of money. The housekeeper of this witness had often lent money to *Andres*, and *Andres* came once to this witness with a ring which he valued at 30 guilders, which he pawned for him at Ehenheim with the Jews for 5 guilders. This witness, moreover, said that he knew well that, in the autumn, he had put two half-omens of sodden wine into two vessels and sent one half-omen to *Johann Gutenberg*, and presented the other half to *Midehart*, and also presented *Gutenberg* with a quantity of beer. *Andres* also requested this witness at one time to buy him two half-measures of wine, which witness did, and of these two half-measures *Andres Dritzehn* and *Andres Heilman* presented one to *Hans Gutenberg*.

Hans Niger von Bischoviszheim het geseit das|| Andres zu jm kam und sprach er bedörffte gelts, dar-|| umb so müste er jm und andern sinen lehenluten|| dessen getrangen dun, wenn er het ettwas under henden|| daruff kunde er nit gelts genug uffbringen, Also|| do frogte diser gezug was er schaffen hett, Antwurt|| er, er wer ein spiegelmacher, Also do stalte diser|| gezuge tröschen und furte sin korn gon Molssheim und|| Ehenheim und verkouffte das do und bezalt jn. Diser|| gezug het ouch geseit das er und Reimbolt jm zu einer|| zit II. halb fuder wines kouffen und furte es diser gezug|| har, und also er kam bi Sant Arbegast do

Hans Niger von Bischoviszheim has said that *Andres* came to him and said 'that he was in want of money, wherefore he had to appeal to him and his other money-lenders, as he had something in hand on which he could not spend money enough.' Therefore this witness asked him what he was doing, to which he replied '*he was a manufacturer of looking-glasses.*' Then this witness had his corn ground and took it to Molssheim and Ehenheim, where he sold it, and paid him [the money]. This witness has also said that he [*Dritzehen*] and *Reimbolt* bought from him at one time two half-measures of wine, and he effected the trans-

[1] andren, Schoepflin.
[2] das, Schoepflin.
[3] hant, Schoepflin.

hatt er|| ouch ½ omen gesottens wins uff dem wagen, den nam|| Andres und trug jn Johann Gutenberg heim, und ouch|| ettwie vil biren, und von denselben II. halben fudern|| verschanckte Andres selige und Andres Heilmann|| Johann Gutenberg I. halb fuder wins.||

port of it; and when he came to St. Arbegast he had also half an omen of sodden wine on his cart, which *Andres* took and carried it in to *Johann Gutenberg*, and also a good deal of beer; and of these two half-measures the blessed *Andres* and *Andres Heilmann* presented one half to *Johann Gutenberg.*

In bywesen Böschwilrs.

In the presence of *Böschwilr.*

Item Fridel von Seckingen hat geseit, das Gutenberg[1]|| ein kouff geton habe und das er fur jnen bürge würde und das er nit|| anders wust dann das es Her Anthonie Heilman ouch|| anging,[2] und das aber darnoch die schulde|| von des selben kouffs wegen bezalt worden sy. Er hat|| ouch geseit, das Gutenberg[1] Andres Heilmann[3] und Andres|| Dritzehen jnen gebetten haben jr bürge zu werden, gegen Stoltz|| Peters dochterman[4] vür CI. guldin, das habe er geton,|| also, das sü drye jm deshalb[5] einen schadeloss brieff geben|| soltent, der ouch geschriben und mit Gutenbergs[6]|| und Andres Heilmans Insigeln versigelt würde, Aber|| Andres Dritzehem hette jn alles hünder jm und kunde jm|| von jm nit versiegelt[7] werden, doch so habe Gutenberg|| solich gelt darnoch alles bezahlt[8] in der vastmesse nehst vergangen.|| Dirre gezuge hat ouch geseit, das er von der obgenannten[9] dryer gemeinschafft|| nit gewisset habe, dann er nye dar zu gezogen noch|| dabei[10] gewesen sy.||

Item *Fridel von Seckingen* has said that *Gutenberg* had made a purchase, and that he had become surety for him, and that he did not know otherwise but that it concerned Mr. *Anthonie Heilman* also, and that afterwards the debt concerning this purchase had been paid. He also said that *Gutenberg, Andres Heilmann,* and *Andres Dritzehen* had requested him to become their surety with *Stoltz,* the husband of Peter's daughter, for 101 guilders, which he did, in this way that these three should give him, on this account, a letter of indemnification, which indeed had been written and sealed with the seals of *Gutenberg* and *Andres Heilman.* But *Andres Dritzehen* always delayed the matter, and he could not induce him to seal it. *Gutenberg,* however, paid afterwards all the money at the time of the fair of last Lent. This witness has also said that he did not know of the partnership of the above three, because he had never been joined to it, nor had been present.

1 -burg, Schoepflin.
2 angieng, Schoepflin.
3 -man, Schoepflin.
4 doht-, Schoepflin.
5 deshalp, Schoepflin.
6 -burgs, Schoepflin.
7 versigelt, Schoepflin.
8 bezalt, Schoepflin.
9 obgenanten, Schoepflin.
10 dobei, Schoepflin.

[*Second* entry.]

Gutenbergs Worheit wider Jörge Dritzehn. In bywesen Franz|| Berner und Böschwiler.||

Item Herr[1] Anthonie Heilman hat geseit Als er gewar wurde das Gutenberg|| Andres Dritzehen zu einem dirten teil wolte nehmen[2] in die Ochevart zu den Spiegeln|| do bete er jn gar flisseclich das er Andres sinen bruder ouch darin neme, wolte er|| zu mol gern umb jn verdienen[3], do spreche er zu jm, er enwuste Andres Fründe[4]|| möhten morn sprechen es were göckel werk[5], und were jm nit wol zu willen,|| do über bete er jn und mahte jm einen zedel, den solte er jnen beden zoigen und|| sollten[6] daruff gar wol zu rate werden,[7] den zedel brehte er jnen und wurdent zu|| rote das sü es also woltent tun, was im zedel verzeichent stunde, und ginge es|| also mit jm[8]. In disen dingen bäte Andres Dritzehen disen gezugen|| jm umb geld zu helffen, do spreche er, hette er gut underpfant, er wolte jm balde|| helffen und hülffe jm also zu leste umb LXXXX. ℔ und brehte jm das gelt hinuss|| zu Sanct[9] Arbgast, und domit loste er den Frowen Sant Agnesen II. ℔ geltz abe,|| und sprehe[10] dirre gezuge was sol dir so vil geltz du bedarffst[11] doch nit me

Gutenberg's testimony against *Jörge Dritzehen.* In the presence of Franz Berner and Böschwiler.

Item Mr. *Anthonie Heilman* has said: When he became aware that *Gutenberg* would accept *Andres Dritzehen* for a third part in the pilgrimage to Aix-la-Chapelle about the looking-glasses, he requested him urgently to accept also his brother *Andres* if he wished to render him [*Anthonie*] a great service. He [*Gutenberg*] then said to him, 'he was afraid that the friends of *Andres* would speak of it as sorcery, which he would not like.' On that account he [*Anton*] requested him again, and drew up a contract which he should show to both, and which they should discuss carefully; he brought him the contract, and they resolved to do according to the contract, which was, therefore, agreed upon. In the midst of these arrangements *Andres Dritzehen* requested this witness to help him with money; to which he replied that, if he had a good pledge, he would soon help him, and at last assisted him with 90 ℔s., and brought him the money at St. Arbgast, whereby he redeemed 2 ℔s. of money from the St. Agnes nuns; and this wit-

---

1 Her, Schoepflin.
2 nemen, Schoepflin.
3 De Laborde has here a star, but does not explain what it means. Schoepflin's text runs on.
4 frunde, Schoepflin.
5 werck, Schoepflin; but wrongly. See Laborde's facsimile.
6 solten, Schoepflin.
7 De Laborde places here two stars without explaining what they mean.
8 Schoepflin adds: in.
9 Sant, Schoepflin.
10 spreche, Schoepflin.
11 bedarfft, Schoepflin.

dann LXXX.|| guldin, do antwurte er jme, er müste sust ouch gelt han,|| und das wer II. oder III. tage in der fasten vor unser Frawen[1]tage|| [d]o gebe er LXXX. guldin Gutenberg, So gebe dirre gezuge ouch LXXX. guldin, wann|| die beredunge were LXXX. guldin jegelichem teil, umb das übrige[2] dirte teil|| so dann Gutenberg noch hette, und wurde das gelt Gutenberg, umb den teil|| und um die kunst, und wurde in kein gemeinschafft geleit. Darnoch|| so habe Gutenberg zu disem gezugen gesprochen Er müste ein anderes[3] gedenken[5]|| das es in allen sachen glich würde, sit er jn vor so vil geton hette und gantz|| mitenander in eins kement, nit das einer vor dem andern ut verhelen möhte,|| so dienet ouch es wol zu dem andern.

Der rede was dirre gezuge fro|| und rümete es den zwein, und darnoch über lang do spräche er aber dieselbe|| rede, do bäte in dirre gezuge aber als vor, und spräche er wolte es umb|| jn verdienen.

Darnoch so mehte er jm ein zedel uff dieselbe rede und spreche|| zu disem gezugen, heiszen sü wol zu rote werden, obe es jr gefug sy, das|| dete er und wurdent daruff etwie lange zu rate, Sü nement in joch ouch|| zu rate, do spreche er sit dem mole das yetz so vil gezüges do ist, und|| gemaht werde das uwer teil gar nohe ist gegen uwerem gelt, so wurt uch|| doch die kunst vergeben.

Also gingen[4]

[1] Frowen, Schoepflin, and, perhaps, also Laborde.

[2] überige, Schoepflin.

[3] anders gedencken, Schoepflin.

[4] gingent, Schoepflin.

ness asked, 'what do you ask so much money for, as you don't want more than 80 guilders?' He replied that 'he wanted still more money, and that it was two or three days in Lent before Lady Day that he had to give 80 guilders to *Gutenberg*.' This witness also gave 80 guilders, as the agreement was 80 guilders for each share, and the other third part, which *Gutenberg* still had, would become *Gutenberg's* property, as his share and for his art, and would not be put into any partnership. Afterwards *Gutenberg* spoke to this witness that 'he had to mention something else, namely, that there should be equality in everything because he [*Anton*] had done so much for him, and that they should understand each other well that the one should conceal nothing from the other, and that it should serve also the others.'[1] This witness was pleased by this conversation, and spoke highly of it to the other two, and long afterwards he [*Gutenberg*] repeated this conversation, and this witness requested him as before and said that he wished to make himself worthy of it. After this he made a contract according to this proposition, and said to this witness: 'Tell them that they should consider it carefully whether this be convenient to them.' This he did, and they discussed this point a long time, and even consulted him [*Gutenberg*], who said afterwards at a certain time: 'there are at present so many tools ready and in course of preparation that your part is very near your own money [which you advanced], and so the art will be confided to you gratuitously.' In

[1] Schoepflin has here *idque ad reliquum opus pertinere.*

sü die sache mit jme in, umb zwen punten, den einen gar abe zu tunde, und den andern, bass zu lüternde. Der punt abe zu tunde was, das sü nit wolten, verbunden sin, von Hans Riffen wegen gross oder clein, wan sü nit von' jme hettent, was sü hetten das hetten sü von Gutenbergs wegen. | Der ander punte zu lüternde was, wer es das jr einer[1] von todes" wegen abeginge, das das bass gelütert würde, und wart der also, gelütert, das man des erben so abeginge, solte vür alle ding gemaht, oder ungemaht vür gelt geleit so sich jegelichem teil gebürt zu kosten; zu zu legen und formen und allen gezügk nützit usgenommen, noch,| den fünff joren geben hundert guldin, do dett er jn gross vorteil;' wer es das er abeginge, wan er liess jn ouch darin gon, alles so er für| sinen kosten solte voran han genommen zu sinem teil, und solten doch| sinen erben nit me dann[2] hundert guldin geben für alle ding," als der andern einer. Und geschach das uf das, wer ess das jr einer,' abeginge, das man nit muste allen erben die kunst wisen und uffen; sagen oder offenboren, und das were alles eime also gut als dem'| andern.

Darnoch so habent die zwene Andres disem gezugen under den Kürsenern geseit, das sü mit Gutenberg eins worden sient von des' zedels wegen, und hette jnen den punten von Hans Riffen wegen,| abegelon und wolte jnen den lesten punten bass lütern, so in dem, nehsten artickel stet, und seitent ouch doby das Andres Dritzehen hette, Gutenberg geben XL. guldin, und dis gezugen bruder jm L. guldin, ; wann die beredunge uff das zil was fünfzig guldin, als der' zedel wiset, und darnach in

this manner they agreed with him on two points, one of which was to be quite done with, and the other to be explained well. The point which was to be regarded as settled was that they wished to be under no obligation to *Hans Riffen*, either great or small, as they had nothing from him; what they had they had it from *Gutenberg.* The matter which was to be explained was that, if one of them happened to die, exact explanation should be given; and they decided that, at the end of the 5 years, they should pay to the heirs of deceased, *for all things made or unmade*, for the money advanced, which every partner had to pay in the expenses, and *for the forms* and *for all tools, nothing excepted*, 100 guilders. In case, therefore, of his death, it would be a great advantage to them, because he left them everything which he could have taken as his part for the expenses, and yet they had not to pay his heirs more than a hundred guilders for everything, just as one of the others. And this was stipulated in order that, if any one died, they should not be under the necessity of *teaching, telling, or revealing the art* to all the heirs, which was as favourable to the one as to the others. Thereupon the two *Andreses* told witness [i.e., *Anton Heilmann*], at the reunion of the furriers, that they had agreed with *Gutenberg* regarding the contract, and that he had settled the point regarding *Hanns Riffen*, and wished to explain to them the last point further as it was put in the next article. They also said that *Andres Dritzehen* had given 40 guilders to *Gutenberg*, and the witness's brother [*Andres Heilmann*] had given him 50 guilders, as the agreement was 50 guilders for this

[1] keiner, Schoepflin.
[2] wann, Schoepflin.

den nehsten Winahten XX. guldin, und das|| syent die Winahten nehst vergangen, und dann darnach|| zu halbvasten aber gelt als der zedel wiset do sich dirre gezuge uff-|| gezuhet, und spricht ouch[1] diser gezuge das er den zedel bekenne by den|| zilen, und würde das gelt nit in gemeinschafft geleit|| es solte Gutenberges sin. So habe ouch Andres Dritzehen|| kein burse mit uns geleit und nye kein gelt usgeben, do usse|| für essen und trinken[2] so sü do usse dotent.

Dirre gezuge hot[3] ouch|| geseit das er wol wisse das Gutenberg unlange vor Wihnahten|| sinen kneht sante zu den beden Andresen, alle for-

[1] auch, Schoepflin.
[2] trincken, Schoepflin.
[3] hat, Schoepflin.

term, as was shown by the contract, and afterwards, the following Christmas, 20 guilders, which was Christmas last, and then afterwards, at mid-Lent [the fourth Sunday in Lent], as much as the contract showed which witness had signed. And witness also said that he acknowledges the contract by the terms, and the money was not put into the association, but was to belong to *Gutenberg*. Neither had *Andres Dritzehen* lived in common with them, and had never spent any money, not even for the food and drink which they took outside [the town, *i.e.*, at St. Arbogast, where *Gutenberg* lived]. This witness also said that he knew very well that *Gutenberg*, shortly before Christmas, had sent his servant to the two *Andreses to*[1]

[1] Schoepflin translated: "ut omnes formas peteret, quæ in conspecu ejus *disjectæ*, quod nonnulla in illis emendanda reperiret." Meermann (Orig. typogr., II., 76) has: "ut omnes formas peteret, easque in conspectu eius dissolutas, et complures etiam formas defectu laborasse." De Laborde translates: "pour chercher les formes, afin qu'il pût s'assurer qu'elles avaient été *séparées* et que même plusieurs formes lui avaient donné du regret." Dr. Van der Linde (Haarlem Legend, p. 27) translated: "om alle formen te halen; deze werden voor zyn oogen *versmolten*, wat hem van ettelyke formen leed deed;" *i.e.* in English: "to fetch all the forms; these were *melted* before his eyes, which he regretted on account of several forms." Why does Dr. Van der Linde use here the word *melted*, whereas it appears plainly enough from the depositions of the other witnesses that there is question of taking something to pieces? He explains in his Haarlem Legend, p. 36: "*Zurlossen* = *zerlassen* means 'to melt.'" On p. 27 of his "Gutenberg" he maintains this explanation and illustrates it with the Dutch *laten*, *ontlaten*, which

men zu holen|| und würdent zur lossen das er ess sehe, und jn joch ettliche formen|| ruwete. Do noch do Andres selige abeginge, und dirre gezuge|| wol wuste das lüte gern hettent die presse gesehen, do spreche Gutenberg|| sü soltent noch der pressen senden er fohrte[1] das man sü sehe, do sante|| er sinen kneht harin sü zur legen, und wann er müssig were so|| wolte er mit jn reden, das entbot er jn. Er hat ouch geseit das von|| Reimbolt Muselers wegen und von sinen wegen synie[2] gedaht worden.||

fetch all the forms, and that they were taken asunder before his eyes, which he [either witness or *Gutenberg*] *regretted on account of several forms.* At the time that the blessed Andres died and this witness well knew that *people would have liked to see the press, Gutenberg said they should send for the press, as he feared that any one should see it, whereupon he sent his man to take it to pieces ;* and when he had the time he would talk with him, which was what he proposed to him. He has also said that on the part of *Reimbolt Museler* and on his own part they had never been summoned.

Item Herr[3] Anthonie Heilman hat anderwerbe geseit, das der lengeste|| zedel under der[4] zwein zedeln gewesen sy von dem in siner obegemelten sage|| stet, so Gutenberg den zwein Andres geben liess sich daruff zubedenken,[5]|| und von des andern zedels wegen

Item Mr. *Anthonie Heilmann* has also said that the longest of the two contracts was that mentioned above which *Gutenberg* caused to be given to the two *Andreses* to consult about it ;

and of the other contract, which was

[1] forhte, Schoepflin.
[2] sy nye, Schoepflin.
[3] Her, Schoepflin.
[4] den, Schoepflin.
[5] -dencken, Schoepflin.

means to thaw, to melt (said of snow). On p. 515 he returns to the word and tells us: "*zerlassen* means *to melt*, and not (!) *to take asunder, to distribute* a page [of type]' (*zerlassen* ist *schmelzen* und nicht *auseinandernemen*, einen schriftsaz distribuieren). After this follows the opinion of an educated printer . . . .

I have translated *zurlossen* by *taken asunder*, and not by *melted*. *Zurlossen* is a dialectic pronunciation of *zerlâssen*, which is a past part. of *zerlassen*, which means *to take asunder, to separate*, just as well as it may mean *to melt* (*cf.* Lexer, Mittelhochdeutsches Handwörterb., iii., 1072, i.v. *zerlâszen*) ; and I may observe that the first meaning is the prevailing one: *cf.* Leo, Angels. Glossar, col. 452 ; Mor. Heyne's Heliand, Paderborn, 1866, Glossar, voce *lâtan*, &c., &c. With respect to the words *und—ruwete*, De Laborde and Dr. Van der Linde seem to be right.

der der erst gewesen sin sol, do|| weis dirre gezuge nit obe er es sy oder nit, dann es sy jm usser|| synne gangen. Er hat ouch geseit, das Andres Dritzehn[1] und Andres|| Heilman dem obgenanten Gutenberg ein halb[2] fuder wins geben hant|| vür das sü by Im du usse gessen und getrunken[3] hant. So habe ouch Andres|| Dritzehn[4] Im besonders geben I. omen gesottens wins und by hundert Regelsbiern|| So hat er ouch geseit, das er sinen bruder darnoch gefraget habe w a n n[5]|| sü anfingent zu leren, do habe er jm geantwurt, Gutenberg breste|| noch X. guldin von Andres Dritzehn,[4] an den funftzig|| guldin so er an r u c k e s[5] geben solt han.||

said to have been the first, witness did not know whether this was the case or not, as he had forgotten it. He has also said that *Andres Dritzehn* and *Andres Heilman* had given to the said *Gutenberg* half a measure of wine in return for what they had eaten and drunk with him outside [the town]. *Andres Dritzehn*, in particular, presented him with one omen of sodden wine and nearly a hundred flasks of beer. He has also said that he asked his brother *when* they commenced to learn, to which he replied that *Gutenberg* still claimed 10 guilders from *Andres Dritzehen* of the 50 which he had to pay on St. Henry's day.

Item Hans[6] Dünne der goltsmyt hat geseit, das er vor dryen|| joren oder doby Gutemberg by den hundert guldin abe verdienet habe|| alleine das zu dem trucken gehöret.||

Item *Hans Dünne*, the goldsmith, has said that three years ago or thereabout he had earned from Gutenberg nearly 100 guilders *merely for that which belonged to printing.*

Item Midehart Stocker hat geseit[7] dass er wol wisse das Andreas xiij|| den vj. [8] gelts versetzet habe vür CXX. ℔. und das|| das selbe gelt Claus xiij. sinen brüd worden sy, und das der|| selbe Claus solich gelt den von Bischoffsheim by Rosheim geben habe|| vür xij. L. gelt lipgedinge[9] und das er

Item *Midehart Stocker* has said that he knew well that *Andreas Dritzehen* had mortgaged the . . .[1] VI [℔.] . . .[1] of money for 120 ℔s., and that this same money had become the property of *Claus Dritzehen* his brother, and that the same *Claus* had given this money to those of Bischofsheim near Ros-

---

[1] -zehen, Schoepflin.
[2] halp, Schoepflin.
[3] getruncken, Schoepflin.
[4] -zehen, Schoepflin.
[5] Laborde spaces these words; Schoepflin prints them in the ordinary way.
[6] Hanns, Schoepflin.
[7] Schoepflin prints here five dots, and omits all that follows till and including the next *geseit* in this paragraph.
[8] The same space is left in Laborde's text.
[9] De Laborde has liszgedinge, but erroneously, I suppose.

[1] There seems to be a *lacuna* here in the manuscript.

andres xiij. auch zu im|| gesetzet habe, Also wer es das er es abginge dan er so solte Andres|| die selbe lipgedinge sinn lebetage auch nyessen, Und[1] das gelt das|| er in gemeinschafft legen solte wurde beret zu zilen zu geben,[2]|| Er hat auch geseit das er von Andres xiij [i. e. Dritzehen] gehort habe, das er|| spreche hülff In got das das gemahte werk[3] in[4] der gemeinschaft[4] vertriben wurde, So hoffte|| und truwete er vsz allen sinen nöten zu kummen||

heim for 12 ℔s. of money of a life-annuity[1] . . . . .

when *Andres* would enjoy the same life-annuity during his lifetime. And it was agreed that the money which he would put into the association should be paid by instalments. He has also said that he had heard from *Andres Dritzehen* that he said may God help him that *the work made in the partnership might be sold*, in which case he hoped and trusted that he would get out of all his needs.

[*Third* entry: Querimonia of Lorentz Beildeck.]

ICH Lorentz Beildeck clage uch Herren der meister abe Jorg Dritzehen, Als hatt er mir für uch mine gnedigen Herren meister und Rath[5] gebotten Ime ein worheit zu sagen, da ich ouch by minem geswornen eide geseit habe was ich davon wuste, Als ist nu der egenannt Jörg Dritzehen darnoch aber für uch komen und hatt einen botten anderwerbe an mich gevordert jme eine worheit zu sagen und hat damit geret ich habe vor nit wor geseit. Darzu hat er ouch zu mir offenlich geruffet, hörestu worsager du must mir wor sagen solte ich mit dir uff die leiter kommen, und hat mich damit frevenlich geschuldiget

I, *Lorentz Beildeck*, complain before you, Lords magistrates, on account of *Jorg Dritzehen*, that he —having summoned me before you, my gracious Lords magistrates and council, to give him a testimony, and I having said on my sworn oath what I knew of the matter—that yet the said *Jörg Dritzehen* has again come before you and forwarded a messenger to me to give him a testimony, and has said that at first I have not spoken the truth. He has also publicly said to me: hearest thou, witness, thou shalt have to tell me the truth even if I should have to go to the gallows with thee; and has therefore criminally accused

[1] Und—kummen has been given here according to De Laborde's facsimile, not according to his printed text.

[2] There is a sign in Laborde's facsimile, by the side of the line which he has omitted in his text, probably because he thought that the sign indicated that the line was to be deleted; but it appears to be nothing but a letter inadvertently written by the scribe and afterwards struck through.

[3] werck, Schoepflin.

[4] in—gem. added in the margin.

[5] Rat, Schoepflin.

[1] After this first life-annuity (Germ. *lipgedinge*) follow 19 words, of which I am unable to make out the exact meaning.

und gezugen das ich ein meincidiger bösewicht sye, da er mir doch von den gnaden Gottes unrecht geton hatt das doch swer böse sachen sint, etc.

me and represented that I am a perjured criminal, and has, by the grace of God, done me wrong, which is a bad affair.

[*Fourth* entry: List of Gutenberg's witnesses against Jerge Dritzehen.]

Dis ist Gutenbergs Worheit wider Jerge Dritzehen.

Item Her Anthonie Heilman.—Item Andres Heilman. — Item Claus Heilman. — Item Mudart Stocker.—Item Lorentz Beldeck. —Item Wernher Smalriem.—Item Fridel von Seckingen. — Item Ennel Drytzehen.—Item Conrat Saspach.—Item Hans Dunne.—Item Meister Hirtz.—Item Her Heinrich Olse.—Item Hans Riffe. —Item Her Johans Dritzehen.

This is *Gutenberg's* truth against *Jerge Dritzehen.*

Item Mr. *Anthonie Heilman.*—Item *Andres Heilman.* — Item *Claus Heilman.*—Item *Mudart Stocker.*—Item *Lorentz Beldeck.*—Item *Wernher Smalriem.*—Item *Fridel von Seckingen.*—Item *Ennel Drytzehen.*—Item *Conrat Saspach.* —Item *Hans Dunne.* — Item *Meister Hirtz.*—Item Mr. *Heinrich Olse.*—Item *Hans Riffe.*—Item Mr. *Johans Dritzehen.*—

[*Fifth* entry: List of Jerge Dritzehen's witnesses against Hans Gutenberg.]

Dis ist Jerge Dritzehen Worheit gegen Hans Gutenberg.

Item Lütpriester zu Sant Martin.—Item Fridel von Seckingen. —Item Jocop Imeler.—Item Hans Sydenneger.—Item Midhart Honöwe.—Item Hans Schultheis der holzman.[1]—Item Ennel Dritzehen sin husfröwe.—Item Hans Dunne der goltsmit.—Item Meister Hirtz. —Item Heinrich Bisinger.—Item Wilhelm von Schutter.—

Item Wernher Smalriem.—Item Thoman Steinbach.—Item Saspach Cunrat.—Item Lorentz Gutenbergs kneht und sin fröwe.—Item Reimbolt von Ehenheim.—Item Hans IX jor von Bischoffsheim.—Item Stöszer Nese von Ehenheim. —Item Berbel das clein fröwel.—

This is *Jerge Dritzehen's* truth against *Hans Gutenberg.*

Item the parish priest at St. Martin.—Item *Fridel von Seckingen.*—Item *Jocop Imeler.*—Item *Hans Sydenneger.*—Item *Midhart Honöwe.*—Item *Hans Schultheis,* the wood-merchant.—Item *Ennel Dritzehen,* his wife.—Item *Hans Dunne,* the goldsmith. — Item *Meister Hirtz.*—Item *Heinrich Bisinger.* — Item *Wilhelm von Schutter.*—Item *Wernher Smalriem.*—Item *Thoman Steinbach.*—Item *Saspach Cunrat.*—Item *Lorentz,* the servant of *Gutenberg,* and his wife.—Item *Reimbolt von Ehenheim.*—Item *Hans IX jor* (i.e., *nine year*) *von Bischoffsheim.* —Item *Stöszer Nese von Ehenheim.* —Item *Berbel,* the little

[1] holtzman, Schoepflin.

Item Her Jerge Saltzmütter.—Item Heinrich Sidenneger.—Item ein brieff über X. ℔ gelts hant die Herren zum jungen Sant Peter her Andres versetzt.—

Item ein brieff über II. ℔ gelts hant die Wurmser ouch.—Item Hans Ross der goltsmit und sin fröwe.—Item Her Gosse Sturm zu Sant Arbegast.—Item Martin Verwer.

woman.—Item Mr. *Jerge Saltzmütter.*—Item *Heinrich Sidenneger.*—Item a letter about 10 ℔s. of money, which the Canons of St. Peter jun. have pawned to Mr. *Andres.* — Item a letter about 2 ℔s. of money is in the hands of the people of Wurms.—Item *Hans Ross*, the goldsmith, and his wife.—Item Mr. *Gosse Sturm*, at St. Arbegast.—Item *Martin Verwer.*

[*Sixth* entry: Sentence of the Council.]

WIR Cune Nope der Meister und der Rat zu Strassburg thun kund[1] allen den die disen brieff sehent oder hörent lessen, dass für uns kummen ist Jerge Dritzehen unser burger im namen sin selbs und mit vollem gewalt Clauss Dritzehen sins bruders, und vorderte an Hans Genszfleisch[2] von Mentz genant Gutenberg, vnsern hindersosz, und sprach alss hette Andres Dritzehen sin bruder selige ein erber gut von sime vatter seligen geerbet, und desselben sins vetterlichen erbs und guts etwa vil versetzet und darus ein trefflich summe gelts broht, und wer also mit Hans[3] Gutenberg und andern zu einer gesellschafft und gemeinschafft kommen, und hett solch gelt in dieselbe gemeinschafft zu Hans Gutenberg geleit, und hettent gut zit Ir gewerbe mittenander gemacht[4] und getriben des sie auch ein mychel teil zusammen broht hettent, So were auch Andres Dritzehn[5] an vil enden do sie bli und anders das darzu gehört kaufft hettent, bürge worden, das er auch vergolten und bezahlt[6] hette, Alss

We, *Cune Nope*, the Master and the Council at Strassburg, announce to all who will see this letter, or hear it read, that before us has appeared *Jerge Dritzehen*, our citizen, in his own name, and with full power of *Claus Dritzehen*, his brother, and laid a claim against *Hans Genszfleisch von Mentz genant Gutenberg*, our inhabitant, and said: *Andres Dritzehen*, his blessed brother, had inherited some goods from his blessed father, which paternal inheritance and goods he had rather heavily mortgaged, and thereby procured himself a good deal of money; and he had also entered into a society and partnership with *Hans Gutenberg* and others, and had put this money into this partnership to *Gutenberg*, and that *for a considerable time they had made and exercised their trade* with each other, of which they had derived a good deal of profit. And *Andres Dritzehn* had remained security in many places when *they bought lead and other things belonging to it*, which [securities] he had redeemed and paid.

[1] kunt, Schoepflin.
[2] Genszefleisch, Schoepflin.
[3] Hansz, Schoepflin.
[4] gemaht, Schoepflin.
[5] Drytzehen, Schoepflin.
[6] bezalt, Schoepflin.

nu derselbe Andres von tode abgegangen[1] were, hette er und sin bruder Clauss ettwie dick an Hansz[2] Gutenberg gefordert, das Er sie an Irs bruder seligen stat, in die gemeinschafft nemen solte, oder aber mit Inen überkommen umb solich ingeleit gelt, so er zu Im in die gemeinschafft geleit hette, das er aber alles nie getun wolte, und sich domit behülffe, das Andres Dryzehen solich gelt in die gemeinschaft[3] zu Im nit geleit haben solte, do er aber hoffte und truwete erberlich su erzügen wie er dovor geret hette, dasz das also ergangen were, und darumb so begerte er noch hütbitage dass Gutenberg In und sin bruder Clauss in Ir erbe und in die gemeinschaft[3] an Irs bruder seligen stat setzen, oder aber solich ingeleit gelt, von Irs bruders seligen wegen wider harus geben wolte, Alss Inen das von erbes und rechtes wegen billig zugehörte; Oder aber seite warumb er das nit tun solte.

Dagegen antwurt Hanns Gutenberg, dass Ime solich vorderunge von Jerge Drytzehen unbillig neme, Sit er doch durch etlich geschrifft und zedel so er und sin bruder hinder Andres Drytzehen[4] Irem bruder noch tode funden hätte wol underwissen were, wie er und sin bruder sich mittenander vereiniget[5] hettent, Dann Andres Drytzehen[4] hette sich vor ettlichen Jahren[6] zu Im gefüget und understanden ettlich kunst von Im zu leren und zu begriffen, Dess hett er In nu von siner bitt wegen geleret, Stein bollieren das er auch zu den ziten wol genossen hette, Donoch über gut zit, hette er mit

Now, when the said *Andres* had died, he and his brother *Claus* had often demanded of *Hansz Gutenberg* that he would take them into the partnership in the place of their blessed brother, or to make an agreement with them regarding the money which he had brought into the partnership; which he [*Gutenberg*] declined to do, and excused himself by saying that *Andres Dryzehen* had never brought such money to him in the partnership; as he, however, hoped and trusted to show honestly that the matter had passed, as he had said before, and on that account he still desired that *Gutenberg* should put him and his brother *Clauss* into their inheritance and into the partnership in the place of their blessed brother, or to pay back the money which their blessed brother had contributed, because it reasonably belonged to them as an inheritance and by right; or to say why he would not do this.

Against this *Gutenberg* answered, that he considered such a demand on the part of *Jerge Drytzehen* unreasonable, because he could know, through many writings and contracts, which he and his brother must have found after the death of their brother *Andres Drytzehen*, how he [*Gutenberg*] and his brother [*Andres Dritzehen*] had associated with each other: namely, *Andres Drytzehen* had come to him *some years ago with the understanding* to learn and comprehend some arts from him; for which reason *he had taught him, in consequence of his request, to polish stones*, of which he had enjoyed [some] good [profits] at the time. Yet, after a consider-

[1] abegangen, Schoepflin.
[2] Hannsz, Schoepflin.
[3] -schafft, Schoepflin.
[4] Dryzehen, Schoepflin.
[5] vereyniget, Schoepflin.
[6] Jaren, Schoepflin.

Hanns Riffen vogt zu Lichtenow ein kunst understanden Sich der uff der Ocher heiltumsfahrt[1] zu gebruchen und sich des vereinigt[2] dass Gutenberg ein zweiteil und Hans Riffe ein dirteil daran haben solte, Dess were nu Andres Dritzehen[3] gewar worden, und hette In gebeten Inen solich kunst auch zu leren und zu underwisen, und sich erbotten dess[4] noch sim willen umb In zu verschulden. In dem hette Her Anthonie Heilmann Inen deszglichen von Andres Heilmanns sins bruders wegen auch gebetten, do hette er nu Ir beden bitt angesehen und Inen versprochen Sie des zu leren und zu underwissen, und ouch von solicher kunst und afentur das halbe zu geben und werden zu lassen, also dass sie zween ein teil Hans Riff den andren teil und er den halben teil haben solte, Darumb so soltent dieselben zwene Im Gutenberger hundert und lx. gulden geben in sinen seckel von der kunst zu leren und zu underwisen, Do Im auch uff die zit vom jr jeglichem lxxx. gulden worden were, Als hettent sie alle vor Inen dass die heiltumsfart uss[5] dis Jar solte sin, und sich daruff gerüstent und bereit mit Ir kunst, Alss nu die heiltumbfart sich eins Jares lenger verzogen hette, hettent sie fürbas an In begert und gebetten Sie alle sin künste und afentur so er fürbasser oder in ander wege mer erkunde oder wuste, auch zu leren und des nicht vür Inen zu verhelen, Also überbatent sie Ine dass sie des eins wurdent und wurde nemlich beret dass Sie Im zu dem ersten gelt geben soltent II½ᶜ. gulden, das were zusammen 410. gulden, und soltent Im auch des hundert gul-

[1] -fart, Schoepflin.
[2] vereynigt, Schoepflin.
[3] Dryzehen, Schoepflin.
[4] dass, Schoepflin.
[5] uff, Schoepflin.

abletime, he and *Hanns Riffen*, Provost of Lichtenow, came to an understanding *about an art which was to be used on the occasion of the Ocher pilgrimage* [to Aix-la-Chapelle], and they had united on the condition that *Gutenberg* should have two parts, and *Hans Riffe* a third part in this undertaking. Now, *Andres Dritzehen* had become aware of this, and requested him to teach and show him also this art, promising him to pay for it whatever he should desire. Meantime Mr. *Anthonie Heilmann* requested him also on the part of his brother, *Andres Heilmann*, and he had considered the request of both, and promised them to teach and instruct them in it, and also to give and transfer to them the half of *such art and undertaking*,[1] so that they two would get one part, *Hans Riff* the other part, and he [*Gutenberg*] the half. On that account the two would have to pay to *Gutenberg* 160 guilders into his purse, for his teaching and instructing them in the art. He had received, indeed, at that time, 80 guilders from each of them, as they imagined that the pilgrimage would take place that year, and *they had prepared themselves with their art*. But when the pilgrimage was put off for one year, they further desired from him and requested *to teach them all his*[2] *arts and undertaking*[2] *which he might further, or in another way learn, or knew at present, and to conceal nothing from them.* Thus they persuaded him and came to an understanding, and it was agreed that in addition to the first sum they should give him 250 guilders, which would make together 410

[1] The German word *afentur* implies an *undertaking liable to some risk.*
[2] Schoepflin translates: *artes mirabiles atque secretas.*

den geben als bar, dess Im auch uff die zit 50. gulden von Andres Heilmann und 40 fl. von Andres Dryzehen worden werent, und stundent Im von Andres Dryzehen des noch 10. fl. uss. Darzu soltent die zwene Ir jeglicher Im die 75. fl. geben zu dryen zilen noch dem dann dieselbe zil deszmols beret worden werent, Do ober Andres Dritzehen[1] in solichen zilen von tode abegangen were und Ime solich gelt von sinet wegen noch usstünde, so were auch uff die zit nemlich beret, dass solich Ir affenture mit der kunst solt weren fünff gantze Jar, und wer es dass ir einer under den vieren in den fünff jaren von tode abeginge, so solte alle kunst, geschirre und gemaht werck by den andern bliben, und soltent des abegangenen erben dafür noch ussgang der fünff jor werden hundert gulden, Das und anders auch alles zu der zit verzeichent und hinder Andres Dryzehen kommen sy darüber einen versiegelten[2] brieff zu setzen und zu machen, alss das die zeicheniss luter uswisset, und habe auch Hans[3] Gutenberg sie sithar und daruff solich afentur und kunst gelert und underwisen, dess sich auch Andres Dryzehen an sine todtbett[4] bekannt[4] hette, Darumb und wile di zedel so darüber begriffen und hinder Andres Dryzehen funden werent, das luter besagen und innhalten, und er das auch mit guter kuntschaft[5] hoffte[5]

[1] Dryzehen, Schoepflin.
[2] versigelten, Schoepflin.
[3] Hanss, Schoepflin.
[4] tot bett bekant, Schoepflin.
[5] kuntschafft hofte, Schoepflin.

guilders. Of this he [*Gutenberg*] was to receive 100 guilders in ready money; and he did receive 50 guilders from *Andres Heilmann*, and 40 guilders from *Andres Dryzehen*, so that *Andres Dryzehen* had still to pay him 10 guilders. Besides this the two should each pay him 75 guilders in three instalments, as had been previously agreed upon. But as *Andres Dritzehen* had died within these terms, and the money was still due from him, it was decided that their *adventure with the art*[1] should last for five whole years, and in case one of the four died within the five years, *then all their art, tools, and work made already should remain with the others*, and after the expiration of five years the heirs of deceased should receive 100 guilders. This and other things were written down at the time, and after the [death of][2] Andres Dryzehen they had agreed to prepare a sealed letter about the matter as is clearly shown by the act[3] and *henceforth Hans Gutenberg had taught and instructed them in such undertaking and art*,[4] *which had been acknowledged by Andres Dryzehen on his death-bed.* Therefore, and because the contracts which concern it, and were found with *Andres Dryzehen*, clearly declare and contain it, and he [*Gutenberg*] hoped to prove with good witnesses, he desired

[1] Schoepflin translates: *pro exercenda arte mirabili.*

[2] The sense is not quite clear here: *hinder* means after; therefore, perhaps to be supplied *the death of.* There is further in the original: Andres Dryzehen kommen sy darüber einen versiegelten, &c., where we might have expected the word *ein* after *darüber.*

[3] *or* signature?

[4] Schoepflin translates: *hanc secretam & mirabilem artem.*

byzubringen, so begerte er dass Jörge Dryzehen und sin bruder Clauss Im die 85. gulden so Im von Irs bruder seligen wegen noch also ussstünden, an den 100. gulden abeschlahent, so wolle er Inen die übrigen[1] 15 gulden noch geben, wiewol er des noch etliche jahr zit[2] hette, und Inen darumb tun noch wisunge solicher zedel davon begriffen, Und alss Jerge Dryzehen fürbas gemeldet hette wie Andres Dryzehen sin bruder selige etvvie vil sins vatters erbe und guts gehebt, versetzet oder verkauft habe, das gange Ine nicht an, und Im sy von Im nit me worden, dann er vor erzält habe, ussgesat ein halben omen gesotten wins, ein korp mit bieren und er und Andres Heilmann haben Im ein halb fuder wins geschencket, do sie zwene east[3] me by Im verzert hettent, darumb Im aber nützit worden were, Darzu als ir[4] fordert Inen in sin erbe zu setzen, do wisse er deheim[5] erbe noch gut do er Ine insetzen solle oder dovon er Im iht zu thun sy. So sy auch Andres Dryzehen nirgent[6] sin bürge worden, weder für bli oder anders, ohne[7] ein mol gegen Fridel von Seckingen, von dem habe er Ine noch sime tode wider gelidiget und gelöset, und begert darumb sin kundschaft[8] und worheit zu verleien.

that *Jörge Dryzehen* and his brother *Clauss* should deduct the 85 guilders, which he had still to claim from their blessed brother, from the 100 guilders, whereupon he should give them the remaining 15 guilders, though he had still some years' time to do this in, according to the contents of the act. And as to *Jerge Dryzehen* having further said how *Andres Dryzehen*, his blessed brother, had raised much upon his father's inheritage and property, or had mortgaged or sold it, this did not concern him [*Gutenberg*], for he had never received more from him than he had related before, except half an omen of sodden wine, a basket with beer, and he [*Dritzehen*] and *Andres Heilmann* had presented him with half a measure of wine, though the two had almost more consumed with him, and for which he had obtained nothing. Moreover, when he demands to put him into his inheritance, he did not know of any inheritance or property into which he could put him, or with which he had anything to do. Nor had *Andres Dryzehen* become his security anywhere, *either for lead or for anything else*, except once with *Fridel von Seckingen*, from whom he had redeemed and relieved him after his death, and on that account requests to bring forward his witnesses and truth.

Alss nachdem[9] Wir Meister und Rat obgenannt forderunge und antwurt, rede und widerrede, auch kuntschafft und worheit so sie

We Master and Council having heard the aforesaid demand, and response, the discussion for and against, also the witnesses and

[1] überigen, Schoepflin.
[2] zil, Schoepflin.
[3] fast, Schoepflin.
[4] er, Schoepflin.
[5] dehein, Schoepflin.
[6] niergent, Schoepflin.
[7] one, Schoepflin.
[8] kuntschafft, Schoepflin.
[9] nochdem, Schoepflin.

beder site fürgewant habent und besunder den zedel wie die beredung vor Uns gescheen, verhörtent, do komment Wir mit recht urteil überein und sprochent es auch zu recht: wile ein zedel da ist der da wiset in welcher masse die beredunge zugangen und geschehen sin soll. Sy dann dass Hanns Riff, Andres Heilmann und Hanns Gutenberg schwerent einen eit an den Heiligen, dass die sache ergangen sient, alss das der obgemelt zedel wiset, und das derselbe zedel daruf[1] begriffen wurt dass ein besigelter brieff daruss gemaht sin solt ob Andres Dryzehen by sinem leben bliben were, und dass Hanns[2] Gutenberg domit sweret, dass Im die 85. gulden von Andres Dritzehen noch unbezahlt[3] usstont, so sollen Im dieselben 85. gulden an den abgemelten[4] 100. gulden obegon,[5] und soll die übrige 15 gulden gemelten Jörge und Clauss Dryzehen harus geben, und sollent die 100 gulden domit bezalt sin noch innhalt der obgemelten zedel, Und soll Gutenberg fürbas von dess wercks und gemeinschafft wegen mit Andres Dryzehen all nützit zu tun noch zu schaffen haben. Solichen eit Hans Riff, Andres Heilman und Hanns Gutenberg vor Uns also geton habent, ussgenommen dass Hanns[6] Riff geseit hat dass er by der beredung am ersten nit gewesen[7] sy, so bald er aber zu In kommen und sie Im die beredung seiten, da liesz er das auch daby bliben, daruff gebieten Wir diese verheiszung zu halten. Datum vigil. Lucie et Otilie Anno XXXIX.

truth, which both parties have brought forward, and having especially seen the contract and the convention, we have agreed with a correct judgment, and pronounce it also as right: while there exists an act which shows in what form the convention has come about and has taken place. Let, therefore, *Hanns Riff*, *Andres Heilmann*, and *Hanns Gutenberg* swear an oath by the Saints, that the matters have taken place as the aforesaid act indicates, and that this same act had contained a provision that a sealed letter should have been made of it if *Andres Dryzehen* had remained alive; and that *Hanns Gutenberg* also take an oath that he has still to claim 85 guilders from *Andres Dritzehen*; so that these 85 guilders may be deducted from the above-mentioned 100 guilders, and he shall pay the remaining 15 guilders to the said *Jörge* and *Claus Dryzehen*, wherewith the 100 guilders shall have been paid in conformity with the contents of the said act; and *Gutenberg* shall henceforth have nothing to do or to arrange with *Andres Dryzehen*, on account of the work and the partnership. This oath having been taken before Us by *Hans Riff*, *Andres Heilman*, and *Hanns Gutenberg*, except that *Hanns Riff* has said that he had not been present at the first convention; but as soon as he came to them and they showed him the convention, he altered nothing, wherefore we command to maintain this convention. Datum vigil. Lucie et Otilie Anno XXXIX (12 Dec. 1439).

[1] daruff, Schoepflin.
[2] Hanss, Schoepflin.
[3] unbezalt, Schoepflin.
[4] obg-, Schoepflin.
[5] abegon, Schoepflin.
[6] Hans, Schoepflin.
[7] gewessen, Schoepflin.

8 (VI). An act, with dates (secundo ydus Jan.; quarto ydus Febr.; xii kalend. Marcii; viii kal. April. i.e.) Jan. 12, Feb. 10, Feb. 18, and March 25, 1441, in which the Knight Luthold von Ramstein, and *Johannes dictus Gensefleisch alias nuncupatus Gutenberg de Maguntia* (later on *Johannes Gutenberg*), both living at Strassburg, remain surety before the judge of the *Strassburg* cury, for 100 guilders (about 400 fr.), which a certain Joh. Karle, armiger, had borrowed from the St. Thomas Chapter at 5%.

This act and document 10 were, according to Schoepflin (Vindiciæ, p. 12), discovered by Prof. Jo. Geo. Scherz, in the Archives of the Church of St. Thomas, at Strassburg, in 1717, who communicated extracts from them to some friends, who in their turn communicated them to Schellhorn, who mentions them, *for the first time*, in 1720, in his "Amœnitatum Literar." tom. iv. p. 304. Schellhorn did not publish them, but only quotes from them the words "Joannes dictus Gensfleisch, alias nuncupatus Gutenberg de Maguncia Argentinæ commorans," for the purpose of showing that Gutenberg and Gensfleisch were one and the same. He says, however, that both documents were communicated to him by "Generosissimus Dominus Marcus Antonius de Krafft, Reip. Ulmensis, Senator, & . . . . Patronus meus demisse colendus," who copied them at Strassburg while on a tour. Schellhorn's quotation was evidently copied, in 1727, by Joannis in his Scriptt. Hist. Mogunt. tomus novus, p. 456. The documents (8 and 10) were published *in extenso* in 1760, by Schoepflin, in his Vindiciæ (8 as Num. V., ex libro salico ecclesiæ Thomanæ Argentoratensis, N°. B., fol. 293 *a*; 10 as Num. VI., ex libro salico eccl. D. Thom. Argent., N°. B., fol. 302 *b*.) Cf. Schaab, Erfind. der Buchdruckerkunst, i. 27, 28, 31, where we read that

"in 1826, the Strassburg Librarian Schweighäuser found the documents in the place mentioned. Volume B is a large folio, for the most part written on paper. It contains contemporary copies of documents, and a table of contents, written on parchment, is bound at the beginning of the volume." Schaab adds: "The four important documents (Nos. 4, 7, 8, 10) are preserved at Strassburg, and it would be audacious to entertain the slightest doubt as to their genuineness."

Cf. C. Schmid (Nouv. détails sur la vie de Gutenberg) who says that the original of doc. 8 does no longer exist, but that the entry found in Reg. B, fol. 293[a] is a copy.

9 [A.D. 1441]. A piece of oak, of which Dr. Van der

Linde (p. 87) tells us that "it is 3 ft. in length and provided with a screw-hole; that it was *discovered* in Gutenberg's first printing-house at Mentz, *im Hofe zum Jungen*, on the 22nd of March, 1856, in the afternoon at five o'clock, at the digging of a cellar 24 ft. under the ground. This piece of wood had done service as a press, and bore the inscription J. MCDXLI.G." (a ridiculous inscription according to Dr. Van der Linde, p. 517). He adds:—

"It was found among a heap of smaller and larger pieces of wood of the same kind, so that with these fragments a whole press might have been constructed; not a single piece of iron or other metal was found near them, but close by to the right were found eight baked, round, perforated stones (as they are sometimes found in Roman tombs), four Roman coins of copper of Aug., Trajan, Marc. Aurel., and two fragments of Roman vases of terra-sigillata. A couple of feet further on the right, Roman stoves were discovered in their original situation (Dr. Van der Linde places here an ?), &c. &c."

Dr. Van der Linde says that he himself has been on the spot and has seen these interesting objects, and remarks that it is obvious to the most superficial that in this falsification ignorance and impudence vie with each other for mastery, and he refers us to "a contemptible apology of K. Klein, Professeur au Collége Grand-Ducal de Mayence, &c. &c.," entitled, Sur Gutenberg et le fragment de sa presse, trouvé dans la maison où il a établi sa première imprimerie, Mayence, 1856, 8vo.

In *Notes and Queries*, Sec. Series, vol. xi. p. 23, an article on the above interesting discovery, by the well-known Mr. Francis Fry, may be found. He saw the objects in 1860. There were *then*, beside the principal block (which he calls "precious relic"), and preserved in a glass case, some other pieces of wood, supposed to have been parts of the press, a few stone mulls, used no doubt for grinding the ink, and four coins, one of each of the reigns of Augustus, Trajan, and Marcus Aurelius, one illegible. [The Roman portion of the find reveals Gutenberg to us as a *numismatist* and a general *antiquary;* but why does Mr. Fry not mention the stoves?]

Mr. Fry goes on to say:

"Gutenberg, on his return from Strassburg about the year 1445, settled in a portion of the house of his paternal uncle, John Geinsfleish, the Hôtel du Jungen, where he erected his press; and from the date on the beam it must have been used in Strassburg, where Gutenberg resided in 1441, in the production of prints from wood-blocks, which he is known to have executed in that town. The locality in which the discovery was made confirms the opinion generally held that he worked in secret. . . . . &c. &c."

Any one desirous of reading an enthusiastic and romantic notice of this discovery may consult Madden, "Lettres d'un Bibliographe," 5e Série; Cf. also Bernard, Origine de l'Impr. i. 157.

10 (VII). An act, dated (xv kal. Dec., i.e.) Nov. 17, 1442, whereby *Johannes dictus Gensefleische alias Guttenberg de Maguncia*, and Martin Brechter, a citizen of Strassburg, obtain a loan of 80 guilders from the Chapter of St. Thomas Church at Strassburg, for which they pledge their salvation (seligkeit), and Gutenberg's inheritance from Johannes Richter, otherwise Leheymer, the secular judge of the town of Mentz, his great-grandfather. Gutenberg's seal, still intact, is attached to this document, as well as those of the episcopal court, and of Martin Brechter. (Cf. Le Bibliographe Alsacien, 1869, p. 203, and Lempertz' Bilderheften, 1858, tab. i.). This document, which formerly belonged to the Archives of St. Thomas, is at present deposited in the Library of the Protestant Seminary, at Strassburg, Cf. No. 8 (VI). Cf. Schaab, Erfind. der Buchdruckerkunst, i. 28; and see above, doc. 8.

The following particulars deserve to be translated from C. Schmid, Nouv. détails sur la vie de Gutenberg:—

"Martin Brechter offers himself as codebtor, and on the 17th Nov., 1442, Johann called Gensefleische . . . and he present themselves before the episcopal judge. For the Chapter appear the Canons Nic. Merswin and Conrad Hüter to treat with Gutenberg, who sells to the Chapter a rent of 4 livres (=16 fr.), payable each year on St. Martin's day, on a revenue of 10 florins on the town of Mentz, which he had inherited from his uncle, Johann Richter, called Leheymer, secular judge in his native town. This sale is effected for 80 livres (=320 fr.), which the two canons handed to the buyers, and which money was entirely for the use of Gutenberg. The latter gives mortgage to the Chapter on the said revenue of 10 florins.—This document, like No. 8, was published from a copy in the registers of St. Thomas (Reg. B. fol. 302[b]), but some years ago (Schmid writes in 1841) the Librarian Jung discovered the original document among the ancient papers preserved in the magazines of the Grandes-Boucheries (Cf. Le Bibliographe Alsacien, 1869, p. 204). Martin Brechter belonged to a family which was afterwards ennobled; Cf. Schœpflin, Alsatia ill., ii. 639."

In perusing the old books of the Chapter of St. Thomas Schmid found "that Gutenberg paid his interest till 1458, even after his return from Strassburg to Mentz in 1444. The accounts of the years 1443, 1444, '47, '48, '49, '51, '52, '54, '56 are wanting. In the quires of 1445, '46, '50, '53, '57, it is each time said :

Item Johan Gütenberg d[t] (dat) iiij lib.

or Item Johan Güttenberg und Martin Brechter d[t] iiij lib. As no observation is made in the registers, it is to be assumed that the interest was paid also in those years of which the registers are wanting. Gutenberg therefore paid his debts even after 1448, when his cousin and friend Arnold Gelthus of Mentz had borrowed 150 florins to assist him, and even after 1455 when Fust deprived him of his presses. But after 1455 Dr. Humery began to advance him money and after St. Martin's day of 1458 Gutenberg began to forget (*oublia*) what he owed to the Chapter and the 4 livres interest were no longer paid. In the contract it was stipulated that after a certain time had elapsed before any rent had been paid, the Chapter would have the right to seize the goods of Gutenberg and his surety. The Chapter allowed two years to elapse before using their rights ; and only in the spring of 1461 they decided to take action against Gutenberg and Brechter. The Chapter brought their complaint before the Imperial Chamber at Rottweil in Suavia, and on the 10th of April 1461 wrote to the Count Jean de Sultz, the president of this chamber the letter," which will be found below as document No. 18. Cf. Bernard, Origine de l'Imprimerie, i. 149.

11 (VIII). Some items in the Strassburg Helbelingzollbuch (a register of the *hellerzoll*, *i.e.* a tax of a heller or penny), in the first of which it is said that *Hans Gutemberg* paid a tax in July, 1439, but remained in debt for 12 shillings, which he paid on the 24th of June, 1440. He pays again on the 21st of Sept., 1443; and again March 12, 1444.

In this same register appeared the entry in which it is said that "Ennel Gudenbergen diesen Zoll zahlt habe" (cf. Schaab, Erfind. der Buchdruckerkunst, i. 44), of which entry we have seen Dr. Van der Linde speak under document 6 as being *a forgery*. The several items were published for the first time in 1760, by J. D. Schoepflin, Vindiciæ typogr., documenta, N°. VII, p. 40.

[It will not be superfluous to remark that after this last item of 1444 no further trace of Gutenberg is said to be found at Strassburg, and he is considered to have been dissatisfied with his results in that town and to have quitted it as soon as possible to try his fortune in his native town. Some authors quote, in support of their opinion that he emigrated in 1443, a document of the same year by which Johan Gensfleisch hired, at Mentz, the house *zum Jungen*, which Gutenberg occupied afterwards (see above, p. 16). But this

Johan Gensfleisch is called the *alte* and is Gutenberg's oncle (Cf. Köhler, *Ehren-rettung*, p. 67, 82; Schaab, *Erfind. der Buchdruckerk.*, ii. 250; Bernard, *Origine de l'Imprimerie*, i. 155.]

12 (IX). A letter relating a transaction which had taken place (Inne deme Jare . . . Dusent vyerhundert vyertzygk und Echte Jare vff sant Gallen tag des heyligen Confessors, i.e. in the year 1448 on the day of St. Gall, the holy Confessor, i.e.) the 16th Oct., 1448, and published (Anno prenotato feria quinta proxima post diem beati galli confessoris, i.e.) the 17th Oct. 1448, by which Arnolt Gelthuss gives security to Reinhart Brömser and Johann Rodenstein for a loan of 150 guilders, contracted by him in behalf of *Henn* (*Henchin*) *genssefleisch, called gudenbergk*, who now resided *at Mentz.*

This letter we only know from a later document of the secular court of Mentz, dated (mitwuchen nehist nach sant Bernharts tagk des heyligen abbtes, i.e.) 23rd Aug., 1503, in which the letter is repeated and authenticated in behalf of Dhiel Hepp von breythart, a tailor and citizen of Mentz, and Elsse, the widow of the blessed Clese fresenheimer.

This latter document is preserved in the town library at Mentz, and Bodmann (who forged at least three documents in behalf of Gutenberg's biography) has written on it, "Ad Historiam Typographiæ inventæ."

Schaab, after he had come into the possession of Bodmann's papers, published it *for the first time* in 1830 (Gesch. der Erfind. der Buchdr. ii. 253) and calls it "the most interesting document of his collection, because (cf. his vol. i. p. 165) it fills up the epoch 1445–1450, which had hitherto remained the darkest of Gutenberg's existence, and the document shows us that during this time Gutenberg was in Mentz, had no property and no credit, and was supported by his rich relatives by means of borrowed money"—cf. further his vol. i. 461 sqq.

In this letter Gutenberg is spoken of as *Henn genssefleisch* den man nennet *gudenbergk*, and *Henchin genssefleische.* We find also mentioned *Hans von Sorchenloche* genante *genssefleische—hanss von Sorgenloche gnante genssefleisch*, a distant relation of John Gutenberg. Schaab (i. 32) says of it: "The vidimused document lay before the eyes of the tribunal. They examined the writing, seals, &c., and described it correctly. The precious document is written on a large sheet of parchment, with Latin characters. The five seals which had been attached to it have, indeed, come off, but the slits at the bottom of the parchment still prove this number. In one of the corners is written, in a newer hand : *das Haus Zum alten Rath belangend. Ist selbiger Zinsz von Meister Jörge Hofsattler im Jahr* 1666 *abgelegt worden.*"

13. "A notarial document, dated 3rd July, 1453, in which *Johann Gudenberg* is mentioned as a witness, and in which Hans Schumacher von Selgenstadt, brother and servant of the convent of St. Clara, gives and bequeathes to this convent all his possessions, outstanding debts, &c. From the original, or copy."

The above note was found among the papers of the well-known Bodmann, but Schaab tells us (ii. 267) that he has in vain looked for the notarial document or the copy.

14 (X). The Notarial Instrument of the Law-suit of *Johann Fust* against *Johann* (*Johan*) *Guttenberg* (*Gutenberg; Guttenbergk*) alleged to have been decided on the 6th Nov., 1455 (cf. Schaab, Erfind. der Buchdruckerkunst, i. 47, 58 &c. &c.).*

---

* I think it necessary to state that the history of this document was written and in type before I had an opportunity of making researches for the original in Germany. I found it needful to make these researches, because every author on the invention of printing speaks of an *original* or *autographum*, yet when I compared what they said with the circumstances under which they published their text, there was in some cases a certainty, in other cases a strong suspicion, that they had printed from a *transcript* which emanated, in the seventeenth century, from Joh. Friedr. Faust von Aschaffenburg, the very man who wrote a long discourse to demonstrate that Johan Fust was the inventor of printing, and his ancestor. It is true, Joh. David Köhler stated plainly enough, in 1741, that he printed the document "from an original on vellum in forma patente," but in his preface he declared that he had obtained *all* his documents from Johan Ernst von Glauburg. As it will be seen from the latter's own words (on pp. 74, 75, 93) that he, on two occasions, contented himself with transcribing this document from the *Faust von Aschaffenburg* transcript, and never even speaks of an original, it was to my mind out of the question that *he* could have supplied Köhler with an *authentic* copy, while he himself preferred to deal with a *transcript*.

I have failed to find the original used by Köhler, but I saw, in the Darmstadt Archives (Oct. 9, 1880) a letter written by him in 1728 to this very Joh. Ernst von Glauburg informing him that he had obtained *the original* from a relation (*Vetter*) of von Glauburg's. Who this relation was or where his literary property is now preserved, I have been unable to ascertain, but Köhler's letter must set at rest, at least for the present, all doubts as to the source of his text.

The external history of the document does not seem ever to have

The contents of the document are well known. It is sometimes called the Helmasperger document, because in it the Mentz Notary Ulricus Helmasperger testifies to have drawn it up for and on behalf of Johan Fust, and it bears his name and notarial mark.

Allusion is made in *this* document to another one which has not come down to us—namely, the contract (*czettel*, mod. Germ. *Zettel*, see line 43 of the Instrument) made between Gutenberg and Fust, at the commencement of their association (see Schaab i. 169, 170).

This association is calculated to have commenced in the second half of the year 1450, because, in the Instrument, Fust reckons the interest of the first advanced 800 guilders to amount to 250, which is exactly the amount (at 6 per cent.) for five years and two-and-a-half months, and points to the 26th Aug., 1450, as the day on which the 800 guilders must have been advanced. After two years this money appears to have been spent, and about the 6th of December, 1452, Fust advanced another 800 guilders.

At the time the first loan was advanced, Gutenberg seems to have had no printing tools, but was to make them with Fust's money, and to pledge them to Fust for the money advanced (Dass ym Guttenberg—Johann Fust 800 Gulden verlacht solt hain, mit solchem Gelde er sin gezuge zurichten und machen solte—und solche gezüge des genanten Johann—Fust—pffant sin solten). Schaab (Erfind. der Buchdruckerk. i. 174), from whom these particulars are copied, adds:—

"As there is question of a new manufacture of printing tools, it follows that Gutenberg *did not bring any with him to Mentz from Strassburg*, and did not procure them even at Mentz, until the contract of association had been concluded. Fust acknowledged that it was

---

had any attraction for writers on the origin of printing. It is not given anywhere, and German authors who ought to know publish particulars regarding this external history and the whereabouts of the document which are most perplexing to foreigners, as I have found to my cost. For these reasons I publish the result of my reading and research unaltered, however confused it may appear, in the hope that the extraordinary errors to which I allude will be removed and the attention of Librarians and Archivists may be directed to the matter, and a search for the original or originals made without delay. The results of my researches at Hamburg, Frankfurt on the Main, Höchst on the Nidder (in Baron Carl von Günderrode's library), and Darmstadt, as far as they bear on this subject, have been stated in notes or in paragraphs preceded by ¶.

Gutenberg's invention and only advanced the money for the making of the tools. . . . Gutenberg presumably commenced with the tools which we have partly seen in the house of Andreas Dritzehn at Strassburg, namely a press, cut characters, forms for putting them together, and wooden blocks." *

On p. 313 Schaab argues that—

"Peter Schöffer must have married Fust's daughter before 1455, and I see in this close relation between Fust and Schöffer the cause of the law-suit and the breaking up of the association. Fust and Schoeffer knew by that time Gutenberg's secret; the latter had fully equipped his printing-office; Schoeffer's improvements in the casting of type had been effected; Gutenberg could be dispensed with; he had spent the remainder of his property in the printing-business, and they knew that he was unable to repay the money advanced to him. It was now the most favourable moment not only to exclude Gutenberg from the partnership and to secure his printing-office, but also to make him harmless for the future. A pretence was soon found, namely the costs of the Latin Bible. . . . . Fust was a rich man, but had purposely borrowed the money, which he lent to Gutenberg, from Jews and Christians, in order to excuse his usury and to be able to claim six per cent. Gutenberg was summoned by Fust before the tribunal, and —according to the document of which we treat—the tribunal decided, 1st. that Gutenberg should furnish an account of all receipts and expenses concerning the work which he had prepared for their mutual profit; 2nd, that when it resulted that he had received more money than he had spent, and had devoted this not to their common use, but to his own profit, he was to pay this to Fust; 3rd, if Fust proved by oath or legal evidence—legal testimony—that he had obtained the sum mentioned on interest, and had not lent it from his own money, Gutenberg was to pay him this interest, according to the contents of the contract. The notarial Helmasberger Instrument does not say that Gutenberg produced the account, but as he replied that he would account for the second 800 guilders, we may conclude that he drew it up and produced it. The tribunal awarded interest at *six per cent., a rate which was forbidden by the then secular and ecclesiastical*

* "Da hier von einer neuen Zurichtung des Druckgezeugs die Rede ist, so muss Gutenberg keines von Strassburg nach Mainz gebracht, und auch daselbst nicht vor Abschliessung des Gesellschaftsvertrags sich angeschafft haben. In diesen Akten ist von Fust anerkannt worden, die Erfindung gehöre unserm Gutenberg an und Fust habe das Geld vorgelegt, damit Gutenberg sin gezüch mit solchem zurichten und machen solle; es sich also nicht anders denken lasse, als dass Gutenberg gleich nach dem mit Fust abgeschlossenen Gesellschaftsvertrag die Hand ans Werk gelegt, um neue Druckwerkzeuge zu verfertigen, und dass er dabei von seinem Gesellschafter seye unterstützt worden. Vermuthlich hat er mit den Werkzeugen angefangen, welche wir zum Theil in Strassburg in der Wohnung von Andreas Dritzehn gesehen haben, nemlich einer Presse, geschnittenen Buchstaben, Formen zu ihrer Zusammensetzung und hölzernen Tafeln."

law ; it even awarded interest on interest, or, as Gutenberg called it, usurious interest, which it was forbidden to take ; finally it awarded the full payment of interest for the capital sum which had only been advanced from time to time." *

Schaab goes on :—

Which tribunal pronounced this judgment, which is so remarkable in many respects, and *when* it was pronounced, are matters about which the notarial document and Mentz history are silent.

---

* Die Epoche der Verheirathung Schöffers mit Fustens Tochter Christina läst sich um so gewisser für die Jahre 1453 und 1454 annehmen, als. . . Da ich den Beweis geliefert zu haben glaube, dass die Epoche von Peter Schöffers Verheirathung vor das Jahr 1455 falle, so sehe ich in dieser nahen Verbindung zwischen Fust und Schöffer die Ursache zur Erhebung des Prozesses gegen Gutenberg und zur Trennung der Gesellschaft. Fust und Schöffer befanden sich im Besitze eines Geheimnisses, dass Gutenberg so lang und sorgfältig bewahrt hatte, die Druckerei war von ihm vollständig eingerichtet, Schöffers Verbesserungen des Gussverfahrens waren geschehen, Gutenberg war ihnen entbehrlich, er hatte den Rest seines Vermögens in die Druckeinrichtung verwendet, sie wusten, dass er sich ausser Stand befand, die ihm vorgeschossenen Summen auf der Stelle zu ersetzen. Der günstigste Moment war eingetreten, den geheimen Plan auszuführen, um sich den alleinigen Besitz der ganzen Druckerei zu verschaffen und nicht allein Gutenberg daraus zu verdrängen, sondern ihn für die Zukunft ganz unschädlich zu machen. . . . Ein Vorwand war bald gefunden. Die Kosten der lateinischen Bibel mussten ihn abgeben. . . Fust war ein reicher mann und doch hatte er absichtlich das Geld bei Juden und Christen aufgenommen, um seinen vorgehabten Wucher zu beschönigen und eine Aufforderung von sechs Prozent durchzusetzen. . . . Gutenberg wurde von Fust vor Gericht geladen. . . . Das gericht erkannte : (1) dass Gutenberg eine Rechnung stellen solle über alle Einnahmen und Ausgaben, welche er auf das Werk zu beiderseitigem Nutzen gemacht habe ; (2) wenn sich daraus ergebe, dass er mehr Geld empfangen als er ausgegeben und nicht in ihren gemeinen Nutzen, sondern zu seinem eignen Profit gekommen, das solle er an Fust herauszahlen ; (3) würde Fust durch einen Eid oder rechtlichen Beweis—rechtliche Kundschaft—darthun, dass er das angegebene Geld auf Zinsen genommen und nicht von seinem eignen dargelichen habe, so solle Gutenberg ihm solche Zinsen auch bezahlen, nach Inhalt des Zettels. Das Helmasberger'sche Notariats Instrument erwähnt mit Keinem Worte, ob Gutenberg die auferlegte Rechnung gestelt habe. Da er aber antwortet, dass er wegen der weitern 800 fl. Rechnung thun wolle, so lässt sich darauss schliessen, dass er sie auch gestelt und übergeben habe. Das Gericht erkannte Zinsen zu 6 vom Hundert, nach einem Zinssfuss, der durch die damals bestandenen weltlichen und geistlichen Gesetze proskribirt war, es erkannte sogar auf Zinsen von Zinsen oder wie Gutenberg sie nennt, auf Wucherzinsen, welche zu nehmen verboten sind, es erkantte endlich auf eine volle Zinsszahlung von einem Kapital, dass doch nur nach und nach geschossen worden."

Our old law-books do not go further back than 1550. It could not have been any other tribunal but the secular court of this place, which consisted of a treasurer (kämmerer), justice of the peace, and four judges. In 1455, Johann Münch of Rosenberg was treasurer; Ditherich Billung was justice of the peace; and the judges were Clas Schenkenberg, Endres Weyse, Degenhard von Cleberg, and Friedrich von Weyler. A judge of this court was Niklas Fust (a brother of Johann Fust) from 1439 to 1442 or 1443. In the latter year he was transferred from this Court to the Council of the town. The Fust family belonged to the richest and most distinguished plebeian citizens of Mentz. Their members were in the Council, and the goldsmith Jacob Fust, the brother of Johann Fust, was, seven years afterwards, Burgomaster of the town. . . . . The Fusts belonged to the first corporate families of Mentz. Their reputation and power were great and *they were feared.* The honest Köhler already remarked 'that Faust knew well that the Court had to connive at his proceedings' (dass Faust wohl bekannt gewesen, dass ihm das Gericht durch die Finger sehen müsse). Bergel, who obtained the materials for his beautiful Latin poem from old and honest Mentz citizens, calls the Court a forum pavidum, a timorous tribunal, and thereby points unequivocally to the fear which it must have felt for the powerful Fust family. Fust took the oath, which the judgment required from him, on the 6th Nov., 1455, before the Notary Ulrich Helmasberger, in the Refectorium of the Convent of the bare-footed friars, in the absence of Gutenberg, but in the presence of several persons, and desired and obtained an act of the same. After this taking of the necessary oath, Fust probably did not neglect to present the copy which he obtained from the notary to the secular tribunal, and to insist on possession on the pledge assigned to him in the contract. That this possession followed, and Fust became proprietor not only of the printing tools, but also of the sheets of the Bible already printed off, the parchment and paper in stock, is evident (1) from the fact that Gutenberg possessed no printing-office after the law-suit, and only with the money of the Mentz Syndic, Dr. Humery, could he procure another one, the possession of which was, however, reserved to Dr. Humery (see below, document No. 23); (2) from the fact that the types of the 42-line Bible are afterwards in the possession of Fust and Schœffer, &c. &c.—Fust and Schöffer were not satisfied with the possession of Gutenberg's printing-office, but continued their judiciary persecutions against him and, even after his death, against his heirs, probably because that which they found was not sufficient to pay the amount awarded them by the verdict. The law-suit lasted for several years, and had not come to an end about the middle of the 16th century. This is proved by a letter which Peter Schœffer wrote on the 22nd of July, 1485, from Frankfort, to his dear godfather Johann Genszfleisch, secular judge of Mentz, in which he urgently asked him for payment of his debt, with which he had had so much patience [this letter was published by Köhler, Ehren-Rettung, 1741, p. 94, from Lersner's Franckf. Chronicle, p. 438]; and the long duration of the law-suit is also referred to by Bergellanus, lines 261 and 262.

I am unable to say on what authority Schaab makes the above statements; but, assuming that he represents the case correctly, three of his points deserve attention:—(1) *The tribunal,* which had to decide in the cause, *stood in fear of the Fust Family;* (2) it awarded *a rate of interest* which was *forbidden* both *by the secular and ecclesiastical law;* (3) there exist at present no Mentz Law-registers earlier than the year 1550; hence we see (*a*) that the original *public Registers* which would contain the official record of any suit of the kind at Mentz are long since lost; and (*b*) that we are at present compelled to deal only with an insulated document which, however authentically drawn up as a *Notarial Instrument,* at once passed from public custody into private hands.

Our Notarial document relates the transactions which took place at the taking of the oaths in the refectory of the convent of the Minorites, or Franciscans, at Mentz, in the street which is at present called Schustergasse. Schaab (Erfind. der Buchdruckerk. i. 170) explains that at that time it was an old custom at Mentz to transact all judiciary and even administrative public affairs in the churches and monasteries or their surroundings. Fust caused Gutenberg to be summoned to the conventual-room of the Minorite convent, because this was situated opposite his own house. The transaction had to take place in the refectory, as the ecclesiastics were still in the conventual-room. Johann Fust appeared with his brother Jacob in person, accompanied by three citizens, the notary Ulrich Helmasperger, and his two witnesses. Johann Gutenberg did not appear in person, but sent Heinrich Chünther (Günther), pastor at St. Christopher, Mentz, Heinrich Keffer, and Bertolff (Bechtolf) von Hanau, his servant and workman, in order to hear and see what was to happen in the matter.

The Notarial document was published *for the first time* in **1734**, by Senckenberg, Professor at Giessen, in his Selector. Jur. et Hist. Anecdot. (Frankf. 1734–1742, 6 vols. 8vo.) tom. 1. p. 269, with the heading:—

> "Laudum inter Jacobum & Johannem Faustios ex una, & Johannem Guttenberg ex altera parte, agens de pecunia in librorum impressionem insumta."

In the margin Senckenberg prints: "1455. Ex orig." The document is Num. xxxvii. of Senckenberg's 3rd part of vol. i., which, on the top of the pages, bears the general heading *Diplomatarium Francofurt*[*ense*] *Miscellum,* while at the commencement we read *Manipulus documentorum res Francofurtenses et viciniam illustrantium.*

This third part of vol. i. contains 40 documents, and Senckenberg, in his preface to the first volume (p. 47), declares that they are

"*partim ex ipsis*, quæ vocant, *Originalibus*, partim ex Authenticis, partim etiam nudis copiis decerpta. Hæc maximam partem nostra penus (cabinet) servavit, pars eorum aliis debetur, queis hic publice gratias agimus."

By the side of every document we find *ex authentico*, except at Nos. 20, 36, 40, where only the dates 1336, 1430, 1484 are given, while at Nos. 26, 27, 28, 37 (our document), 38, 39, we find *ex orig.* and the respective dates of the documents.

Senckenberg does not specify the sources whence he obtained his documents, but on p. 9 of his preface to the first vol., where he enumerates the persons who had written on Frankfort and those whose collections or works he used, he says :—

"Advoco Johannis Friderici Faustii ab Aschaffenburgo, Viri diligentissimi *Collectanea Francofurtensia*, III Voluminum in fol. parte I res gestas, duabus sequentibus Genealogias familiarum Nobilium Francofurtensium & lapides sepulcrales percurrentium. Vastum hoc opus, multum boni, nullius fere pretii plurimum sistit, a rerum cognitione & studio in patriam, caeteroqui laudem promeritum. Nescio vero, an non huic Viro tribuendum sit, *Corpus diplomaticum Francofurtense*, in forma quarta, quod nonnullibi spectare contigit, certe aliqua sunt, hunc auctorem olentia."

Let us now see what happened before and after Senckenberg's time.

Polydore Vergil says, in 1499, that a certain Peter, a German, had invented the art of printing, as he had heard from the latter's countrymen (Van der Linde, p. 288).

Johann Schœffer, the son of Peter Schœffer, and the grandson of Johann Fust, represents himself in 1503 (in the Mercurius Trismegistus) as one of the most distinguished citizens of Mentz, descended from the most fortunate race, who, favoured by fortune, invented the almost divine art of printing (Van der Linde, p. 288).

In 1505, in the German translation of Livy, published by the same Johann Schœffer, the dedication to the Emperor Maximilian (probably, says Van der Linde, from the hand of Ivo Wittig) mentions "Johan Güttenbergk as inventor of printing (1450) and Johan Faust and Peter Schöffer as improvers of the art."* This work was reprinted *six* times with the same dedication; yet in 1509 the *Breviarium Moguntinum* says it (the *Brev.*) was printed "at the expense and trouble of Johann Schœffer, whose grandfather [i.e. Johann Fust] was the first inventor and author of the art of printing" (Van der Linde, p. 288).

In 1515 the same Joannes Schœffer, the grandson of Joannes Fust, published Joh. Tritheim's *Compendium sive Breviarium historiæ francorum*, in the colophon of which he says that—

"This Chronicle is printed and completed in the year 1515, on the eve of St. Margaret, in the town of Mentz, *the first inventress* of the art of printing, by Johann Schoeffer, grandson of the late honourable Johann Fust, a Mentz citizen, the first author of the said art, who, *finally*, from his own genius, commenced to excogitate and to investigate the art of printing in *the year* 1450, in the 13th indiction, under the reign of the Roman Emperor Frederic III., and of the archbishop and elector at Mentz, Theodoric Schenk von Erpach. But in the year 1452 he perfected it and brought it (under favour of the Divine grace) to the work of printing; with the assistance, however, and by means of many necessary additional inventions of Peter Schoeffer von Gernsheim, his servant and adopted son, to whom he also gave his daughter, Christina Fust, in marriage, as a worthy remuneration of his labours and many by-inventions. Both, however, Johann Fust and Peter Schoeffer kept this art secret, binding all their servants and domestics by oath never in any manner to reveal it; which art at last, in the year 1462, was spread by the same domestics into divers countries and increased not a little."†

* . . . "In welicher stadt (Mentz) auch anfengklich die wunderbare kunst der Trückerey, vn*d* Im ersten von dem kunstreichen Johan Güttenbergk, Do man*n* zalt nach Christi vnsers heren gebürth 1450 Jare erfunden, un*d* darnach mit vleyss, kost vnd arbeyt Johan Fausten vnd Peter Schöffers zu Mentz gebesserth, vnd bestendig gemacht ist worden . . ." [A copy of this work is in the Brit. Mus., pressmark 1308. l.]

† "Impressvm et completvm est presens chronicarum opus, anno D*omi*ni MDXV in uigilia Margaretæ uirginis. In nobili famosaq*ue* urbe Moguntina, huius artis impressoriæ inuentrice prima. Per Ioannem Schöffer, nepote*m* quo*n*da*m* honesti viri Joannis fusth ciuis Moguntin*i*, memorate artis primarij auctoris Qui tande*m* imprimendi arte*m* proprio ingenio excogitare specularique coepit a*n*no d*omi*nic*æ* natiuitatis MCCCCL. indictio*n*e XIII. Regnante illustrissimo Ro. imperatore Frederico III. Præsidente sanctæ Moguntinæ sedi Reuere*n*dissimo in chr*ist*o pa*t*re domino Theoderico pincerna de Erpach pri*n*cipe electore Anno aut*em* MCCCCLII perfecit

On the 9th of December, 1518, the Emperor Maximilian accords to Johann Schœffer the privilege of printing the Livy (1518–1519), and in this privilege says that—

"He has learned, and been advised on the faith of worthy testimonies, that the ingenious invention of chalcography was effected by his grandfather." *

In 1519 (cf. Meerman, Orig. typ. ii. 158) Joh. Thurmayer Aventinus (who was born in 1474, and died in 1534) writes that—

"In 1450, Joannes Faustus, a German, a citizen of Mentz, conferred a great and almost divine benefit on the human race; he invented a new kind of writing, which people use to call chalcography (cutting, printing), and completed it in two years . . . This celestial work, kept secret by Faustus and Peter Schoeffer de Garensheim, his son in law, to whom he betrothed his only daughter Christina . . . was divulged in Germany, ten years afterwards, by Faust's servant, Johannes Guttenberger, a Strassburger. The latter's countrymen, Ulricus Han,

---

deduxitq*ue* eam (diuina fauente gratia) in opus imprime*n*di (Opera t*ame*n ac multis necessarijs adinuentionibus Petri Schöffer de Gernsheim ministri suiq*ue* filij adoptiui) Cui etiam filiam suam Christinam fusthin*am pro* digna laboru*m* multaru*m*q*ue* adinue*n*tionu*m* remuneratio*n*e nuptui dedit. Retinueru*n*t aute*m* hij duo ia*m* prænominati Joannes fusth et Petrvs Schöffer ha*n*c artem i*n* secreto (om*n*ibus ministris ac familiaribus eor*um* ne illa*m* quoq*uo*modo manifestare*n*t, iurejura*n*do astrictis) Quo tande*m* de a*n*no *domi*ni MCCCCLXII p*er* eosdem familiares i*n* diuersas terrar*um* p*ro*uincias diuulgata haud parum sumpsit i*n*crementum .·. Cum gratia et privilegio Caesaree Maiestatis iussu & i*m*pensis honesti Joannis Haselperg ex Aia maiore Constantien*sis* diocesis." A copy of this work is in the Brit. Mus., King's library (Pressmark 183. c. 1). The privilege of the Emperor Maximilian, which is dated 10 Nov. 1514, is granted to Joannes Haselberg.

* Maximilianus . . . honesto nostro et sacri Imperii fidelino bis dilecto Joanni Scheffer chalcographo Moguntino, gratiam nostram Caesaream et omne bonum. Cum, sicut docti et moniti sumus fide dignorum testimonio, ingeniosum chalcographiae, authore avo tuo, inventum, felicibus incrementis in universum orbem promanaverit . . . Proinde, volentes tibi tum ob avum tuum, omni vel ob hoc divinum inventum favore et commendatione dignum, tum pro damni tui recuperatione . . . succurrere . . . omnibus . . . chalcographis & librorum impressoribus . . . inhibemus . . ." This edition was edited by Nic. Carbachius, who commences his letter to the reader thus: "Joannes Scheffer Chalcographus, a cuius avo chalcographice in hac primum urbe inventa, exercitaque est . . ." It also has a preface of Erasmus, who says, "laudis praecipua portio debetur huius poene divini dixerim opificij repertoribus, quorum princeps fuisse fertur, totius aevi memoria celebrandus Joannes Faust, avus eius, cui [i.e. Joan. Scheffer] Livium hunc . . . debemus."

Xystus Reisius, brought it to Rome and Italy, &c." (Annal. Boior., lib. vii.) *

In 1526 the German printer Cromberger published at Sevilla *Visiones deleitables por Don Alfonso de la Torre*, in which it is said that the art was invented in Germany, at Mentz; a noble, very rich citizen of this town, Peter Fust, invented it; it spread in the year of our Lord 1425; afterwards, in 1431, a dispute arose between two archbishops: one took the town and killed nearly all the inhabitants, and also that important man, Peter Fust, was killed. Cf. Meerman, Orig. typ. ii. 163.

In 1541 a Mentz press-corrector, J. Arnold (Bergel *or*) Bergellanus (of Bürgel, near Frankfurt-a.-M.), published his *Encomion chalcographiæ*, Mogunt., Fr. Behem, 1541, 4to., in which he is admitted on all hands to *allude for the first time to a law-suit* between Fust and Gutenberg. He dedicates his work to Albert, the Archbishop of Mentz, and tells him:—

"I have seen the historical books of Johannes Tritheim of the past century, and read his eulogy on chalcography and the invention thereof, which he ascribes to a noble citizen of Mentz, Johan Gutenberg, as the first author, with two coadjutors, Johan Faust and Peter Schoefer. I have heard this confirmed in conversations with Mentz citizens. Moreover, some old tools prepared for this work by the originators are still in existence, and have been seen by me." †

* "Hoc anno magnum ac vere divinum beneficium Joannes Faustus Germanus, civis Moguntinus, generi humano contulit, novum scribendi genus haud dubie coelitus revelatum (quod chalcographiam excusoriam impressoriamque vocare solent) invenit et biennio complevit . . . Hoc coelestissimum munus a Fausto et Petro Schoeffer de Garensheim genero suo, cui unicam filiam Christinam desponderat, inter secreta, adactis omnibus sociis ad silentii fidem iurisiurandi religione, habitum, decimo post anno Fausti minister, Johannes Guttenberger, Argentoratensis, in Germania vulgavit. Municipes huius Ulricus Han, hoc est Gallus, Xystus Reisius Romae Italiaeque intulere, &c." [The Ann. Boior. appeared in 1522 at Nuremberg under the title: *Bayerisches Chronikon in Latein.* I have only been able to consult the edition of 1554, published at Ingolstadt. J. H. H.]

† "Incidi in Joh. Trithemii proximi saeculi historicos libros, in quibus elogium quoddam de *Chalcographia* ejusque inventione deprehendi, qui Moguntinae urbis incolae, equestris dignitatis virtutisque nobilissimo, *Joanni Gutenbergo*, primo auctori, ejusque coadjutoribus *Joanni Fausto, Petroque Schaefero*, hujus admirabilis artificii, certis formulis libros excudendi, acceptam refert. Id quod et a nonnullis Moguntiae civibus mihi postea in familiari colloquio, cum ea de re mentio inter alia incideret, certo certius relatum est. Accedit et hoc

In the poem itself Bergel says:—

"Johan Gutenberg invented the new art in 1450, at Mentz, under the reign of Frederic III.; but being on the point of abandoning the work, his means being exhausted, he was *assisted* by Faust, who gave light to the undertaking and *bore the costs.* Afterwards Petrus, cognomine Schæffer, came to their assistance; he *invented* the *matrices;* their hope revived; the work was carried on in secret places without witnesses; they published several little books. Afterwards, when they saw the gain their work produced, they made a compact that the gain and labour should be divided among them; but, as is often the case, the authors of this compact begin to quarrel; they separate; the partnership is dissolved, and each was henceforth to work with his own press and to obtain profits. Gutenberg could not bear the unjust quarrel; he calls God to witness that the compact was broken; the *cause was brought before a timorous tribunal,* and a *horrible process was instituted;* the matter was treated for a long time in a wordy strife, and is even now (1541) in the hands of the judge." *

---

quod et hodie vetustissima quaedam, in eum usum ab auctoribus comparata, quae vidi, instrumenta ibidem extant" (Jo. Christoph. Wolf. Mon. typ. I. 1; Van der Linde, p. 278).

* . . . Sed cedat magno quicquid in orbe nitet ;|| Artis namque novae natum est opus, arte magistra,|| Id quod divini numinis instar erit,|| Conflatis docuit libros quae cudere signis,|| Et praeli dociles exprimit apte typos.|| . . . Hanc peperit captis antiqua *Moguntia* muris|| . . . *Saecula bis septem numerabant* ordine fati|| Christigenae, hinc illis *lustra decem*que dabant,|| Tertius ac orbis Fridericus frena regebat,|| . . . Clarus *Johannes* en *Gutenbergius* hic est,|| Aquo, ceu vivo flumine, manst opus.|| Hic est Aonidum custos fidissimus, hic est,|| Qui referat latices, quos pede fudit equus.|| Quam veteres nobis *Argenti* voce notarunt,|| A puero fertur sustinuisse virum ;|| Illa sed huic civi largita est munera grata,|| Cui clarum nomen *Mogus* habere dedit.|| *Primitias illic* coepit formare laboris,|| Ast *hic maturum* protulit artis *opus.*|| . . . . *Annulus in digitis erat illi occasio prima,*|| . . . Illum tentabat molli committere cerae,|| Redderet ut nomen littera sculpta suum.|| . . . Robora prospexit dehinc *torcularia Bacchi,*|| Et dixit, preli forma sit ista novi.|| . . . Necque erat ulla dies Eoas vecta sub auras,|| Qua non sit vigili littera sculpta manu ;|| Atque notas vocum finxit de *duro orichalco,*|| . . . . Altera sed rebus succrescit cura renatis,|| Inventis uti mens generosa nequit.|| Implorat placidos zephyros, et carbasa pandit.|| Haeret et in scopulis nescius auxilii.|| Cumque illi starent *caelata toreumata magno,*|| Et labor angustas attenuabat opes,|| Artis nec poterat certos extundere fines,|| Inceptum statuit jamque relinquere opus.|| *Consiliis tandem Fausti persuasus amicis,*|| *Viribus exhaustis qui tulit auxilium,*|| *Addidit ac operi lucem sumtumque laboris,*|| *Faustus, Germanis munera fausta ferens*|| *Ex levi ligno sculpunt hi grammata prima,*|| Quae poterat variis quisque referre modis.|| Materiam bibulae supponunt inde papyri,|| Aptam quam libris littore Nilus alit,|| Insuper aptabant mittit quas sepia guttas,|| Reddebat pressas *sculpta tabella* notas.|| Sed quia non poterat propria de classe character|| Tolli, nec variis usibus aptus erat,|| Illis succurrit *Petrus cognomine Schaeffer,*||

We need not speak here of the manner in which Bergellanus says the invention came about.

These few quotations, which show that John Fust became in course of time to be regarded as the inventor, are sufficient to explain the use which, as we shall see, was afterwards made of the Notarial Instrument to establish a genealogy.

Joh. Frider. *Faust* von Aschaffenburg, *the father*, is said "to have copied, about the year 1600, from the original, which was at that time still in the possession of the family, *the instrument of the law-suit* of the first inventor of the art of printing, Junckher Johann Guttenbergk, of the family zum Jungen, with Johann Fausten, the first publisher of the said printing-office, about the costs of publishing." *This transcript* of Joh. Frider. Faust von Aschaffenburg, *the father*, is said to be, in 1712, among his manuscripts (sub lit. O., fol. 159), and on the 3rd of March of that year Joh. Ernest von Glauburg "copies it diligently and correctly."

These two assertions were found written on a transcript of the Notarial Instrument which was, in 1736, in the possession of Joh. *Christoph.* Wolf (*Conspectus svpellectilis epistolicae et literariae manv exaratae quae exstat apud* Jo. Christoph. Wolfium, 8vo., Hamburg, 1736.) This Hamburg pastor

Quo vix caelando promptior alter erat.|| Ille sagax animi praeclara toreumata finxit,|| Quae sanxit *matris* nomine posteritas; || Et *primus vocum fundebat in aere figuras*,|| Innumeris cogi quae potuere modis.|| Hic nova spes oritur, redit in praecordia sanguis,|| Exultant animc, pectoris inque sinu.|| Abdita tecta petunt, agitur res testibus absque,|| Ne fieret populo sordida praeda levi.|| . . . Hoc opus exegit sic quoque sancta Trias.|| Illo primus erat tunc Gutenbergius in albo,|| Alter erat Faustus, tertius opilio.|| . . . Hinc inter sese magnis hi viribus instant,|| Atque opus exercent nocte dieque novum.|| Componunt certo certas pars ordine voces,|| Pars forti torquent prela sonora manu. || Emittunt varios, cudunt quos aere, libellos,|| . . . Hic dum cernebant *raras procedere merces*,|| *Sanxerunt dextris foedera pacta suis*: || *Quae Deus, aut fortuna dabit, communia sunto*,|| *Aequalis nostrum sitque laboris onus*.|| Foedera sed lucri raro concordia nutrit,|| Indiga sunt pacis, dissidioque patent.|| Sic postquam *autores quaestus spes cepit habendi*,|| *Ad lites vertunt pectora capta leves*.|| *In partes abeunt, sinceraque pacta resolvunt*,|| Et promissa cadunt, irrita fitque fides; || *Cuilibet ut propriis serviret pergula prelis*,|| Et sibi multijugas quisque pararet opes.|| Non tulit *injustas* mens Gutenbergica *rixas*,|| Testatur Superos *foedera rupta* Deos.|| Caussa *fori* tandem *pavidi* defertur ad ora; || Scribitur ac illis dica nefanda fori.|| *Tempore sed longo res est tractata dicaci*|| *Lite, hodie pendet judicis inque sinu*.||

describes in this volume a collection of manuscript letters and other documents which he had bought from the heirs of Zacharias Conrad von Uffenbach, a distinguished magistrate and collector of literary treasures at Frankfurt, who died in 1734.

This collection consisted of A) *Epistolae manuscriptae*, of which Wolf describes 71 volumes in *folio*, and 62 volumes in *quarto* and B) *Apparatus manuscriptus qvi historiæ literariæ & librariæ inservit*, of which he describes 21 volumes in *folio* and 29 volumes in *quarto* and *octavo*. Vol. XII. (in fol.) of the second division contains, according to Wolf (p. 278):—

"1) Catal. Msstorum Bibliothecæ S. Màrtini Rev. Capituli Archiepiscopalis Metropolis Moguntinensis, . . . an. 1654 confectus; 2) Laur. Odhelii Bibliotheca Philologica Græca et Latina; 3) Catalogus MSS. Bibliothecæ Carolinæ Tigurinæ; 4) Delineatio operis cujusdam medici manu exarati . . . auctore Judæo, qui . . . scripsit opus A.C. 1430; 5) Eliæ Hofmanni Consilium de tollendis nævis et mendis Scholæ Francofurtanæ, germanice scriptum."

Immediately upon this Wolf says :—

"Here follows, after some things placed between, *the transcript of an ancient vernacular instrument*, from which we may learn the law-suit between Joh. Guttenberg and Joh. Faust, decided in 1455. This instrument has been transcribed by Jo. Ern. von Glauburg, on the 3rd of March, 1712, from a manuscript codex of Jo. Frid. Faust, who in 1600 had brought together many authentic documents, respecting this cause, which he had received from his ancestral inheritance. Its title runs :—"Copia eines alten Instruments, den process des ersten Erfinders der Buchdrucker-Kunst, Junckherrn Johann Guttenbergk, des Geschlechts derer zum Jungen, mit Johann Fausten, dem ersten Verleger gemeldter Buchdruckerey, wegen der Verlags-Kosten betreffend, aus Joh. Frider. Fausten, der solche circa an. 1600 von deme damahlen bey der Familien annoch vorhanden gewesenen original abgeschrieben, Manuscriptis ausgezogen, und sub lit. O. fol. 159 befindlich, von mir Joh. Ernst von Glauburg Anno 1712, den 3 Mart. von gemeldten mit Lit. O. bezeichneten MSto J. F. Fausten fleissig und richtig abgeschrieben." *

[¶ I have examined this vol. xii. at Hamburg, and can say that it contains not *one* transcript, but *two* transcripts

* Sequitur, post interjecta alia, copia *Instrumenti* antiqvi, vernaculi, ad cognoscendam litem, inter *Jo. Guttenbergium* et *Jo. Faustum*, an. 1455 disceptatam, pertinentis. Instrumentum illud ex codice MS. *Jo. Frider. Fausti*, qvi an. 1600 authentica documenta multa, quæ ad hanc causam spectant, ex avita hæreditate accepta, congesserat, descriptum est à *Jo. Ernesto von Glauburg* an. 1712. 3 Mart. Titulus iste est : Copia, &c.

of the Instrument, both written by Von Glauburg on the first same 3rd of March, 1712, for Z. C. von Uffenbach. One transcript is No. 9, the other No. 16 in the volume; they differ from each other in small matters only. The "title" *Copia*, &c., of which Wolf speaks is, of course, one made by Von Glauburg. In the "title" of the second transcript Von Glauburg seems to have considered it necessary to insert above the word "Verleger" the two words "Erfinder und."]

In 1740, Joh. *Christian* Wolf, the brother of Christopher, published his *Monumenta typographica* (Hamburg, 1740), and on p. 471 of Vol. I. gave the Notarial document of the Lawsuit as an Appendix to a Discourse on the Invention of Printing, of which I shall speak presently. He printed the document from the transcript which his brother Christopher possessed as an Appendix to this Discourse, as we shall see presently [p. 90]. In Christian's *Monumenta* we read after the Discourse:—

> "Here follows the copy of a judicial instrument *from the autographum* (the document has been taken from the original word for word), whence it appears that Johann Guttenberg was in nowise the first originator of this noble art, but furnished Johann Faust, by whom he had been taken into partnership, with money."*

Christian Wolf makes it plain to us that he did not print the Instrument from one of the two separate transcripts made by Von Glauburg in 1712, which were in the possession of his brother Christopher (see above), because, not only does he tell us that he had seen this transcript (qu. both?), but also gives its title (Copia eines alten, &c.) and the *variants* contained in it. Moreover, as Christian Wolf also adds to his text the variants found in Senckenberg's text, we are led to believe that the transcripts made by Von Glauburg in 1712, and the texts published by Senckenberg in 1734 and by Christian Wolf in 1740 are totally independent of each other.†

* Sequitur exemplum Instrumenti judicialis *ex avtographo* (Documentum hoc ex Originali de verbo ad verbum sumtum), unde apparet, *Johannem Guttenbergium* nequaquam artis hujus nobilis primum auctorem esse, sed à *Joh. Fausto* in consortium adscitum, pecuniam ei suppeditasse.

† Christian Wolf says: "Oculis usurpavi aliud hujus instrumenti exemplum, quod inscribitur: *Copia eines alten*, &c. [see p. 75]. Exstat etiam illud typis expressum in V.C. *Henr. Christiani Senckenbergii* Selectis Juris et Historiarum Tom. I. pag. 269–277 ubi inscribitur: *Laudum inter* Jacobum et Joannem Faustios *ex una*, et Johannem

[¶ A personal visit to Hamburg enables me to say that Christian Wolf printed the text of the Instrument and of the Discourse (of which I shall speak afterwards, see below, p. 91) from the transcript made for Von Uffenbach in 1715 from the *apographum* made by Joh. Max. Zum Jungen (†1649). Von Uffenbach had the whole copied in a codex, and wrote on the first page: "Faust ab Aschaffenb. De origine atque inventione artis Typographicae. Ex apographo Viri Illustris Jo. Max. Zum Jungen quod generos. Dn. Jo. Ernest. a Glauburg benevole concessit hanc sibi copiam per amanuensem fieri jussit Z. C. ab Uffenbach Ffurti ad Moenum. Mens. Jan. MDCCXV."]

In 1741 Joh. Dav. Köhler, Hist. P. Prof. Ord. at Goettingen from 1735 to 1755, again published the Notarial document on p. 54 of his *Ehren-Rettung Johann Guttenbergs* (4to, Leipz., 1741). He prints it, line for line, and states that he takes it

"from the original on parchment, in forma patente, in folio." *

After the text Köhler adds (on p. 57) a note, in which he states :—

a) That Arn. Bergellanus (see above, p. 72) was the first who mentioned the lawsuit between Guttenberg and Faust ; b) that a more detailed account of this lawsuit was given by Joh. Friedr. Faust von Aschaffenburg in the Discourse on the Origin of Printing [of this I speak below], to which was added, for the first time, the Instrument of the Notary Helmasperger, though in a manner of writing entirely altered and modified according to modern usage ; c) that a copy of this Discourse must have come into the hands of the Amberg Syndic, Heinrich Salmuth, as his *De Typographiae sive Artis Impressoriæ inventione verissima historia*, which appears as an Appendix to *Tit. xii. de Typographia*, in *Guid. Pancirolli Nova reperta*, is scarcely anything but a Latin translation of the Discourse, in which he also refers to the Instrument in question, and says of it, p. 312, ed. Francof. 1646 [it appears already in an ed. Francof. 1631, p. 312—J.H.H.] 'sicut ex archetypo Instrumenti, quod etiamnum superest, & anno 1455. 6. Novembr. à Joh. Ulrico Helmaspergero Notario ea de re confectum fuit, liquido demonstrari potest ;' d) that Philip. Ludov. Authaeus, in his *Warhafftige Historia von Erfindung der Buckdruckereykunst* (An. 1681), which is an extract from Faust's Discourse, and is of exactly the same import as Salmuth's narrative, also refers to this Instrument ; e) that, because Faust's Discourse has always remained in writing, the said *Instrument in forma* has never been seen in print until Senckenberg, Councillor and Professor

---

Guttenberg *ex altera parte, agens de pecunia in librorum impressionem insumta.* Ex utroque varietates lectionis diligenter notavi."

* "Aus dem Original auf Pergament, in Forma patente, in folio."

at Giessen, published it in 1734 for the first time, in tom. I. of his Select. Jur. &c. [see above, p. 68]. f) that Prof. [Jo. Christian] Wolf, at Hamburg, published it again [in 1740] in his Monum. Typogr., together with a Latin translation of Faust's Discourse, to which, as has been said before, it was attached, while he [Wolf] added, as far as was necessary, 'variantes lectiones' from the copy which Mr. Joh. Ernst von Glauburg had diligently and correctly made, on the 3rd of March, An. 1712, from the MSS. of Joh. Friedr. Faust, who had copied it, circ. An. 1600, from the original, which at that time was still in existence in the family, while Wolf also collated the Senckenberg copy; g) that, whereas he (Köhler) had *also obtained an authentic copy written on parchment in forma patente—of the correctness of which we could doubt the less because in line* 66 *Johann Faust desires the Notary Ulrich Helmasperger to prepare one or more open Instruments as many and as often this would be necessary* —he had thought it necessary to add this in a new copy, regularly prepared by him according to the numbered lines, with correct observation of all letters, syllables, abbreviations, and the few interpunctions occurring in it.

If we did not know it from another quarter, it would be clear from Köhler's statement b) that the Instrument to which he alludes, as being annexed to the Discourse, was *a transcript*, in nowise directly emanating from the Notary Helmasperger. His statement e) seems to imply that Senckenberg printed his text (said to be taken *from the original*) from *this transcript* annexed to the Discourse.

Köhler does not say how and whence he obtained *his* own copy, which he declares to be "*authentic, written on parchment in forma patente.*" On p. 23 he speaks of "the original, on parchment, as lying before him."

Dr. Van der Linde naïvely says (p. li.), "V. Glauburg gave also to Köhler an authentic (!) copy on parchment." If Dr. Van der Linde believed this to be a fact, the worthlessness of Köhler's copy should have been clear to him from the circumstance that v. Glauburg himself declares in 1712 that he makes his transcript merely from *the transcript* made about 1600 by J. Fr. Faust v. Aschaffenburg, and that, therefore, he (v. Glauburg) could not be expected to supply any one with an *authentic* copy.

If Köhler really obtained his copy from v. Glauburg, it could only have been a transcript, in which case his reference to line 66 of the Instrument [see above Köhler's statement g] would not only be absurd, but misleading, as it cannot mean anything but that he declares his copy to be an *authentic one drawn up by the Notary Helmasperger himself, at the request of Fust.* And yet—one can hardly avoid the conclusion that von Glauburg *was* the man who supplied Köhler with his copy of the Instrument; for the latter, in the preface to his "Ehrenrettung," says:—

"I myself had, for a long while, been unable to extricate myself from the many entangled accounts and contradictions concerning the person, the genealogy, and social position of Johann Guttenberg, *until*, in 1723, *I had the honour and the pleasure to make the acquaintance of the late Johann Ernst von Glauburg, of Nieder-Erlenbach.* This gentleman, possessing much knowledge of History, Genealogy, and Heraldry, and especially of affairs concerning Mentz, had the kindness, in a very busy correspondence with me, to supply me, from the papers of the noble and baronial Family Zum Jungen, of whom he was a near relation, with a clue which fortunately enabled me to escape from this labyrinth. Therefore, whatever substantial evidences concerning Johann Guttenberg, extracted from contemporary documents, the reader will find in this work, *he owes them solely to the industry and friendly communication of this obliging nobleman* to whom he, together with me, will render thanks for having set this obscure matter in such clear light, *in the same manner as Prof. Senckenberg* [the italics are mine, J. H. H.], in his preface to vol. 1 (pp. 41, 43), and vol. 2 (p. 31), of his Select. Jur. & Histor., very much praises the assistance with which [von Glauburg] enriched his magnificent collections of old documents." ¶

[¶ I have already explained on p. 63 why I deemed it necessary to have a little more security as to the origin of Köhler's text. The only difficulty was where researches were to be made. All that could be gathered from the latest authors on the invention of printing (Wetter, Van der Linde) was that the original of the Instrument and of the Discourse (of which I shall speak presently) were *thought* to be at Frankfurt on the Main, in a collection brought together by Z. C. von Uffenbach († 1734), who, *it was said*, had come into possession of the MSS. and papers of Johan Ernst von Glauburg († 1733), Johan Maximilian Zum Jungen († 1649), Johan Friedr. Faust von Aschaffenburg († 1621), &c. In June last I requested Dr. Haueisen, the Librarian at Frankfurt, to tell me whether these collections were still there and would be accessible to me, and this request was repeated twice, but for some reasons, which I must leave him to explain, he never replied to any of the three letters. In my uncertainty I commenced, in Sept. 1880, my researches at Hamburg, where I knew for certain that some of the Uffenbach MSS. were preserved, and afterwards went to Frankfurt on the Main. My difficulties at the two places were considerable in spite of Dr. Isler's great kindness at Hamburg. To mention but *one* incident; at *Hamburg* I found two folio volumes, which were evidently *indexes* to a collection of letters written to, and by, Von Uffenbach from A.D. 1706–1732; but where were the letters themselves? A search of three days at Hamburg enabled me to say that they were *not* there, and that they would *probably* be at Frankfurt. I therefore copied from the indexes at Hamburg all that I thought could help me at Frankfurt, and I then went to the latter place, where I actually found 16 volumes containing the letters and Uffenbach's replies. Among these were a great number written by Köhler, von Glauburg, Senckenberg, Schelhorn, Geo. Chr. Joannes, &c., all persons who

In 1878 Dr. Van der Linde writes a life of Gutenberg and reprints the Instrument, apparently from Köhler's text, without having seen either an original or any of the transcripts, and on p. 292, speaking of "an extremely solid ground, the Mentz notarial instrument of 1455," he actually

occupied themselves at that time with the question. In many of these letters allusion is made to the work which Köhler was preparing on Gutenberg. E.g. Von Glauburg wrote to Von Uffenbach already on the 30th Nov. 1723, about "Vindiciae Guttenbergicae" which he himself had long intended to bring out, and which they now expected from Köhler's pen, to whom he (Von Glauburg) had transmitted some documents bearing on the subject. Of the original of the Notarial Instrument nothing was said in all these letters that could give me any light. From a remark made to me by the Archivist of Frankfurt, Dr. Grotefend, I was led to go to Darmstadt. In the Archives there some of Köhler's letters to Joh. Ernst von Glauburg are preserved, two of which made it evident to me that he had really found an *authentic* copy of the Instrument. But, in whose possession? On the 14th of April 1727 he wrote to Von Glauburg that he had already asked for "an accurate orthographic copy of the original of the Faust Instrument." And on the 7th January following he writes to the same: "The original Instrument in the Guttenberg and Faust process, which *your cousin in Frankfurt* has communicated to me, has fortunately enabled me to correct several false readings and has served me greatly as regards the old orthography." This phrase, "your cousin (Vetter) in Frankfurt," is thus the sole clue we possess.

It is strange that Köhler, who is very particular in his "*Ehrenrettung*" in mentioning the sources of his other documents, is silent about this, the most important of his whole collection. He mentions this relative of Von Glauburg's nowhere, and merely says the Instrument "had come into his hands" (p. 58) and "it was lying before him" (p. 23). This last statement is corroborated by Christian Gottl. Schwarz, who says (Dissert. de origine typographiae, Altorf. 1740; reprint. Norimb. 1793, p. 304) "he had seen with his own eyes the *autographum* written on vellum, in Köhler's hands," but, curiously enough, he suspected that Köhler had obtained it from Senckenberg! It is fortunate, however, that we have Köhler's own evidence for the authenticity of his document, for Schwarz was possessed of rather strange eyes and a strange memory. E.g., he declared in the same dissertation (p. 314) that in 1728 he had seen in the Carthusian monastery at Mentz a copy of the [36-line] Bible, of which he had read in the old catalogues of the monastery that this Bible had been presented to the monastery by Johann Gutenberg and some others whose names he had forgotten. Schaab (I. 264) has demonstrated that Schwarz could not have seen this Bible at Mentz, as the Carthusians had sold the copy ten years previously, and that the old catalogues which Schwarz *could* have seen merely speak of the Bible of 1462 as printed by Fust and Schoeffer. See Madden, Lettres d'un bibliogr. iii. 57, who contradicts Schaab, but the latter seems to be correct.

Another strange circumstance is that Köhler worked at least 18 refers his readers to the title (Copia eines alten, &c.) which von Glauburg prefixed to the *transcript* which he made in 1712 from a *transcript* said to have been made in 1600 by Joh. Friedr. Faust von Aschaffenburg from the original! Cf. Dr. V. D. Linde's "Gutenberg," at the end, p. li., where he also says that another copy, also on parchment and with the notarial mark, is in the Mentz town-library—(No, says he, on p. 524, it is *not* there).

Strange that Dr. Van der Linde should have been under the impression that he was writing history!

We may now turn to the *Discourse* mentioned before, which is said to have been written by Joh. Friedr. Faust von Aschaffenburg, *Junior.* But before we examine this document, it will not be superfluous to examine some utterances of the other Joh. Friedr. Faust von Aschaffenburg, mentioned before, who is said to have been his father.

Achill. Aug. von Lersner published, in 1706, *Chronica der Stadt Franckfurt-a.-M.* (Franckf. 1706, fol.). In his Preface he says that—

"the basis of his work is Gebhard Florian's Frankfurter Chronik, published in 1664, and a second vol. by Geo. Fickwirth, ed. by Joh. Friedr. Faust von Aschaffenburg [the *son*], first published in 1660, and reissued, with a new title-page, in 1664 as a *continuation* of Florian's Chronicle. That, moreover, he made use of the 'many *Collectanea* of the celebrated and laborious Joh. Friedr. Faust von Aschaffenburg [the *father*], which he, according to his own handwriting, collected during a period of 25 years.'"

Lersner devotes Chapter XVIII. of the first volume to the noble Families of the House Limpurg and on p. 299 he says:—

"The noble families here [Frankfurt] are famous for their inventions of new sciences; and especially Mr. Zumjungen zu Gudenberg invents printing, which Johannes Faust von Aschaffenburg (*sic!*) assists afterwards in cultivating." *

---

years (1723-41) at his "Ehrenrettung Guttenbergs," a book of not more than 124 pages, and that in spite of his receiving great assistance from Von Glauburg, Von Uffenbach and others. The former supplied him with nearly all the documents and accompanied them by notes which Köhler inserted in his work almost word for word, as may be seen from the sketch which Von Glauburg kept for himself and which is still preserved in the Darmstadt Archives.]

* "In Erfindung neuer Wischenschafften seynd hiesige Adliche Familien auch berühmt; und sonderlich Herrn Zumjungen zu Gudenberg, erfindet die Druckerey, welche Johannes Faust von Aschaffenburg hilffet nachmahls excoliren."

In Ch. XXVIII. he treats of the question of the invention of printing. He first quotes Phil. Lud. Authaeus' *Warhafftige Historia von Erfindung der Buchdruckerey-Kunst* (typis Blasii Ilsneri, 1681), which is nothing but an extract from the *Discourse* of which we are going to treat. As this ascribes the invention of printing to Faust, Lersner, in refutation of this account, quotes Tentzel's *Discurs von der Buchdruckerey*, where Gutenberg is said to be the inventor, and adds (p. 437):—

"Johann Friederich Faust von Aschaffenburg [the father], who published the Lübeck and Franckenberg Chronica, as well as the Fasti Limpurg, does not accept, *in his manuscript*, the invention of printing for his Family, but attributes it equally to Gutenberg, of the Family Zum Jungen, in these words:—'The Fausts von Aschaffenburg are a very old, honest, and distinguished family, who have always existed on their income or have been in the employ of great lords and towns. Where the first lived cannot be well indicated; I deplore the negligence of my ancestors in this respect, but it may be that through the length of time the documents have been lost. I have to regard Johann Faust, who died 1420, as the founder of the family; his son was joint-proprietor in the printing-office in the town of Mentz. *Some would have and make him, against his will, an inventor, though he only helped with his means and good advice in the thing*; it seems (!) that he had a daughter, named Christina, whom he gave to Mr. Peter von & zu Gernszheim named Schäffer, as wife, on account of his qualities, especially on account of facilitating the printing, and adopted him as son; these begat Johann von Gernsheim, whose son, of the same name, the last of this name, died without heirs.'" *

* "Johann Friederich Faust von Aschaffenburg, welcher nebst der Lübeckischen und Franckenbergischen Chronica auch die Fastos Limpurg. durch den Druck der Welt hat mitgetheilet, lehnet die Erfindung der Buchdruckerey in seinen MS. also von seiner Familia ab, da er seine Familiam beschreibet, und eignet sie gleichfals dem Gutenberg von der Familien derer Zumjungen zu, in diesen Worten. Es seynd die Fausten von Aschaffenburg ein sehr altes, ehrliches und vornehmes Geschlecht, so sich iederzeit ihren Renten und Zinsen ernehret, oder in grosser Herren und Stadt Diensten sich gebrauchen lassen. Wo der erst gelebt, ist nicht wohl anzuzeigen; Ich beklage die Nachlässigkeit meiner Vor-Eltern in diesem Stück. Zwar kan es auch seyn, dass durch die Länge der Zeit die Documenta seynd verlohren gangen. Johann Fausten, welcher 1420 gestorben, muss ich vor den Stammvater halten. Dessen John gleiches Nahmens, ist Mitverleger der Buchdruckerey in der Stadt Mentz, *etliche wollen wider seinen Danck ihn zu einen Inventorem haben and machen, so aber nur mit seinen Vermögen und guten Rath in der That geholffen.* Er soll eine Tochter gehabt haben, Nahmens Christina, welche er Herrn Peter von und zu Gernsheim, genannt Schäffer, zur Frauen gegeben, wegen seiner Qualitäten, in specie wegen der facilitirung der Buch-

Nothing is said here of the Instrument of the law-suit.

After this quotation from Faust's papers Lersner adds:—

"Maximilian Faust von Aschaffenburg [a son of Johan Friedr., born 2 Sept. 1593, died 5 June 1651] says in his *Consilia pro Ærario*, Clas. 16, Ord. 1193, p. 694 (published at Francof. 1641), that he had the Faust documents concerning this point in hand, and quoted many authors who had written on the art of printing, saying at the same time that the first printing commenced in 1446 with the Officia Ciceronis. The documents of both these families were put by Johann Schäffer in his Roman history of Livy, and published March 6, 1505, with the old Faust and Schäffer arms."

This Johann Friedr. Faust von Aschaffenburg, the *father*, (who is said to have *copied*, about 1600, the Instrument of the Law-suit from the *original*, and who published a Chronick von der Stadt Limpurg, at Heidelberg, in 1617 and 1619, and a Franckenbergisch and Lubeckisch Chronick at the same place in 1619), is said to have died at Franckfurt, in 1619 (cf. Lersner's Chron. der Stadt Franckfurt, I. 281; J. Christoph. Wolf, Mon. typ. I. 453; Van der Linde, Gutenberg, 291), and Dr. Van der Linde says (p. 522) that he had remained silent [about the origin of printing] because he was too sincere!

Very well; *but let us see whether Dr. Van der Linde is right.* There is in the Brit. Mus. (Pressmark, 172, i. 3): "Lubeckische Chronick. . . . . zusammen getragen durch Hans Regkman. . . . . an tag gegeben è MSS. Johann Friederichs Fausten von Aschaffenburg. . . . Verlegt durch Gotthard Vögelin [without place, but G. Vögelin lived at *Heidelberg*, J. H. H.]. Im Jahr 1619". After the title follows a dedication to the Mayor and Council of Lubeck, which is signed "*Johann Friederich Faust, von Aschaffenburg &c. L*[*ubecensibus*] *M* [*agistris*] *DD.*", and it is dated "from Nidercleen, situated in Tripoli Giessen, Wetzlar and Butzbach, in the year 1620, the 20th day of April."* In this dedication we find on the second page:—

"Meantime had He [i.e. God] prepared the way and given to the whole world an unheard-of gift, namely, the noblest art of all

druckerey, und ihn in filium adoptiret haben. Diese zeügen Johann von Gernsheim; dessen Sohn ejusdem nominis der letzte dieses Nahmens stirbt ohne Erben."

* "Gestellt zu Nidercleen in Tripoli Giessen, Wetzlar vnd Butzbach gelegen, im Jahr der Geburt unsers Erlösers Jesu Christi M.DC.xx den zwantzigsten Tag Aprill."

the arts, printing, out of the distinguished town of the Holy empire, Mentz, through a distinguished citizen there, called *Johan Faust*, who in the year 1450, brought this art to light, and through the assistance of *Peter Schäffer von Gernsheim*, a clerk, his servant, afterwards the husband of his daughter, improved it to such an extent that every one, especially the Italians and French could not wonder enough about it, and out of jealousy tried in vain to scratch out and destroy these writings by means of lye and scratching-brushes." *

After the dedication follows the privilege accorded to the printer by Frederic, Pfaltzgraff bey Rhein, dated "Haidelberg, the 19th of July, 1619."

Now, if Johann Friedrich *the father* died in 1619, as it is asserted, then this dedication *could* not have been dated by *him*. But I doubt whether the father *did* die in 1619. In Lersner's Chronica (mentioned above), p. 278, we find a "List of Frankfurt magistrates," and it is to this List that J. Chr. Wolf refers (Monum. typogr. i. 453) when he speaks of Faust's death as having taken place in 1619. The List commences with the year 1570, and in it we find it stated, indeed, that J. F. Faust v. Aschaffenburg died in "1619," but it is clear that the compiler of the List did not derive this year from any authentic or sure source, as he does not say on what day of the year Faust died, whereas this is done with a great many other magistrates mentioned in the List. It is, therefore, not so certain that J. F. Faust, the *father*, was no longer alive in 1620; and that it is the *father* and *not*

* "Inmittels aber hatt Er, zu einer bequemlichen Gelegenheit Weg vnd Baan bereitet, vnd der gantzen Welt ein ohnerhörte Gaben geschenckt, nemlich die Edleste Kunst aller Künsten, die Buchdruckerey, aus der damals noch des H. Reichs vornemen vnd genandten Güldenstadt Meintz, durch einen vornemen Bürger daselbst, Johan Faust genandt, welcher in Anno 1450 solche Kunst an tag gebracht, vnd durch hilff Petri Schäffers von Gernsheim Clerici, seines Dieners, hernach Tochtermans, dermassen verbessert, dass sich jedermänlich, vorab die Wahlen vnd Frantzosen, nit genug darüber verwundern können, vnd aus vergunst, mit laugen vnd kratzbürsten solche Schrifften auszukratzen vnd zu vernichtigen, vnd verruft zu machen, aber vergebens, vnderstanden. Die doch hernach, als Meintz von dem Reich in Anno 1462. vnd also vmb diese vortrefliche gaben, die sie allein vor sich behalten können vnd mögen, nit ohne sonderliche schickung Gottes, kommen, vnd dahero die Burgerschaft ausgejagt vnd zerstört, vnd also auch der Druckerey Diener ausgetrieben, vnd anderswohin sich zu begeben verursacht worden, derselbigen am meisten gebrauchet vnd ihren nutzen damit geschaft haben."

the *son* who dated and signed the dedication, seems clear when we find it said towards the end, by Faust, that he had had the Chronicle in question "a long time among his MSS." This could not have been said by the *son* in 1620, if his father had died in 1619. That the title-page of the Lubeck Chronicle bears the year 1619, and the dedication is dated 1620, is probably owing to the printing of the book having been finished before the preface was written.

Strange to say, after the Chronicle follows an appendix of 17 pp. on Wissmar affairs. Quite at the end of this appendix, on p. 17, we read :—

"How long is it that the noble art of printing books or prenterey was found? In the year 1440 after the birth of Christ the printing of books arose under the Emperor Frederic by Johann Genssfleisch, at Mentz, though several ascribe the invention of this art to Johan Guttenberg, of and at Strassburg. Others say the art was invented and raised by Johan Guttenberg, a knight at Mentz, Anno M.CCCC.L." *

Did this passage, perhaps, emanate from Hans Regkman, the compiler of the Chronicle, who lived in the sixteenth century?

[¶ A personal visit to the Hamburg Library enables me to state that the Low German MS. from which Faust von Aschaffenburg edited the Chronicle in a High German version is preserved there, and contains the passage quoted. The MS. seems to have been continued by H. R. till 1537, but was, in 1551, in the possession of one who calls himself Reynier Cock. I cannot say how far and what the latter added to the MS. vol., but I found no later date in it than 1560, and the whole is of about the same period.]

It is plain that if the dedication is the father's dedication, he could scarcely be the author also of the statement about his Family published by Lersner from his MSS.; otherwise Faust v. Aschaffenburg would not have spoken of his reputed ancestor, in one place, as not being the inventor, and in another place as the inventor.

* Wie lang ist, dasz die Edle Kunst der Buchtruckerey oder Prenterey erfunden sey? Nach Christi geburt 1440. jahr hat sich erreget vnder Kayser Fridrich das Buchtrucken im Teutschland von Johan Genszfleisch zu Mentz: wiewol etliche dieser Kunst erfindung zuschreiben Johan Guttenberg von vnd zu Strassburg. Die dritten sagen die Kunst sey erdacht vnd vfkommen von Johan Guttenberg, eim Ritter zu Mentz Anno MCCCC.L.

An examination of the MS. vol. in which Faust v. Aschaffenburg is said to have written the statement about his Family, can alone satisfy us as to this note being written by himself.¶

It is to be observed, however, that in neither of the above statements, ascribed to the elder Faust v. A., do we find *any mention of the Instrument of the Law-suit of* 1455.

And now as to the *Discourse*, which is a more detailed account of the invention of printing considered to have been written by the *son*, also called *Johan Friedrich Faust von Aschaffenburg.* (Cf. Wolf, Mon. typ. I. 452; Van der Linde, Gutenberg, 292.) It must have been written after 1620, at least after the publication of Chr. Besoldus' *Dissertatio de inventione typographiæ*, which appeared in 1620

[¶ Dr. Grotefend, the Archivist at Frankfurt, kindly informed me that Baron von Günderrode, who resides at Frankfurt, but whose ancestral seat is at Höchst on the Nidder in Ober-Hessen, possessed some MSS. of Joh. Friedr. Faust von Aschaffenburg. Having obtained the permission of this nobleman to make researches in his library at Höchst, I went thither and found a great number of genealogical tables all written by J. F. Faust v. Aschaffenburg himself. I failed to find the *passage quoted by Lersner.* But I *did* find some lines which make it superfluous, I think, to look for Lersner's quotation any further. Tracing the genealogy of himself, J. F. Faust v. A. wrote:

Johann Faust Typographiæ author vixit 1454 cum fratre laut vertrags, mit Johan v. Gutenberg seins Gemeins getroffen. Christine.	Christina F. Peter v. Gernsheim zum Schöfer . author typographicæ impressuræ &c.

In another table he says again:

Jacob Faust.
vixit 1454.
Johan F.
Typographiæ
inventor, vixit
cum fratre 1454.

In the face of these statements no one will be anxious, I suppose, to search for Lersner's quotation. If it is still in existence, it could not, I think, have been written by the same man who wrote the tables in Baron v. Günderrode's possession. And I am positive that these are in the handwriting of Joh. Friedr. Faust v. Aschaffenburg, *senior*, because I have been able to study his writing from a letter of his preserved at Hamburg, dated 14 April, 1617.]

at Tübingen, as this treatise is referred to in the Discourse. The writer says:—

"Authors are uncertain as to the place and time of the invention and the person of the inventor, and on that account I have thought it necessary to narrate and to prove somewhat more in detail the whole course and commencement of this art, partly as I have accepted it from trustworthy old testimonia and documents, as also from my blessed father, and he from his parents and ancestors, quasi per aures et manus, and partly as it has been written down. First it is affirmed that there lived at Mentz, a citizen of a respectable family, named Joh. Faust, who, devoted to literature, comprehended that the scarcity of books (for the writing of which a long time and immense costs are required), which very few can bear, is often the cause of the most superior intellects becoming dull, and being withdrawn from study. He, therefore, laboured to devise a commodious way of multiplying various useful books with less trouble, and of placing them within the reach of many at a small and fair cost. God, favouring such benevolent wishes and intentions, showed him the means and a model, so that he first cut an alphabetical table with raised characters. He bestowed much thought on the discovery of a peculiar ink, because the common ink flows together when put on letters cut of, and in, wood, and confounds the characters. Lamp-black produced a tolerable, but not a lasting impression, until a tenacious black and durable ink was discovered. When, by means of this material, such tables were printed with small presses, every one with great surprise, bought them for a small sum, and admired them, and he [Faust] was thereby induced to go on and to produce the Donatus. But as this was cut on entire blocks and with unequal characters, and not many copies could be printed of it, the inventor deemed it more commodious to compose a book with single and separate letters, than to cut it with entire columns and pages. He, therefore, cut the blocks asunder and took from them all the characters, and in this manner commenced composition, and replaced the worn-out characters by new ones. But as this could only be effected by great labour and slowly, the inventor met with great obstacles in the new art, also on account of the presses. Now, he employed several servants who printed for him and assisted him diligently in other necessary things as preparing ink, composing, &c. Among them was a certain Peter Schöffer, of Girnsheimb, who learning his master's intentions and liking the work himself, by God's favour invented the art of cutting letters into puncheons and casting them, which enabled him to multiply them continually, and not to cut each letter separately. This assistant secretly cut the puncheon for a whole alphabet, and showed them with the matrices and the cast letters to his master Johann Faust, who was so much pleased with them that he promised him his daughter Christina in marriage, which very soon took place. But the impression or casting of these characters gave as much trouble as the wooden ones, until some mixture was found which could bear the pressure of the press for some length of time. In order that such a noble gift of God might be kept secret, the father-in-law and his son-in-law bound their assistants with an oath to keep all the matters a secret, and the blocks, wooden types, and other early instruments, they put together with some cord and showed them now and then to their friends. A MS. left to us* testifies to my grandfather, Dr. Johann Faust, having seen these first beginnings, among which was the first part of a Donatus. God, however, disposed that the art should not remain a secret. The next-door neighbour of Johann Faust, called Johann von Guttenberg (it is also thought that Johann Faust and Guttenberg lived together in one house named Zum Jungen in Mentz, wherefore it afterwards obtained the name of Printing-office), having learned that this noble art not only created great glory in the whole world, but also produced good and honest profits, behaved friendly towards the said Faust, and offered his services with advances of the necessary money, which was readily accepted by Faust, because the work which he intended to print on parchment required considerable expenses. They therefore agreed, and settled by a legal (*aufgeschnitten* = indented) contract, the contents of which follow, that they would bear together the costs and share the profits. But because Faust had borrowed more money and the expenses ran higher than Guttenberg had anticipated, the latter would not pay his half share, and they therefore, came together before the secular court at Mentz, which inquired into the matter; and when Johann Faust declared on oath that the money borrowed had been devoted to the work, Guttenberg was compelled to pay. To this sentence Johann Faust rendered satisfaction in the refectory at Mentz in the Convent of the Barefoot Friars, *as may be seen profoundly and truly from the instrument which is annexed herewith in copy.* But Johann von Guttenberg was very angry, and, therefore, did not come to hear the oaths taken, and very soon went from Mentz to Strassburg, where he had probably his own printing, and several men followed him, and a complete separation happened, so that this glorious art was no longer kept secret, but *spread since the date of the said instrument, which was dated Ao.* 1455. And Hans von Petersheim, a servant of Johannes Faust and Peter Schœffer, settled in 1459 at Frankfurt; and others, especially when Mentz was treacherously conquered in 1462, settled elsewhere, and exercised, revealed, and made common the said art. Also this misfortune happened that, when they had taken to Paris, in France, an important law book printed on parchment, the foreigners were jealous of such art, and tried, but in vain, to put the book in lye and to scratch out [the letters] with scratching-brushes. Thereupon all copies were confiscated on the pretence that the printer had imported into France strange goods without special permission of the king. But he obtained indemnification from the Emperor Frederic III., and the affair was at last settled by the monarchs of both countries, and Peter Schœffer obtained satisfaction."

The last clause may be compared with the father's narrative in the Dedication to the Lubeck Chronicle.

It should not be overlooked that the Author of this Discourse himself says that he subjoins the Instrument to his compilation *in copy.*

* I am not aware that this manuscript has ever been traced.

It is, as has been remarked above, uncertain when this narrative was written, though it could not have been *before* 1620; *it was not published* by the younger Faust, its reputed author, when, in 1660, he himself published a work, entitled *Der Stadt Franckfurt Herkommen und Aufnehmen.*

The Discourse, however, must have been known in **1631**, because in that year Henr. Salmuth, the syndic of Amberg, published an edition of Guid. Pancirolli *Rerum Memorabilium recens inventarum pars post.*, Francof. 1631,* 4to (in Br. Mus., Pressmark, 461, b. 1), and there we find as an Appendix to the 12th chapter de Typographia, an abridged *Latin* translation of the Discourse, but without the name of the author; the Instrument of the law-suit is thus referred to:—

"Sicut ex archetypo Instrumenti, quod etiamnum superest, et anno 1455, 6 Novembr. à *Joh. Ulrico Helmaspergero Notario* ea de re confectum fuit, liquido demonstrari potest."

In **1641** the papers and documents of the Faust family were in the hands of Maximilian Faust von Aschaffenburg, who, in that year, published *Consilia pro ærario civili, &c.* (Francof., 1641), of which Class 108, ord. 1193 is devoted to a history of typography, and in which, enumerating some authors on this subject, e. gr. Cardanus (lib. 17 de Subtil. et de Variet. lib. 13 c. 64), Joh. Bodinus (in Methodo, c. 7), Steph. Forcatuli (lib. 4 de Imp. et Phil. Gallor.), Phil. Melanchthon (in Chron. lib. 5), he says the invention is ascribed to Johan Faust, in the year 1440, adding "the original documents about this point are in my hands." †

In **1650**, Jacobus Mentelius in his *De vera typographiæ origine parænesis*, p. 54, refers to Salmuth's work, and calls the Instrument "a forged and fictitious public instrument" (ementitum fictumque Instrumentum publicum). But he gives no reasons for his opinion; and it is well to bear in mind that his work is an attempt to ascribe the honour of the invention to his name-sake of Strassburg.

In **1681**, Phil. Lud. Authaeus published: *Warhafftige Historia von Erfindung der Buchdruckerey-Kunst*, ex MSS.

* Dr. Van der Linde only knows the ed. of 1646 as the earliest, a date which he no doubt took from Köhler.

† "Inventum tribuitur, Anno 1440. Johanni Faustio de quo mihi documenta originalia in manibus sunt."

Phil. Lud. Authæi: Typis Blasii Ilsneri, MDCLXXXI. He dedicated the work to two brothers, Joh. Hector and Frid. Jacobus Faust von Aschaffenburg, and gave the Discourse in German, without mentioning the name of the author. In his work the reference to the law-suit is in these words:—

"Solchem Rechts-Spruch hat Johann Faust ein Genügen gethan wie auss einem noch in Archivis verhandenem Instrument Anno 1455 gründlich und warhafftig zuerweisen."

The original pamphlet of Authæus I have been unable to find in any library, nor is it mentioned in Theoph. Georgii *Bücher-Lexicon* (Leipz. 1742) or the Supplements, or in Jöcher's *Gelehrten-Lexicon;* but it is reprinted, probably *verbatim*, in Achill. Aug. von Lersner's *Chronica der Stadt Franckfurt* (1706), p. 435 sqq., where we find also an extract from Joh. (Aventinus) Turmaier († 1534), in which also Johannes Faust appears as inventor in 1450, having as servants Petrus Schöfer von Gernssheim and Johannes Gutenberg, a Strassburger, the latter revealing the art in 1460 (see above p. 71).

In 1736 Joh. Christopher Wolf published, at Hamburg, his *Conspectus supellectilis epistolicae*, which I have mentioned above, p. 74. Vol. 2 (in quarto) of the second division of this collection contains, according to Wolf (p. 284), a

"Commentatio ad investigandam artis typographicæ originem, with the Title: *Discurs vom Ursprung der Druckerey, wer, auch wann, und an welchem Orte solche erstmahls erfunden, aus denen ad familiam der Fausten von Aschaffenburg gehörigen documenten*, commencing with a Latin preface to the reader, which is followed by various opinions and testimonies regarding the invention of the art of printing and its first author, till p. 31. After this, till the end (p. 68), we read an account of the beginnings of this art by Joh. Faust, a learned citizen of Mentz, and Peter Schoeffer, of Gernsheim (first his servant, and afterwards, on account of the increase which he caused to the art invented by Faust), his son-in-law, accompanied by appropriate documents, among which the notarial instrument. . . ."

Wolf, after a further analysis of the Instrument, proceeds:—

"This dissertation deserves to see the light. *It was copied for Uffenbach from the transcript* (ex apographo) *of Joh. Maximil. zum Jungen, which Jo. Ern. von Glauburg had allowed him to use.* Of its author I know nothing certain. At the commencement of the preface he says that the inventor of the art was the brother of his paternal great-great-great-grandfather, and, from what I have said while describing cod. xii. in fol. No. 6 [see p. 75], I gather that his name was Jo. Frid.

Faust, as he is said to have collected, about the year 1600, all the documents which concern this matter, and to have transcribed from them the notarial instrument which is added to this Discourse. I may be allowed to add that Joh. Dav. Köhler, formerly Professor at Altorf, and now at Goettingen, has long ago promised us a treatise, in which he will show, from the most ancient Mentz monuments that Gutenberg is the first inventor of this art, and that what Tritheim relates about the lawsuit between him and Faust is not accurate."

This is the first time that we learn some particulars about this interesting Discourse, added to which was a transcript of the Notarial Instrument. It is to be observed, however, that we have here of both documents *a transcript*, made for von Uffenbach, from the *transcript* of Jo. Maxim. Zum Jungen (born at Frankfurt A.D. 1596; died there A.D. 1649), which latter was in the possession of von Glauburg. All that we can gather from Joh. Christoph. Wolf's description of his collection of documents is that von Glauburg had been in the possession of, or had access to, *two* transcripts of the notarial instrument; *one* said to have been made about 1600 by Joh. Friedr. Faust von Aschaffenburg, senior, to serve as an appendix to his *autograph* MS. of the Discourse, and a *second* made by Joh. Maximil. Zum Jungen, which in like manner served as an appendix to his *transcript* of the Discourse.

[¶ A personal visit to Hamburg and Frankfurt enables me to state three things: (1) that the transcript of the Discourse made for Von Uffenbach in 1715, by an ordinary scribe, from the *apographum* of Joh. Maxim. Zum Jungen, at that time in the possession of Joh. Ernst von Glauburg, *is still preserved at Hamburg* (see above, p. 77); (2) that the *apographum* itself of Joh. Max. Zum Jungen I saw (in October 1880) in the Archives at Frankfurt; but its proper place is, I believe, the Frankfurt Town-Library. It is, if my memory serves me right, the last article in a large thick folio volume of transcripts, all made (I believe) by Zum Jungen himself. (3) That I have been so far unable to ascertain the whereabouts of the *autograph* MS. of Joh. Fr. Faust v. Aschaffenburg.]

In **1740**, Joh. Christian Wolf, the brother of *Christopher*, published, also at Hamburg, his Mon. typogr., and on p. 452 of the first vol. inserted the Discourse in its entirety, but translated into Latin. He evidently prints it from the transcript which Uffenbach had had made for him, and which was then, as we have seen, in the possession of his brother

Christopher Wolf. Christian Wolf quotes his brother's explanation with regard to the Discourse, and adds :—

"To me it seems very probable that the son of Joh. Friedr. Faust is the author of this account, *first*, because he declares himself 'to have collected everything which his blessed father had accepted from his parents and ancestors as it were by ears and hands, and had communicated to himself, partly by word of mouth and partly consigned in writing,' and adds in the margin, 'history of the invention by J. F. F. V. A., from the account of his ancestors'; *secondly*, because our author endeavours to show that Faust was the inventor of the typographical art and Gutenberg his associate, and supplied him with money, while Authaeus, in Lersner's Chronik, p. 437, produces a different account from the MS. of Joh. Friedr. Faust treating of his Family; *thirdly*, because our author quotes the Dissertation of Christ. Besoldus, which was published at Tübingen in 1620, while Joh. Friedr. Faust died already in 1619."

Wolf thereupon refers to the List of Frankfurt Senators in Lersner's Chronic, p. 281, of which I have spoken before; he further quotes the passage from Senckenberg's preface: *Advoco,* &c. (see above, p. 69), and mentions the three chronicles published by J. Fr. Faust von A. in 1619, and also the passage found at the *end*—but, strange to say, not that which is found in the dedication—of the Lubeck Chronicle (see above, p. 83).

In Wolf's text (on p. 471) we read after the Discourse: "Sequitur exemplum, &c. (see note on p. 76), with the note, Oculis usurpavi, &c.," which I have mentioned before (p. 76). It is to be observed from these references that Wolf adds to the confusion by calling the document which he had before him an *original,* though we know from his brother's description that what he had actually before him at Hamburg was professedly *a transcript* made from *a transcript.*

In 1741, Joh. Dav. Köhler (Ehrenrettung Guttenberg's, p. 89), published again the Discourse in German "*ex MSSto. Jo. Maximiliani zum Jungen.*" The note which Köhler adds to his text gives us no further particulars about the Discourse. He does not say whether he obtained *his copy* from the Uffenbach transcript preserved at Hamburg, which was made from Zum Jungen's transcript, or directly from the apographum of Zum Jungen, which is said to have been purchased by the Frankfurt Library in 1690 (see Schaab Gesch. Buchdruckerk. I. 467). One thing is certain: Köhler *printed from a transcript.*

Wetter, in his Gesch. der Erfindung der Buchdruckerkunst (Mainz, 1836), speaking of the Discourse (p. 271), said that—

"The original of this Discourse was contained in the Uffenbach collection of MSS. brought together by Latomus, Joh. Max. Zum Jungen, Ernst von Glauburg, and others, at present preserved in the Town-library at Frankfurt. In the second volume of this collection are found 155 pages containing the *Notabilia Fausti ex annalibus Friedr. Faust ab Aschaffenburg*. The 6th part contains the MSS. of Joh. Max. Zum Jungen, after whose MS. Faust's narrative has been printed in Köhler's *Ehren-Rettung*."

It is plain that Wetter, though he often visited the Frankfurt Library (see V. D. Linde, p. 522), never saw this Uffenbach collection or made inquiries for it; for his references to a "second volume" and a "6th part" show that he speaks of the Uffenbach collection preserved at Hamburg (!), as may be seen from what has been said above (p. 75) with regard to that collection. Wetter printed his text from Köhler.¶

In 1878, Dr. Van der Linde was anxious to publish his book on Gutenberg. He appears to have been perfectly satisfied about the Notarial Instrument, though he only refers us to *a transcript* made from *a transcript*. As regards the Discourse, however, he seems to have *wished* to see *the original*. But he tells us that he was ill. He therefore requested Prof. J. Becker, at Frankfurt, to examine the MS. volume pointed out by Wetter. Becker replied to Dr. Van der Linde (p. 522) that "he had examined the *Notabilia*, written on 224 pages (not 155, as Wetter said), but could

[¶ All that I have been able to find at Frankfurt is (1) a MS. vol. containing, among other things, a transcript of the *Notabilia Fausti* made for Von Uffenbach from I know not what MS.; it is No. 17 of the Frankfurt Town-Library, and contains nothing about printing. (2) A MS. volume, in 4to, containing excerpts from the Collectanea of Joh. Friedr. Faust von Aschaffenburg, made by Von Uffenbach himself in 1712, from the vol. which in Faust's Collection was marked with Lit. O. The title-page, written by Von Uffenbach, runs as follows: "*Collectanea Francofurtensia Joh. Frid. Faust ab Aschaffenburg. Vol. Litt. O. notatum* (*mihi vero Litt. B*). *Ex autographo Faustiano quod Dn. J. E. à Glauburg benevole secum communicavit hanc sibi copiam fecit Z. C. ab Uffenbach, MDCCXII mense Junio.*" The first page commences thus: "*Excerpta ex collectaneis* Frid. Faust ab Aschaff. à Maximil. Faust coept. in ordinem digeri 1 May 1625. Sub Litt. O." Von Uffenbach *excerpted* (on p. 170) the Discourse, and had the Notarial Instrument copied, in this volume, by Joh. Ernst von Glauburg. This, therefore, not find anything German of this kind in it, and that therefore the German Discourse of Faust v. Aschaffenburg *must* be concealed somewhere else among these papers, and that these *must* have been accessible to Köhler."

Dr. Van der Linde thereupon publishes his book of 700 pages large 8vo., professing to be based upon 15 documents, which he prints, the Latin ones in Roman type, the German ones in the Gothic type, but of none of which the author had ever seen, or ever attempted to see, the original, not even the transcripts!

All the above guesses and speculations as to the author of the Discourse were written and in type, when, looking by chance into the Appendix to Lersner's Chronica der Stadt Franckfurt, all my doubts were removed at once by what we there read on p. 218:—

"1569. Aug. 5. n[atus]. Joh. Frider. Faust von Aschaffenburg, a son of Johann and Anna Bromm, married, 1592, Margaretha Jeckel, died 1621, July 14, at Nieder-Kleen; he wrote his own epitaph, as follows . . ."

Lersner adds:—

"Of this Faust von Aschaffenburg I have already said in my Chronicle, in my preface as well as in the 28th chapter, that he was the author of the second part of Florian's Short Chronicle of the City of Franckfurt [this is a mistake of Lersner's], and published in 1619 the Fasti Limburgenses, and the Lubeck and Franckenberg Chronicle."

I think this makes it clear enough that Joh. Friedr. Faust v. Aschaffenburg, *the elder*, died in the middle of the year 1621, at Niedercleen, the very place from which he dates the dedication to the Lubeck Chronicle. As the assertion in this dedication harmonises with the assertions in the Discourse as to Faust being the inventor, there is no reason whatever to assert that *the son* [Joh. Friedr.] wrote the Discourse, who does not even seem to have come into the possession of his father's papers, as we have seen (p. 73) that Maxim. Faust v. A. had them in 1641. Consequently, the Discourse

was the *third* transcript of the Instrument made by Von Glauburg for Von Uffenbach (see for the *two* other transcripts above, pp. 74, 75). This vol. is also in the Town-Library. (3) The transcript of the Discourse and Instrument made by Joh. Max. Zum Jungen before 1649. This transcript I saw (in Oct. 1880), in the Frankfurt Archives as above stated.]

may be safely attributed to Johann Friedrich Faust von Aschaffenburg, the *Father*, the same man who is said to have copied, about 1600, the Notarial Instrument. But when we do this, we have no choice but to say that the extract from the father's manuscripts, printed in Lersner's Chronica, in which he renounces the honour of the invention for his family, must be a forgery (!) perpetrated by some one who had access to the Faust papers.¶

As the foregoing history was written partly before I had an opportunity of making researches in Germany and partly after my return, and is, therefore, somewhat intricate, it will not be superfluous to give a short chronological résumé of what we now know to be *facts* with regard to the Notarial Instrument of the Law-suit of 6 Nov. 1455, and the Discourse on the Invention of Printing, written by Joh. Friedr. Faust von Aschaffenburg, *the elder*, between 1620 and 1621.

A.D. 1541. Bergel speaks, for the first time, of a law-suit between Fust and Gutenberg, conducted [in the year?] before a "timorous tribunal;" this "horrible" process was still [in 1541] in the hands of the judge (see above, p. 73).

A.D. 1600. Joh. Friedr. Faust von Aschaffenburg, *the*

[¶ At Frankfurt I learned, from papers written by Fichart and preserved in the City Archives, that the Joh. Fr. Faust von Aschaffenburg, who published, in 1660, the Frankfurt Chronick, was the *son* of Maxim. Faust von Aschaffenburg, and we know that the latter was the son of Joh. Friedr. Faust von Aschaffenburg, the author of the Discourse, who died in 1621; consequently Joh. Fr. Faust von Aschaffenburg, *the elder*, was the *grandfather* of Joh. Fr. Faust von Aschaffenburg, *the younger*. The latter seems to have enlisted in the Dutch army and to have been killed in 1674 at the battle of Grave.

Meerman informs us (Orig. typ. 1765, II. 216) that "Henr. Christ. Baron von Senckenberg had sent him a similar Discourse, which Ad. Schrag had added with his own hand to his Dissertation *von erfindung der Buchdruckerey in Strasburg*, Strassb. 1640, of which Schrag declared that it had been communicated to him after the publication of his Essay and had been taken from the authentic documents of the Faust Family preserved at Frankfurt on the Main. It varies somewhat, especially in style, from [the one usually cited]; nor is it so full as regards certain circumstances, though in substance it comes to the same. Hence we may conclude that the descendants of Joh. Faust altered and amplified it, and that Schrag had obtained an older, Köhler a more recent, text."

I have inquired of the Librarian at the Hague whether this copy of Schrag's Dissertation had come into the Meerman Westreenen Museum, and have been informed that it is *not* there. It does not seem to have been inserted in the Meerman Sale Catalogue of 1824.]

elder, seems to have been occupied in collecting the papers and documents of his ancestors. Among them is said to have been the *original* of the Helmasperger Instrument of 1455; and J. Fr. F. v. A. is alleged to have made a transcript of it on p. 159 of a volume, which, in 1712, is declared to have been marked with Lit. O and to be in the possession of Joh. Ernst von Glauburg, at Nieder-Erlenbach, near Frankfurt. (See below, A.D. 1712, and above, pp. 74, 75.)

A.D. 1619. In this year J. F. Faust von Aschaffenburg, *the elder*, did *not* die, as is asserted by Wolf, Köhler, V. d. Linde, &c. (see above, pp. 83–85), because—

A.D. 1620, April 20, he himself dedicated the *Lubeckische Chronick*, edited by him from the compilations of Hans Regkman, to the Magistrates of Lubeck, and in this dedication he himself gives a short account of the Invention of Printing, asserting that *Johan Faust* invented it at Mentz, in 1450, and improved it with the assistance of Peter Schäffer von Gernsheim, a clerk, his servant, and afterwards his son-in-law. (See above, p. 83.)

Not before A.D. 1620, but before July 14, 1621, the same Joh. Friedr. Faust von Aschaffenburg, *the elder*, compiles a lengthy discourse on the Invention of Printing (see above, p. 86), from the old *testimonia* and documents left to him by his father and ancestors, in which he repeats his assertion of April 20, 1620, that *Johan Faust* was the inventor. But this time he adds: (1) That his grandfather, Dr. Johann Faust, testifies, in a MS. left by him, to having seen the first beginnings of printing, among them the first part of a Donatus; (2) that Joh. von Guttenberg, the next-door neighbour of Joh. Faust, helped the inventor with money; (3) that a quarrel arose between them, and the secular court at Mentz condemned Guttenberg to pay; (and 4) that he added to this Discourse *a transcript* of the legal instrument, which was dated A.D. 1455, and related the result of the law-suit. *This Discourse was never published by the author himself;* consequently the public knew, as yet, nothing of this notarial instrument; the Discourse was written, it seems, in the codex, marked by Faust v. A. himself with the letter O. (See above, A.D. 1600.) I am unable to say whether this codex is still in existence. For extracts made from it see below, A.D. 1631, 1681, 1706, 1712.

A.D. 1621, July 14 (and *not* in 1619), Joh. Friedr. Faust von Aschaffenburg, *the elder*, dies. (See above, p. 94.)

A.D. 1631. Henr. Salmuth published an edition of Guid. Pancirolli Res Memor., pars post., in which he gives, for the first time, an abridged Latin translation of the Discourse, without mentioning its author's name. The Instrument of the Law-suit is merely referred to as being then in existence. (See above, p. 89.)

A.D. 1641. Maximilian Faust v. Aschaffenburg, the son of J. Fr. F. v. A., *the elder*, says the original papers concerning the points mentioned in the Discourse are in his possession. (See above, p. 93.)

Before A.D. 1649, Joh. Max. Zum Jungen* transcribes the Discourse, including its appendix (the transcript of the Instrument). This Zum Jungen transcript was, in 1715, in the possession of J. E. von Glauburg; in Oct. 1880 I myself saw it in the Archives at Frankfurt. (See above, p. 91.)

A.D. 1650. Jacobus Mentelius declares the Instrument of which Salmuth speaks (see A.D. 1631) to be "forged and fictitious," but gives no grounds for his opinion, and had, evidently, never seen it. (We must remember that he would naturally object to anything derogatory to the claims of his namesake of Strassburg.) (See above, p. 89.)

A.D. 1681. Phil. Lud. Authaeus publishes a short history of the Invention of Printing, and dedicates his little work, which is nothing but an abridgment of the Discourse, to two brothers, Joh. Hector and Frid. Jacobus Faust v. Aschaffenburg. Authaeus neither mentions the name of the author of the Discourse, nor prints the Instrument of the Law-suit. (See above, p. 90.)

A.D. 1706. Lersner publishes "Chronick der Stadt Frankfurt," and on p. 435 reprints Authaeus' work, but refutes it, and professes to quote (see above, p. 82) from the MSS. of J. Fr. Faust v. A. [*the elder?*] a passage in which the latter appears as denying that Joh. Faust is the inventor of printing. (See above, pp. 83, 86 where it is shown that J. Fr. F. v. A. distinctly asserted, on more than one occasion, that John Fust *was* the inventor of printing and that he descended from him.)

A.D. 1712. Joh. Ernst von Glauburg makes two separate *transcripts* of the Instrument of the Law-suit for Von Uffenbach, from *the transcript* which *he* (von Glauburg) says was

* The exact year of the Zum Jungen transcript cannot be given; but as he died in 1649, it must be put before that year.

made (on fol. 159 of vol. O), about A.D 1600 (see above) by Joh. Friedr. F. v. A. [*the elder*], from the *original.* (See above, pp. 74, 75.) These two *transcripts* are now in the Public Library at Hamburg.

A.D. 1712. Von Uffenbach makes extracts from a vol. marked with Lit. O, which contained *Collectanea Franco-furtensia* Johannis Friderici Faust ab Aschaffenburg, and was lent to him by Von Glauburg, the latter himself copying the instrument in Von Uffenbach's manuscript. This Uffenbach MS. I myself saw (in Oct. 1880) in the Town Library at Frankfurt. Von Uffenbach's extract from the Discourse and Von Glauburg's transcript of the instrument commence on p. 170. (See above, p. 93, *note.*)

A.D. 1715. Von Uffenbach had transcribed for him the Discourse and the Instrument attached to it from the "*apographum*" of Joh. Max. Zum Jungen (see above, A.D. 1649), lent to him by Joh. Ernst von Glauburg. This Von Uffenbach transcript was, in 1736, at Hamburg in the Wolf Collection, and it was still there (in the Town Library) in Sept. 1880. (See above, pp. 77, 91.)

A.D. 1734. Senckenberg *publishes, for the first time*, the Instrument of the Law-suit, from (what he calls) the *original.* He does not state whence he obtained it, and I am unable to say whether what he used is still in existence; I have a strong suspicion that he printed from the *transcript* mentioned above (A.D. 1600). (See above, p. 68.)

A.D. 1736. Joh. *Christoph* Wolf publishes a description of the collection of MS. volumes, containing letters and documents, which he had bought from Z. C. von Uffenbach. This collection contained: (1) *the two transcripts* of the instrument made in A.D. 1712 (see above) by Von Glauburg for Von Uffenbach; (2) *a transcript* of the Discourse made for Von Uffenbach in 1715, by some copyist, from the *transcript* of Joh. Max. Zum Jungen (made before 1649), lent to Von Uffenbach by Joh. Ernst von Glauburg. These documents were, in Sept. 1880, still in the Public Library at Hamburg. (See above, pp. 74, 75, 90, 91.)

A.D. 1740. Joh. *Christian* Wolf publishes his *Monumenta Typographica*, and in it gives, *for the first time, the whole* of the Discourse, in a Latin translation, with the Instrument attached to it in German, *from the transcript* made for Von Uffenbach, in 1715, *from the transcript* of Joh. Max. Zum Jungen. (See above, pp. 76, 91.)

A.D. 1741. Joh. David Köhler publishes "Ehrenrettung Guttenberg's," and in this work prints: (1) the Instrument of the Law-suit, from what he calls "*the original in formâ patente*," which he says he had obtained from a cousin of Von Glauburg (see above, p. 63, *note*), not from the latter himself, as Köhler's preface would lead us to suppose; but I am unable to say whether this *original* from which Köhler copied is still in existence; (2) the Discourse "ex MS. Johannis Max. Zum Jungen," therefore (?), from the transcript now preserved in the Frankfurt Archives. (See above, p. 92.)

A.D. 1836. Wetter publishes a book on the Invention of Printing, and, from taking no trouble to verify any of the documents, is in great confusion as to the whereabouts of the Discourse and the Notarial Instrument. (See above, p. 93.)

A.D. 1878. Dr. Van der Linde publishes a book on Gutenberg, and, from taking all his documents at *second*, *third*, or *fourth* hand, and rarely telling his readers on what authority he himself prints any single document, and from not investigating a single point in the whole question, his book presents, as it could hardly fail to present, a more complete chaos on the subject than any of its predecessors. (See his book, p. 521 sqq.)

A.D. 1880, October. I am able to state that *there are still in existence in MS.*—

(1) *At Hamburg in the Town Library:*

(a) (in vol. 28[A], fol.) the two separate *transcripts* of the Instrument made by Von Glauburg, from a *transcript* in Vol. Lit. O, containing the *Collectanea*, or Annals of Joh. Fr. Faust v. A.;

(b) (in vol. 27, quarto) the Uffenbach *transcript* of the Discourse with a *transcript* of the Instrument attached to it, made in 1715 from the "*apographum*" of Joh. M. Zum Jungen.

(2) *At Frankfurt on the Main, in the Archives:*

(c) the Joh. M. Zum Jungen *transcript* of the Discourse (made from the *autographum?*), and of the Notarial Instrument attached to it (made from the "*apographum*," of Joh. Fr. Faust. v. A.);

(d) *at Frankfurt, in the Town Library* in an Uffenbach vol. entitled: Collectanea Francofurtensia Joh. Frid. Faust ab Aschaffenburg: excerpts from the Discourse by Von Uffenbach (from the Vol. Lit. O), with a *transcript* of the Instrument attached to it, made by Von Glauburg (from the Vol. Lit. O).

(3) *At Höchst on the Nidder, in Baron Von Günderrode's library:*

(e) several genealogical tables, written by Joh. Friedr. Faust von Aschaffenburg, *the elder,* from which it may be seen that he distinctly ascribes the invention of printing to Johan Faust, his reputed ancestor. (See above, p. 86.)

A search has yet to be made for

(1) the *original* Register of the Mentz Franciscans, where the trial is said to have taken place in 1455 (see p. 68), and which must contain an account of the proceedings.

(2) *The authentic copy (or copies)* of the Notarial Instrument, of which we find three distinct traces from 1600–1741; namely (*a*) that from which J. Fr. Faust v. Aschaffenburg is said to have made his transcript, in the Vol. Lit. O; (*b*) that from which Senckenberg printed his text in 1734; (*c*) that from which Köhler printed his text in 1741, and which he elsewhere tells us belonged to a Frankfurt cousin of Joh. Ernst von Glauburg.

(3) The *original* volume marked with Lit. O, in which J. Fr. Faust v. Aschaffenburg wrote his Discourse and transcribed the Notarial Instrument.*

* Aug. Bernard says in his *Origine de l'imprimerie,* i. 193 (note) that the Discourse was "*published* at Frankfurt in 1620, in 12mo, under the title: *Relatio de origine typographiæ . . . . . e documentis ad Faustorum de Aschaffenburg familiam pertinentibus hausta, etc.*" I can find no trace of such an edition, and it would be strange, if it had existed so early in print, that so many transcripts have been made of the Discourse. The title given by Bernard to the Discourse is identical with that given to the *transcript* preserved at Hamburg, from which the Discourse was published in Wolf's *Monumenta typogr.* i. 452, and it is most probable that Bernard did not read Wolf's note carefully, and understood Wolf to speak of a *printed* work, whereas he speaks of nothing but the MS. preserved at Hamburg.

(4) The MS. volume which contained the short statement attributed by Lersner (see above, p. 82) to J. Fr. Faust v. Aschaffenburg, *the elder*, and in which he is said to reject the honour of the Invention for his ancestor Johan Faust, but which I suspect could not have emanated from him, as he has said the contrary over and over again. (See above, pp. 83, 86.)

It will be seen that, at present, all *originals* are missing. Under these circumstances I do not think it advisable to reprint the Notarial Instrument from any of the transcripts. Dr. Wyss, the Archivist of Darmstadt, expressed to me his opinion, that some of the documents, which should be preserved at Mentz, must have found their way somehow to Würtzburg or Munich. I visited Würtzburg last October, for the purpose of examining two cartularies containing transcripts of two Gutenberg documents (see below pp. 115, 120), but I had no opportunity to make further researches there, and must leave this task, for the present, to others. It will be seen below that Dr. Wyss has already commenced his researches, and succeeded in finding at least some valuable *transcripts.* It is not impossible that a proper exploration of the German Archives and Libraries may have unexpected results. But inquiries of this kind are best made by persons residing in Germany, for they demand time and an intimate knowledge of local institutions, which it is not very easy to obtain except by persons living in the country itself.

I conclude this history of the Instrument and the Discourse with a genealogy of both.

NOTARIAL INSTRUMENT of 1455.

Ulricus Helmasperger, if we were to take the expressions of Senckenberg and Köhler separately, would seem to have supplied Johan Fust with at least *three* authentic copies; but there is, as I have said before, a strong suspicion that there never was more that one copy.

(Where now?) 1. An original which was ab. A.D. 1600 in the possession of Faust von Aschaffenburg.

2. An original used by Senckenberg in 1734. (Where now, or = No. 1?)

3. An original belonging to Von Glauburg's cousin and printed by Köhler in 1741. (Where now, or = No. 1?)

(Where now?) the transcript made ab. A.D. 1600 by Faust v. Aschaff. attached to his Discourse.

the text published by Dr. Van der Linde in 1878.

the transcript made before 1649 by J. M. Zum Jungen, attached to the Discourse, now in the Frankfurt Archives.

the three transcripts made by von Glauburg in 1712 for Von Uffenbach, of which two are at Hamburg, and one in the Frankfurt town-Library in the vol. marked B. by von Uffenbach.

the transcript made by Von Uffenbach's scribe, with the Discourse attached to it; now at Hamburg.

the text published by Wolf in 1740 in his *Monum. typogr.*

DISCOURSE of FAUST von ASCHAFFENBURG, the elder.

The *original* written not before 1620, but before July 14, 1621, with a transcript of the Instrument attached to it. (Where now?)

the transcript made by Joh. Max. Zum Jungen before 1649 with the transcript of the Instrument annexed to it, and seen, Oct. 1880, by me in the Frankfurt Archives.

the transcript made for Von Uffenbach by his scribe in 1715, with the transcript of the Instrument annexed to it, and now preserved in the Hamburg Town Library.

the Latin translation published by Wolf in 1740 in his *Monum. typogr.*

15. (XI) An instrument of the notary Ulrich Helmasberger, dated 21st June, 1457, recording a sale of the property of a certain Dielnhenne, an inhabitant of Bodenheim, to a purchaser called Johannes Gensfleisch junior. Among the witnesses appears, according to Schaab's text (Erfind. Buchdruckerk. ii. 270), *Johannes Gudenberg.*

It was published, for the first time, by Steph. Alex. Würdtwein (Bibliotheca Moguntina, Aug. Vindel., 1789, 4°, p. 229), but, according to Schaab (i. 29, ii. 270), with such serious errors, that even the Christian name of Gutenberg appears in his text as *Petro,* whereas the original has (according to Schaab) *Johe.* Schaab (ll. cc.) says that he had seen a contemporary transcript of the document, but transcribed his own text carefully from the *original,* which formerly had belonged to the Victor-Chapter, but, *from the Bodmann Collection* had come, and was then (1830), in the Mentz Library.

Dr. Arthur Wyss, the Darmstadt Archivist, has kindly made inquiries for me at Mentz, and wrote to me on the 9th of Jan. 1881, that "the *original* instrument, which is undoubtedly *genuine,* is preserved in the Mentz town-library and had been very inaccurately printed by Schaab." He himself intends to republish it shortly.

16. A copy of the Dialogues of Pope Gregory, printed at Strasburg about 1470 by Henr. Eggestein, preserved at Wilton House, in the Library of the Earl of Pembroke, and having at the end a somewhat cleverly fabricated imprint, intended to convey the impression that the book was printed by "Johan Guttenberg, at Strassburg, in the year 1458."

The first notice of *this* copy of the Dialogues and its forged imprint appeared in Samuel Palmer's "General history of printing from the first invention of it in . . . Mentz . . ." published in London, partly in 1732 and partly in 1733.

In the Appendix (p. 299), Palmer writes that (when the first part of his work was published) they (*i.e.* Palmer and Lord Pembroke) had not the least ground to conjecture that Gutenberg ever practised printing himself.

"But since then the noble lord unwilling to rest satisfy'd with conjectures, has spared no pains or cost to inform himself whether there was any impression extant done by Guttenberg, and has at length procured this curious one, which his lordship has been pleased to communicate to me."

As the present Earl of Pembroke kindly lent the book in question to Mr. Bradshaw, I am able to give a description of it. It is the edition of the Dialogues of Pope Gregory indicated by Hain under No. *7957, and by Brunet, vol. ii. col. 1726. It is a folio of 58 leaves, printed in two columns of 42 lines each, in the same type as the Ludolphus (Meditationes vitae Jesu Christi) printed by Eggesteyn in 1474, and described by Hain under No. *10290; by Brunet, vol. iii. col. 1225. The work has no signatures, no catchwords, no initial directors, no punctuation, except middle and lower point; it has double hyphens not extending beyond the line, as water-mark the oxhead only. The 58 leaves are arranged in 6 quires: a b c d e^{10} f^{8}.

fol. 1^{aa} lines 1–2 blank;
lines 3 & 4: Vadam die nimijs quorū
dam seculariū tumultibꝫ de

fol. 57^{ab} li. 33:
stia fuerimus.
(lines 34–35 blank)
Explicit liber quartus
Dyalagoꝝ (*sic*) gregorij.
(line 38 blank)
Presens hoc op' factum est per Johan.
Guttenbergium apud Argentinam
anno millessimo ccccl viii.
line 42 blank, and leaf 58 (blank?) wanting.

From this description it will be seen that the book agrees in every respect with the edition described by Hain, excepting, of course, the last three lines.

That these three lines (*i.e.* the fabricated imprint) in Lord Pembroke's copy are printed in by hand, in letters *differing* from the type of the book, is evident at first sight. And it is also clear at first sight that they are the result of a rather clever and yet clumsy forgery. The genuine type of the book has been very well imitated, but the forger, whoever he may be, did not take or was unable to take account of the old and blunted condition, and the *exact* size, of this genuine type, and consequently manufactured a *new* and slightly *larger* type than the old one. It is true, the size of the forged letter is *very slightly* larger, but the difference of the two sizes is yet perceptible.

Schoepflin, whose "Vindiciae typographiae" appeared in 1760, mentioning Palmer's work, writes (p. 40) that he had himself

"examined the Pembroke Library in 1728, five years before Palmer published his work, and had, in the constant company of Maittaire, several times inspected its chief books, but the *Dialogues*, printed, as Palmer asserted, by Gutenberg, had escaped his eyes, though the Earl and Maittaire would have pointed out such a book above all others to a Strasburg scholar. Therefore, the book was probably already at that time regarded as spurious, or if the Pembroke Library acquired it after (1728) it is none the less spurious; to which an inexperienced impostor added a rubric."

In a note Schoepflin adds:

"Maittaire, who diligently mentions the rare books in the Pembroke Library, why should he have omitted the rarest of them all?"

As Lord Pembroke bought the book between 1732 and 1733 (before Jan. 1733), it is quite natural that Schoepflin did not find it in 1728.

Bernard (Origine de l'imprimerie, i. 150) speaking of this copy, says

"Palmer asserts that he saw in the Library of Lord Pembroke an edition of the *Dialogues of Pope Gregory*, at the end of which the rubricator had written in red (avait écrit en rouge): 'Presens hoc opusculum factum est per Johannem Gutenbergium, apud Argentinam, anno millesimo cccclviii.' But Schoepflin declares that he never saw this book, though he had, in the company of Maittaire, carefully explored the Pembroke library, &c."

Bernard is not quite correct here. Palmer speaks (p. 300) of "red letters," but says nothing of their being *written*. Schoepflin (l. c.) uses the words "genuina si foret epigraphe, calci ejus (*i.e.* the book) rubro colore adjecta his verbis."

It must be observed that within a few months after the purchase and printed description of the book, both the Earl of Pembroke and Palmer died; hence the break in the history of this palpable forgery.

Dr. Van der Linde, speaking, on p. 182, of this forgery, and of another, also in Lord Pembroke's Library (see Palmer's work, 3rd Book, 3rd chapter, Westminster), attributes them to Palmer himself and calls him a deceiver (*betrüger*), but there is no foundation for such a charge either in the one case or the other.

17. A document dated (*an sand margreden dag der*

heiligen Junckfrawen, i.e., on the day of St. Margaret, the holy virgin, *i.e.*) July 20, 1459, made like letters patent, with four seals, &c., appended to it (*ausgefertigt in der Urkundenform mit vier anhängenden Insieglen*, Schaab i. 29). It represents brothers, called *Henne Genssfleisch von Sulgeloch* genannt *Gudinberg*, and Friele Genssfleisch, as relinquishing, on St. Margaret's-day, 1459, at the advice and with the consent of their relatives Henne, Friele, and Pedirmanne, all claims to whatever their sister Hebele had brought with her into the Convent Reichenklaren, and Henne Genssfleisch in particular promises that the *books* which he has given to the library of the convent shall always belong to it, and that he will give to the same library all the *books* which he, Henne, has caused to be printed, and may print in future.

In 1830 Schaab (Erf. der Buchdr. i. 30) informs us that Fischer (Beschreib. typogr. Seltenh., 1800, i., p. 42) was the first who made this document known in the German language of the original from a *transcript* which he had received from Prof. Bodmann, who pretended to have *discovered* it in the Archives of the University of Mentz. In 1801 Oberlin gave a French translation of it (Essai d'annal. de la vie de Gutenberg, 4), and only remarked (p. 3) that Bodmann had discovered it. Fischer reprinted the German text in his Essai sur les mon. typogr., 46, and added Oberlin's translation. It was frequently reprinted by later authors on Gutenberg, but Schaab (i. 34) *declares it to be one of* Prof. Bodmann's *forgeries*, and Dr. Van der Linde (p. 19) agrees with him. See for other forgeries of the same Professor documents 1, 13.

18. (XIII.) A letter, dated April 10, 1461, from the Chapter of St. Thomas at Strassburg to the Secular Court at Rottweil, by which they authorize Michel Rosemberg, the procurator of that Court, to bring an action against "Johann Guttemberg" for the money he owed them.

A copy of this letter was discovered in 1841 by Prof. C. Schmidt, of Strassburg, in the Archives of the Chapter of St. Thomas of that city, and published by him in the same year (*Nouv. détails sur la vie de Gutenberg, tirés des Archives de l'ancien Chapitre de St. Thomas à Strasbourg*, 8vo., Strasbourg, 1841). Compare what has been said under document No. 10 (p. 60).

19. (XIV.) Some items in an account-book of the same

Chapter of 1461, in which the expenses are specified which the Chapter incurred through their action taken against Martin Brechter and Gutenberg. The result of the proceedings of the Chapter is not known. Prof. Schmidt says that we should have to search for the documents in the Archives of the Aulic Chamber, which was dissolved in 1787. In any case the Chapter obtained nothing, either from Gutenberg or from M. Brechter, because both appear from 1458–1474 as non-paying; commencing with 1468 *vacat* is found after their names. In 1467 M. Brechter was arrested at Hagenau at an additional cost to the Chapter of seven shillings, and in 1474 the items were noticed as *lost*, though the Chapter spent again one-and-eightpence in summoning M. Brechter. But after this year they are no longer mentioned. Cf. C. Schmidt, *Nouv. détails sur la vie de Gutenberg, &c.*, and *Le Bibliographe Alsacien de* 1869, Strasb., 8vo. Compare what has been said under document No. 10.

20. A so-called rubric in a "Tractatus de celebratione missarum secundum frequentiorem cursum diocesis maguntinensis."

A copy of this work is said to have been transferred, in 1781, from the Carthusian Monastery near Mentz to the University Library of that town. Gotthelf Fischer, who gives the title (*Essai sur les monumens typogr. de Jean Gutenberg, Mayence* [1802], p. 81; and *Typogr. Seltenh.*, 1803, iv. 18), asserts that in this library he discovered it bound in one volume with a number of MS. tracts, and that the rubricator had written on it with red ink:

> Carthusia prope Maguntm̄ possidet ex lber
> donacōne Joanis dicti a bono monte opuscu
> mira sua arte s̄c̄ ē Johannis Nummeistēr
> cleric confectū. Anno dm̄ M° cccc°
> LXiij xiij kal Jul (= 19 Juni 1463)

No one seems to have seen this Mentz copy after Fischer. Bernard says (*Orig. de l'impr.*, i. 204), that the book could not be found in 1851 by the then librarian and that he wrote to Fischer, who replied from Moscow (3–15 April, 1851): "Non-seulement j'ai vu de mes propres yeux l'inscription; mais l'ouvrage doit se trouver encore à la bibliothèque [de Mayence]; il est réuni, dans un volume en 4°, à plusieurs autres traités."

Dr. Arthur Wyss, the Darmstadt Archivist, was so kind

as to inquire for me at Mentz, and in Jan. 1881 wrote to me that hitherto the Mentz Librarian had been unable to find the Tractatus. Wyss has, however, on this occasion discovered a copy of this work in the Darmstadt Hof Library, but without any rubrics.

Fischer has given (Essai, p. 78) a facsimile of the two types (1, church type, used for the rubrics; 2, used for the text) employed in the *Tractatus*. That used for the text was employed for printing 6 other tracts, which have since come to light from time to time. As one of these tracts has the place of printing, namely *Moguntia* (*Mentz*), in the imprint, we are enabled to ascribe them all to this city, and as another (a Prognostication) is said to have been printed for the year 1460, this would enable us to fix the approximate date of the printer, whose productions we may group in the following way:

1) A Prognostication or Kalendar said to be for the year [Mcccc]lx, therefore printed in 1459, described by Fischer (Typogr. Seltenh. vi. 69). According to Bernard (i. 206) the six leaves remaining of this tract could not be found in the Darmstadt Museum when he was writing his book (1853), but it has since turned up as it is mentioned (as "Calender von 1460") in Walther's Beiträge zur Kenntniss der Hofbibliothek zu Darmstadt. 8°. Darmstadt. 1867, p. 88.

2) Hermanni de Saldis [Schildis] Speculum Sacerdotum. 16 leaves, 4°, 30 even lines on a page, with hyphens, no printed initials, no initial directors, no signatures. It has the imprint: Speculum p*re*clarum ips*o*rum sacerdotu*m* a pa||tre Hermanno de saldis sacre theologie p*ro*fes-||sore: ordinis heremitaru*m* sancti Aug*ustini* editum.|| maguntieq*ue* imp*re*ssum feliciter finit.||

Fischer has described it in his Typogr. Seltenh. iv. 14. A copy is in the Library at Munich, described by Hain, No. *14519. A *second* copy is preserved in the Paris Library; cf. "Notice des objets exposés," issued by the Department of the printed books, Paris, 1878; p. 15, No. 48; Bernard, Orig. de l'impr. i. 209. A *third* copy is in the possession of the Rev. John Fuller Russell, London.

3) Tractatus de celebratione missarum secundum frequentiorem cursum diocesis maguntinensis.

The copy, which is said to contain the rubric of which we treat, should be in the Mentz Library. Another copy has now been found at Darmstadt, but without any rubric. From this latter copy I have taken the following description;

It is composed of 30 leaves ($a\ b\ c^{10}$), with 28 even lines (of the small type) on a page; no signatures, with hyphens; no space left for initials (all printed). Types: 1 (rubrics); 2 (text).

leaf 1ᵃ: In presenti libello ɔtinentur aliqua pro
cebracōne (sic) missarū scdm freqñtiorē cursū diocesis maguntiñ. directoria ꝑ pte ex registro
ordinario et ꝑ pte ex quibusdā exptis p̄sbi-
teris eiusdē diocesis collecta et ꝑ nouellis et
ruralibꝫ clericis expientiam plenam eorūdeꝫ
non habentibus hic breuiter annotata. Sal
uis tamen cuiuscūqꝫ eccīe consuetudinibus.

leaf 30ᵇ li 24:
ne viuit et regnat. Amen.

4) A work in German, treating of the necessity of councils and the manner of holding them. It is composed of 24 ($a\ b\ c^{8}$) leaves, 4°, 31 mostly even lines on a page, with hyphens, with initials printed in (except the I on the first page), no signatures, no imprint. It is mentioned by Van Praet in his *Catalogue* in folio (1813), p. 34. Bernard (Orig. de l'imprimerie, i. 209) avowed that he was unable to see the book (in 1853), as it could not be found in the Paris Library. Dr. Van der Linde also says that it could not be found. But it is now mentioned in the "Notice des objets exposés," Paris, 1878, p. 15, No. 47, and I myself examined it on the 13th July, 1881. The first line runs: [I]S ist noit das dicke vnd vil Co*n*cilia werden||.

5) Dyalogus inter Hugonem, Cathonem et Oliverium super libertate ecclesiastica. Described by Fischer (Typogr. Seltenh. vi. 74). A copy of it is preserved in the Darmstadt Grand-ducal Library (see Walther's Beiträge, p. 88); another in the Munich Library (see Hain, No. *6140). A third has recently been acquired by the Paris National Library (Acquisition, No. 84697). It is composed of 20 leaves ($a\ b^{10}$; first and last blank), 4°, 30–32 even lines on a page; initials printed in, except on first page; with hyphens; no signatures.

6) Sifridus de Arena, Episcop. Cirens. Determinatio duarum quaestionum. 26 leaves ($a^{10}\ b\ c^{8}$). 4°.

Copies of it are preserved 1) in the Munich Library, described by Hain, *14723; 2) in the University Library of Cambridge; 3) in the Brit. Mus., Press-mark 690. d. 33, No. 1 (see next title); 4) in the Wolfenbüttel Library (Pressmark 177. i. Th.); 5) in the possession of the Rev. John Fuller Russell, London.

7) Sifridus de Arena, &c. Responsio ad quatuor quaestiones sibi propositas. 10 (a^{10}) leaves. 4°.

A copy of this tract is preserved in the Munich Library and described by Hain *14724; another in the University Library of Cambridge, which is bound up together with a copy of the preceding tract; a *third* copy is in the Brit. Mus. (pressm. 690.d. 33, No. 2), which also is bound up with a copy of the preceding tract. The Brit. Mus. copy has, moreover, a year written in in three places, namely (1) 1456 on the top of the first page in a *modern* hand; (2) apparently 1465 under the imprint of the Determinatio, where also Isenburg is written in red with a hand of the 15th cent.; (3) at the end of the second tract either 1446 or 1456; but in all three instances the date has been tampered with, and the numerals 14 alone are plainly visible. A *fourth* copy is in the Wolfenbüttel Library (Pressmark 177. i. Th), bound up with a copy of the preceding tract. The copy of the preceding tract of the Rev. John Fuller Russell, London, has not the Responsiones.

As regards the *printer* of these tracts nothing certain is known. The so-called rubrication in the "Tractatus" has been variously interpreted by those who believed in it. Bernard would read (i. 204) *scientia etiam* for sc̄ ē and translate: "La Chartreuse près de Mayence tient de la liberalité de Jean Gutenberg ce livre, produit de son art et de la science de Jean Nummeister, clerc." Van Praet (Catal., in fol. p. 33) prints (according to Bernard, i. 204) "Mira sua arte p." (*i.e.* per), which would ascribe the printing to Nummeister alone; but Van Praet evidently altered Fischer's rubric, merely to make it suit a plausible interpretation. Others would read sc*ilicet* e*t*, though ē for et is not usual.

Hain, describing the Tractatus (4833) added: "Moguntiae Joh. Nummeister cleric. a. 1463. 13 Kal. Jul. Sic docet subscriptio cuidam exemplo calamo apposita, *at valde dubia*."

To Helbig (*Bulletin du Bibliophile Belge*, tom. xviii. (1862) 2e Série, tom. ix, p. 41, 42) the rubrication appeared more than suspicious.

Dr. Van der Linde remarks (p. 56):

"The authenticity of [the above] note is highly suspicious: (1) the

Latinizing of Gutenberg's name does not occur anywhere so early. (2) The date agrees ill with the catastrophe of 1462. (3) The discoverer was, alas! a friend of Bodmann. (4) Fischer says (iv. 20, vi. 69): I have caused this important inscription to be engraved; it will contribute not a little to the completion of a second edition of my 'Essai.' This second edition never appeared, and though Fischer published afterwards two parts of his *Seltenheiten* with facsimiles, he made, alas! no use of this 'important inscription,' and only remarks (vi. 75) that no one who had examined these objects (the printed colophon in the Speculum Sacerdotum: *impressumque Maguntie*—and the MS. note in the Celebratio missarum of 1463) would pretend that they are false.—It remains always bad that this pretended donation reminds us at once of the donation of 1459 to the Convent of S. Clara, which was also invented by Bodmann."

In spite of Dr. Van der Linde's suspicion, he ascribes this group of books to Gutenberg, and even prints the colophon of the Speculum in very neat Gothic type, probably to make it look all the more impressive.

¶ After having recorded everything of importance said on the above rubric, I wish to say something myself. On the 3rd October 1881 I visited Darmstadt, for the purpose of describing, for the present work, the *Prognostication* or *Kalendar*, which is said to have the printed date [Mcccc]lx. I found only *four* leaves, not *six* as Bernard, following Fischer (i. 206), says, and it is evident from Fischer's description (Typogr. Selt. vi. 69) that he never had more than *four printed* leaves before him, though he speaks of *six* leaves. Fischer declares that Herr Podozzi, a dealer in works of art, discovered the leaves in the binding of a book and forwarded them to him for inspection. The tract is printed in the two types figured by Fischer in his *Essai sur les monumens typogr. de Jean Gutenberg.*

I copied, without any suspicion, the first four lines as follows:

Particula prima de dño āni et significatīs eius ad
que humana ratio ptingere potest.
Consideratis singulis planetarum di
gnitatibus in figura reuolucōis āni lx

So far all was in accordance with Fischer's description. But a mere child could see that after the lx, in the fourth line, there were more numerals, which had been rather carelessly scratched out. With my naked eye I could discern lxx–ii. What there was between the second x and the units (here represented by –) I could not decipher at once. In this uncertainty it occurred to me to read the text, because, I thought, a Prognostication is likely to contain some allusion to an event or person, which might give me some clue to the date. I was not disappointed. The last two lines of the verso of the second leaf run as follows:

> Papa Sixtus quartus hoc anno graues anxieta
> tes sentiet. Incomoda etiā nature pacietur. Jupit̄

I asked for a book which could give me the reigns of the popes. Potthast was brought to me. Eh bien! Pope Sixtus IV. was elected Aug. 9, 1471; consecrated Aug. 25 following; he died Aug. 12, 1484.

I now examined the spot where the scratching had taken place once more, and read without hesitation lxxxii. After the date something more, which concludes the line, has been scratched out, and again one or two letters at the commencement of the 5th line, but I am unable to say what it is.

Is this plain enough? I think it is.

This discovery makes it clear: 1) that the so-called Prognostication for 1460 is, in reality, a Prognostication for 1482 and has, consequently, been printed in 1481;—2) that the rubrication in the "Tractatus" must be a forgery, if it ever has existed at all.*

That Fischer asserted, in 1804, that the Kalendar (= Prognostication) had the printed date (14)60, may now be passed over without comment; but that Dr. Walther, the Librarian of Darmstadt, could describe it, in 1867, in his *Beiträge zur näheren Kenntniss der Hofbibliothek zu Darmstadt* (p. 88), as the "Calender von 1460" is rather too bad. The numerals have so clumsily been scratched out that the detection of the fraud did not require experience or strong eyes.

The two *forgeries*, in connexion with this group of books, cannot this time be ascribed to Bodmann. Fischer says that he himself *discovered* the Tractatus with the rubrication; and the Prognostication was, at all events, sent to him for inspection.

---

* I have said above that a copy of the "Tractatus" was lately found at Darmstadt, without a rubric. Could this be the very copy which Fischer had before him? Fischer's Library was transferred to the Darmstadt Library, and it is just possible that he *intended* to fabricate the rubrication, and with this idea in his mind published it in advance.

I need not add that henceforth the *seven* books described above can no longer be mentioned in connexion with Gutenberg, as they must be grouped round *the true date* (1481) of the Prognostication.

Before leaving this subject I may mention that I have found in the Library at Mentz an *eighth* work, printed in the same types, and therefore belonging to the same set of books. It is a folio book of 236 leaves (collation: a^{12} b c d e f g h i k l m n o p q r s t u x y z A B C^{8} D^{10} E^{6} F^{8}), in 2 columns of 41 (not always) even lines. It has double hyphens, but no signatures, and all initials are printed in, except the A with which the text commences. Types: 1 (rubrics); 2 (text).

Leaf 1^{a} blank; leaf 1^{b}: Nach dem vnd ein yglich mensch dem gesetze vnterdanig||sein soll als geschrieben steet. ff. dele. et senatus con. l. ij. vnder||(&c. 17 lines in all); leaf 2^{aa}: Hernach volgen die Titel||dis' buchs in rechter ordenūg||; leaf 7^{ba}, line 25: vrteyl gebē hat. . ccxxviij.||; lines 26–41 and leaf 7^{bb} blank; leaf 8^{aa} (in the large type): [A] Ctio de hijs q̃ in frau||dem creditorum.||wan der schuldener|| in vntrewe seins cre=|| etc.; leaf 235^{bb} line 7: passis et restitutis ꝛtc.||; lines 8–10 blank; li. 11: Hie enden sich die clagen||vnd nutzliche lere dis' sūder=||lichen buchs aus' gemeynen|| beschriebenen rechten der key||serlichen gesetz vñ den haubt||buchern originalib' in latein|| Pandectarū. ff. C. vnd instit'.||gezogen. so vil vnd der zu||&c. &c.; leaf 236 blank.

The work has no name of author; no printer's name, no place of printing, no date. The place of printing must, of course, be Mentz. Hain has described this edition under No. *3727; its title is: Sebastian Brant, *Richterlicher Klagspiegel* or *Neu geteutscht Rechtbuch.* Hain mentions no less than *five* editions of this work printed before 1500, of which the British Museum has (a) No. *3726, without date (pressmark: 5510. ee); (b) No. *3729 (pressmark: 5310. dd), printed at Augsburg, 1497; (c) No. *3730 (pressmark: 5207. f), printed at Augsburg, 1500. Panzer (Annalen der ältern deutschen Litteratur, p. 33), points out that, in 1516, Brant published the work again, recast and corrected, under the title: *Der Richterlich Clagspiegel;* this work he mentions on p. 389. The British Museum (pressmark: 708. h. 19) has an edition published under this title at Strassburg, 1536. The particular edition described by Panzer I have not been able to find.

The above Mentz edition appears to me to be the *editio princeps*, but even if we give it this place of honour, the date of its printing cannot be far from 1490, as Sebast. Brandt was born at Strassburg in 1458. Therefore *this book alone* would demolish the Gutenberg story with regard to this group of books. All the circumstances connected with this rubrication and the Prognostication show how little the Germans have hitherto done in the Gutenberg case. It seems to suit them to reprint the old documents, and to repeat old stories without even looking at things which they have ready at their elbow.

A copy of the book in question may be seen in the British Museum (King's Library, Pressmark: C. 8. 1. 4) in as good a preservation as that which I saw at Mentz. The Museum copy seems to have been in the possession of Alex. Horn; the lettering on the back has: "Moguntiae per Jo. Guttenberg," but the British Museum Catalogue has, by accident,* the approximately right date [1490?].

21 (XV). A decree of the Elector Adolf II., dated 18 Jan., 1465, by which he appoints "Johann Gudenberg, on account of his grateful and willing service, his servant and courtier (*dkiener und hoffgesind*) for life, promising to supply him with clothing, and each year 20 *malter Korns* and 2 *fuder wins.*"

This decree was published by Geo. Chr. Joannis, Scriptt. rer. Mogunt. (1727), iii. p. 424, without saying a word as to whence he obtained this document. Joh. Dav. Köhler, Ehren-Rettung (1741), p. 100, published it again without telling us whence *he* obtained it, not even mentioning Joannis. Later authors republished it, quoting Joannis as their source. Dr. Van der Linde mentions (p. 526) Joannis and Köhler, but prints his text apparently from Joannis. Cf. Schaab, Erfind. der Buchdruckerk. i. 48, 60, 472.

When I was at Hamburg in September, 1881, I found

* When the British Museum catalogue is correct with respect to the Incunabula, it is a mere accident. In the present instance *Strasburg* is given in the Catalogue as the place of printing, and the following note has been appended to the rather elaborate description of the title of the book: "Without register, pagination, or catchwords, printed in double columns with type resembling (sic) that of the Speculum Sacerdotum of Hermannus de Salis (sic) and of the Tractatus de celebratione missarum said to be printed by Gutenberg."

This is a bad note! Every one seems to lose his head when dealing with Gutenberg.

in one of the MS. Volumes of the Uffenbach collection (No. xxxvii Uffenbach = xxvi Wolf), preserved in the Town Library, a *transcript* of the decree made by Uffenbach's amanuensis in this volume, to which Uffenbach himself wrote the title: "Cl. Virorum Epistolae variae quas ex autographis ab amicis benevole concessis per amanuenses describi fecit Z. C. ab Uffenbach MDCCXVII seq. annis." The transcript of the decree is No. 74 in the MS. volume, and it agrees with the text published by Joannis, Köhler, and Van der Linde, except that it has after: Hoffgesind Kleyden the additional words: "*werden, zu iglichen Zyten, glich unsern Edelen Kleyden,*" which had probably been omitted by Joannis, and consequently by Köhler, &c.

I am unable to say whence Uffenbach procured his transcript. It is immediately followed by a transcript of document No. 24 (q.v.), under which is written in this same volume "Ex Lib. ii. Adolf AEp. p. 85."

Dr. Arthur Wyss, the Darmstadt Archivist, informed me on the 9th Feb. 1881 that he had traced a *contemporary transcript* of this document and of No. 24 (below) in a Mentz-Aschaffenburg Copial-Buch, at present preserved in the Archives at Würzburg. He told me that the texts published by Joannis and Köhler were derived from the same source, but are not correct and that he will publish them anew.

On the 11th Oct. 1881 I visited Würzburg for the purpose of examining this volume to which Dr. Wyss had called my attention. It is a large folio Cartulary, of 415 vellum leaves, which seems to have been compiled in the chancery of the Mentz Archbishop Adolf. On the back of the binding (which is quite recent) it bears the title (equally recent):

"*Ingrossatur-Buch Adolphi II, vol.* 30. *Kgl. Archiv Würzburg M*[*ainzer*] *Ingrossatur-Buch No.* 30.

The date of the documents entered (not always in strictly chronological order) in this volume range from 1463 till 1468. They are all apparently written consecutively by the same scribe, the Cartulary must, therefore, have been commenced after the last-named year; the headings or rubrics of most of the documents have been added by another hand. It seems that, before the copyist commenced, he had numbered quires ready for his use, but other leaves have been inserted, so that the new numbering (which is of recent date) differs considerably from the old, which does not appear to go further than cccxiiij. Documents with the date 1465 begin to occur on fol. 169, and the *transcript* of the Decree of which we treat is found on fol. 172 (new numbering) or fol. cxxv (old numbering). The index to the vol. was written at the end of the 17th or beginning of the 18th century. I have found no grounds to suspect the genuineness of the cartulary in which this *transcript* is preserved.

Dr. Arthur Wyss has explained to me the reason why these Cartularies are at present preserved at Würzburg. When the Mentz Electorate, to the Archives of which the volumes belonged, was abolished, the Cartularies had been already transferred, for greater security, to Aschaffenburg. When the latter place was annexed to Bavaria, this kingdom also appropriated the Mentz Archivalia. The earlier documents were transferred to the Munich Archives; the Acts and Cartularies to the Archives at Würzburg.

22 (XVI). An entry in an *Anniversarium* of the *Dominican* Church at Mayence, at the 2nd of Feb. [1468] which, after expansion of the contractions, runs thus: "Obiit dominus Joh*annes* zum Ginsefleis cum duabus candelis sup*er* lapidem p*ro*pe cadedram predicantis habens arma Ginsefleis."

Val. Ferd. Gudenus, Cod. diplom. (1747), ii. p. 524, in a Syllabus veterum Moguntiae Curiarum sive Aedium, records the following entry:

> "Anniv. D. Johannis zum Gensfleisch, cum duabis candelis super lapidem prope cathedram . ., habens arma Gensfleisch. M. Sept. Anniv. Dne Kittergin; filia Johannis Berwolfi, uxor Johannis Gensfleisch . . que iacet sub . . pedibus . . Ruppels zum Cleman. Et habet . . duas imagines sculptas & 2 clipeos, scil. cornua & Schotten."

This entry had never been applied to Gutenberg until Bockenheimer published his "Gutenberg's Grabstätte (Mainz, 1876)." He had on the Saturday before Whitsuntide, 1876, discovered the *Anniversarium*, from which Gudenus evidently had copied his entry. According to Bockenheimer (p. 11), the *Anniversarium* must have been commenced in the four first decades of the 15th century (on p. 18 he specifies between the years 1430–1440), as he found that previous deaths were briefly entered by one hand and thence onward till the middle of the 18th century all events are properly noticed by a later hand. It was concluded from this entry that Gutenberg was not buried in the Franciscan,* but Dominican Church, under the chancel. The latter convent was burnt down in July, 1793. On its site was erected a fruit-hall, which also was burnt down in 1875. This latter event, says Dr. Van der Linde (p. 76), would probably enable us to find out the spot where "the mortal remains of the immortal master rest."

It has now been shown by Dr. Schenk zu Schweinsberg, the chief Archivist of Darmstadt, that the entry in the Anniversarium, as read by Gudenus and Bockenheimer, has no connexion whatever with Joh. Gutenberg. In an Essay published in the "Archiv des histor. Vereins für das Grossh. Hessen" (vol. 15, pp. 337–357), Dr. Schenk gives the result of his examination of the original Anniversarium, which is preserved in the Registry of the "Deputation für die Armen- und Krankenpflege" at Mentz. The above entry, he says, is

> "actually found on the leaf numbered ix, written by a scribe who also wrote two other entries with the dates 16 Febr. and 16 Oct. 1473, and a third, of Jan. 28, 1462; but it is merely a *repetition of an entry which may be seen immediately above it on the same day*, and which, having partly been rubbed out, is perhaps not quite legible to inexperienced eyes."

This original entry Dr. Schenk was able to read with his naked eyes, but he took the precaution of using some reagent, and read as follows:—

> "Obiit Dominus Johannes zum Ginsefleis, cum duabus candelis et quatuor luminibus, de cujus ex parte conventus debet habere 1 marcham, adhuc non habemus."

Another entry at the 27th of Sept. runs:—

> "Domine Kettergin, filia Johannis Berwolffi, uxor Johannis Ginssfleisch, cum quatuor luminibus et duabus candelis, que iacet sub lapide jacenti sub pedibus lapidis Ruppels czum Cleman, et primus lapis tangit cum pedibus sedes sub ymagine virginis gloriose et habet eciam duas ymagines sculptas et duos clippeos, scilicet cornua et Schotten."

So far the entries had been made, says Dr. Schenk, in a broad, distinct hand, which, when the Necrologium was commenced, wrote out all the anniversaries which were still to be celebrated. But after the last-mentioned entry, a later

* As was hitherto supposed on the strength of the inscription on the memorial slab said to have been erected by Adam Gelthus to Gutenberg.

hand of the 15th century wrote "Require numero IX. sub litera e." These words, not mentioned by Bockenheimer, are of the utmost importance, because when we refer to the page indicated we find, before the feast of Feb. 2, the dominical letter E, and the first and only entry under this day is the original entry about *Johannes zum Gensfleisch*, which has been partly rubbed out.

Dr. Schenk explains that the *first* hand of the Necrologium, i.e. the person who commenced it, and transferred to it from some earlier Necrologium those anniversaries which were still to be celebrated, continued his work till 1418, or till 1421, or perhaps till 1423, at which year the next hand seems to be already at work. As the first scribe also wrote the two *original* entries quoted above, it is clear that these refer to persons who were dead before his time at least and could have nothing to do with Gutenberg. The Johannes Gensfleisch mentioned in the Necrologium is, Dr. Schenk says, most likely the grand-uncle of Gutenberg, who occurs in charters from 1385–1405.

It would seem clear that Dr. Schenk has proved his point, and that Gutenberg was not buried in the *Dominican* church. There remains, therefore, the assumption that he was buried in the *Franciscan* church at Mentz. Dr. Schenk is of opinion that this assumption rests "on good grounds." But here we meet with another difficulty. An epitaph on Gutenberg, apparently composed by a kinsman of his, Adam Gelthus, was published in 1499 at Heidelberg, at the end of a little work issued by the Heidelberg professors in memory of Prof. Marsilius de Inghen, the founder of their University. In this epitaph the "artis impressorie repertor," or "inventor," is called "Joannis Genszfleisch," and it is said that "ossa eius in ecclesia divi *Francisci* Maguntina fœliciter cubant." The reason why this epitaph should have been published at the end of this work, which has no connexion with printing or with Gutenberg, is not quite clear. But as it is followed by the well-known epigram "Fœlix *ansicare*, &c." of Jac. Wimpfeling in honour of John Gensfleisch, it becomes probable that this scholar, who wrote occasionally on the invention of printing, was the editor of the Heidelberg professors, and added, by way of amusement, the epitaph of Adam Gelthus and his own epigram.

Now, Bockenheimer, who was anxious to prove his case

with regard to the *Dominican* church, not unnaturally writes against the *Franciscan* church. He points out that it is assumed on all hands that the epitaph in question could never have been placed on a memorial slab; at least, not on one which covered the remains of Gutenberg, as it would, in such a case, not have been necessary to say where his bones were (*cf.* also Bodmann, Rheing. Alterth. i. 137). He even goes so far as to suggest that Adam Gelthus was not the author of the epitaph at all, but Wimpfeling himself (see above, p. 15). He also points out that the addition in the MS. "Sagen von alten dingen, &c., where the same statement with regard to the "ossa" is made (see above, p. 16) is of no value, as being of a much later date. And finally, Bockenheimer points out that Gutenberg could not possibly have been buried in the *Franciscan* church; (1) because in the war of 1462, between Adolf of Nassau and Diether of Isenburg, the Franciscans had adhered to the latter, and were, on that account, banished by the victorious Adolf, while their church was converted into a stable: (2) a document of 1473 (Gudenus, Cod. Diplom. v. 1071, sqq.) makes it evident that in that year they had not regained Adolf's favour, and that their convent did no longer exist at Mentz; indeed, it had been transferred to other hands even in 1469 (Schaab, Erfind. der Buchd. i. 465). For these reasons Bockenheimer contends that the relatives of Gutenberg, who is said to have died c. 1468, could not have thought of burying him in a church, and under the care, of an order which was so disliked by the prince whose courtier he had been.

If, then, Bockenheimer has proved his point against the *Franciscan* church, and Dr. Schenk has proved his point against the *Dominican* church, the question arises, Where was Gutenberg buried? No one knows. Dr. Schenk says that F. W. E. Roth in *Geschichtsquellen des Niederrheingaus* (i. p. 264, note, and iii. 237), on the authority of a MS. of a certain Kremer, pronounces in favour of Eltvil, but Dr. Schenk does not appear to believe in it.

23 (XVII). A Letter of obligation of Dr. Homery, dated (*uff frytag nach Sant Mathys dag*, i.e.) Friday after Feb. 24, 1468, by which he acknowledges to have received from Adolf, the Archbishop of Mentz, several forms, letters, instruments, implements, and other things belonging to the work of printing which Johann Guttemberg had left after

his death, and which had, and still belonged to him (Dr. Homery) ;—he, on his part, undertaking to use them, but in no other town than Mentz, nor to sell them to any person but a citizen of Mentz, even if a stranger should offer him a higher price for the things.

This document was published (1) by Geo. Chr. Joannis (Scriptt. Hist. Mogunt., *tom. novus* (1727), p. 424), without a word as to whence he obtained it; (2) by Köhler (Ehren-Rettung, 1741, p. 101), the latter adding, "ex libro Archiepiscopi Adolfi, p. 80, in Archivo Moguntino." Cf. Schaab, Erfind. der Buchdruckerkunst, i. 60, 325 (where some particulars about Humery may be found). Dr. Van der Linde, p. xxxvii, publishes it again, without doing more than mentioning Joannis and Köhler, not even repeating where Köhler says he obtained it. Under document No. 22 I have already pointed out that I found a *transcript* of this Letter at Hamburg, and that another *transcript* has turned up at Würzburg.

On the 11th Oct. 1881 I visited Würzburg for the purpose of examining the volume in which this transcript is found. It is a folio paper Cartulary of 158 leaves, arranged in quires as follows: a^{14} b c d e f g^{12} h^{24} i k (leaf 12 cut away) l m^{12}; the index (12 leaves) is of later date. The leaves are numbered 1–156, because leaf 134 is cut away and on leaf 103 the number 102 is wrongly repeated. After leaf 156 another, more recent, quire has been added, of which only the first leaf has been written upon. On the back of the binding (which is quite recent) it bears the title (equally recent): *Ingrossatur-Buch Adol. II. lib. II.* 31. *Kgl. Archiv Würzburg M*[*ainzer*] *Ingrossatur buch No.* 31. The date of the documents entered (not always strictly chronologically) in this volume range from 1463 to 1473. They have evidently been transcribed by different contemporary scribes, though the volume could not have been commenced before 1470, as a document of this date occurs on fol. 3. The quires seem to have been taken one after another whenever material was necessary for new documents.

The *transcript* of Homery's Letter is found on the recto of fol. 85, which commences with the end (five lines) of a document of 1467. The scribe who copied it wrote also the two preceding documents, both of 1467, and occupying fol. 83 verso, second half, fol. 84 recto and verso and the five first lines of fol. 85 recto; on the verso of 85 another hand commences.

The Letter runs thus:

> eynen v*er*phlichtunges brieff
> Doctor Homerij
>
> Ich Conradt Homery doctor Bekennen mit diesem brieff so als der Hockwirdige||furste myn gnedig*er* lieber Her Her Adolff Ertzbischoff zu Mentz mir etliche||formen buchstaben Instrument gezauwe vnd anders zu dem truckwerck||gehorende dass Johann Gutemberg nach sinem tode gelaissen hait vnd myn||gewest vnd noch ist gnediglich folgen layszen hait. Dass Ich dargegen synen||gnaden zu eren vnd zu gefallen mich verphlichtiget han vnd v*er*phlichtige||mit diesem brieff Also weres dass Ich soliche formen vnd gezũge zu||trucken gebruchen worde nũ oder hernach dass Ich dass thun will vnd||sall bynnen der Stat Mentz vnd nyrgent anderswoe dessglichen ob Ich sie||verkeuffen vnd myr eyn burger dauor souiel geben wolte als eyn fromder|| So will vnd sall Ich dasz dem Ingesesszen*en* Burger zu Mentz vor allen|| fromden gonnen vnd folgen layssen vnd han des alles zu vrkunde myn|| Secret zu ende dieser schrifft getruckt der geben ist des Jars alsman|| schrieyb nach der geburt xpi vnsers hrñ Mcccc vnd lxviij Jare vff||frytag nach Sant Mathys dag—||

I have found no grounds to suspect the authenticity of the Cartulary in which this *transcript* is preserved.

As this Letter of Dr. Homery has given rise to much speculation and some unfounded stories, it will be worth while to see what can be said about it.

Schaab (Erfind. der Buchdruckerk. i. 179) tells us that

> in former times (*sonst*) several wooden characters [types] were preserved at Mentz. They were found, in the first years of the 17th century, in the house zum Sewleffel in the Kirschgarten, which appears to have been inhabited formerly (*sonst*) by the printer Friedrich Haumann, born at Nuremberg, the same who bought, in 1508, Gutenberg's printing apparatus from the Mergenthaler Kogelherrn [also called *Fratres vitæ communis*]. The printer Albinus showed them about 1604, in the same house, to the Mentz historian Serarius (Mog. rer., 1604, lib. I., p. 159).* A hundred years later they appear to have been seen at Mentz by Paulus Pater (Dissert. de Germaniæ Miraculo optimo Maximo, Lips. 1710, 10).

Further particulars about wooden types may be found in Schaab (l. c.), Van der Linde (p. 551).

Schaab does *not* here tell us *when* the Fratres vitæ communis came into possession of Gutenberg's printing apparatus, nor on what authority it is asserted that Friedr.

* Serarius speaks of "primi artis hujus modioli."

Haumann bought this same apparatus from the Fratres. But Schaab is more explicit with respect to the second question, on p. 553, where he enumerates some books printed by Haumann or Heumann. He there says that this printer is the same to whom Bodmann asserted (Rheing. Alterth. i. 138, *read* 136) that the Fratres vitæ communis of Marienthal had sold Gutenberg's printing apparatus, which had been transferred to them by the heirs of Hanns Bechtermüntze.

Schaab returns to Bodmann's statement in his third volume (p. 423), where he says :—

"Friedrich Heumann (Haumann, Hewmann), of Nuremberg, announced the sixth printing-office (at Mentz) in 1509 by the publication of five works, after which we hear nothing more of him.* It is said (!) that in 1508, when the *Kogelherrn* at Marienthal ceased to print, they sold to him the new Gutenberg printing-office which they had obtained from the Bechtermüntz heirs. (Bodmann, Rheing. Alterth. i. 136). It is said (!) that his (Heumann's) printing-house was the house zum Saulöfel (zum Sewlefel) in the Kirschgarten. In this house the printer Albinus showed, in the year 1604, to the Jesuit Serarius, the wooden types of Gutenberg."†

Let us now turn to Bodmann, Rheingauische Alterthümer (2 vols. 4to., Mainz, 1819), vol. i. pp. 128 and 134. There we read :—

"Eltvil was the home of several learned men, who either were born in it or inhabited it, and the Gudenberg printing-office,—transferred thither by the assistants of Henchin Genszfleisch called Gudenberg,

* See below (p. 127) where I show that Heumann was still flourishing and printing in 1512.

† When I was at Strassburg, last Sept., I was told that a certain bookseller lived in the house where Mentelin had had his printing-office. Of course, I called on the gentleman, who told me that this was not the fact, but that it was a tradition that he descended (abstammte) from Mentelin. I asked whether he meant that he was a descendant of Mentelin. No, he replied, but there was a tradition that his business was a continuation of Mentelin's. I answered that this was precisely what I had been told, but, I asked, how can you explain your business to be a continuation of Mentelin's if, as you state yourself, he did not live in this particular house? No, he replied, but we have his old marks and types (!). My astonishment was on the increase. Could I see them? A bundle of papers was exhibited to me, as fresh as if they had been printed the previous day; all woodcuts and figures belonging to the 16th century, if not later; Mentelin's types, of course, were not among them. It is not unlikely that Serarius and Paulus Pater were told and shown something similar at Mentz and *believed* in it.

named Heinrich Bechtermünze, his brother Niclas Bechtelmünz [sic], and Wigand Spiesz von Ortenberg, from which several works issued,—gave it a claim to glory and esteem." (p. 134.) "Heinrich Bechtermünz [Bechtelmonze], a pupil and assistant of Henchin Genszfleisch, genannt Gudenberg, also a patrician and related to Genszfleisch, erected a printing-office at Eltvill during the lifetime of the inventor, and indeed with the latter's own types and printing tools, which had been transferred to him (Bechtermünz), not as property, but to make use of them. He died, however, before our Genszfleisch, in the year 1467, and his brother Niclas finished, with the help of Wigand Spies, the Vocabularium latino-teutonicum, 1467, in small 4°, which Heinrich had commenced. Niclas published in 1469 a new edition of this work, with the same types which he had obtained after the death of Henchin from the Mentz town Syndic, Dr. Conrad Homery."

On p. 136 Bodmann continues:—

"Niclas Bechtermünz was sheriff of the court at Hechtsheim, with Wigand Spies, and appears in this quality often in old (leihbriefen). As he died without male heirs, his considerable property came into the possession of his brother's children, as is evidenced by the detailed document of the division of 1476.* After the death of Hans Bechtermünz [*i.e.* Heinrich's son†], the heirs sold the printing apparatus (Druckerzeug) to the Kogelherrn congregated at Marienthal, and when these ceased to print they transferred it to "Friderich Hauman von Norembergk, dem Buchdrucker im Kirsgarten zu Menz (*Ungedr. Urk.* 1508)." It was probably there that it perished entirely."‡

---

* This document I cannot find anywhere, and I may remark that Nicholaus was still publishing books in 1477.—J. H. H.

† He died the 5th of August, 1483; see Bodmann, i. 135.

‡ Sie [Eltvil] war die Heimath mehrerer gelehrten Männer, die theils aus ihr hervorgiengen, theils solche bewohnten; und die von Henchins Gensfleisch, genannt Gudenberg Gehülfen, Namens Heinrich Bechtermünze, seinem Bruder Niclas Bechtelmünz, und Wigand Spiesz von Ortenberg, dorthin versetzte Gudenbergische Buchdruckerey, woraus verschiedene Werke zu Tag gefördert wurden, gab ihr auf Ruhm und Achtung gerechten Anspruch. . . . Heinrich Bechtermünz [Bechtelmonze] ein Schüler und Gehülfe Henchin's Genszfleisch, genannt Gudenberg, gleichfalls Patrizier, und mit Genszfleisch verwandt, errichtete zu Eltvill noch bey des Erfinders Lebzeiten, und zwar mit dessen eigener, ihm jedoch nicht zum Eigenthum, sondern nur nutzniesslich überlassenen Typen und Druckzeuge, eine Buchdruckerey; er starb aber schon vor unserm Genszfleisch im Jahr 1467, und sein Bruder Niclas vollendete das von ihm angefangene, nun äusserst seltene Werk: Vocabularium latino-teutonicum, 1467, in kl. 4. mit Hülfe Wigands Spies v. Ortenberg. Eben dieser fertigte 1469 eine neue Auflage davon mit den nämlichen Typen, die er nach Henchins Tode, vom Mainzer Stadtsyndikus (Kanzler) Dr. Conrad Homery . . . . erhalten hatte . . . . Niclas Bechtermünz war mit Wigand Spies Schöffe des Gerichts zu Hechtsheim, und kömmt in alten Leihbriefen häufig in dieser Eigenschaft vor. Da er ohne männliche Leibeserben starb, so fiel seine

Bodmann did not publish this *unprinted* deed of conveyance of 1508, nor do I find it among the 380 documents which Schaab either mentions or prints in his second volume. If such a document existed in Bodmann's collection it must have come into Schaab's possession, and he could not have failed to see its great importance. In fact, from what Schaab says, it is clear that he did not believe in the existence of such a document.

Authors who ascribe the Catholicon of 1460 to Gutenberg, do not omit to notice that the types with which this work was printed could scarcely be in the possession of Humery in Feb. 1468, as on the 4th of Nov. 1467, the *Vocabularium ex quo*, printed with these very types, was published by Nyc. Bechtermüncze and Wygand Spyess, at Eltville, near Mentz, who declare in the colophon that the book was commenced by Henr. Bechtermuncze, the brother of Nicolaus. Schaab (Erfind. der Buchdruckerk., i. 454) endeavours to explain this difficulty in this way:

As the Elector Adolf II. did not trust the Mentz citizens, whom he persecuted, he took up his residence at Eltville among his beloved Rheingau subjects, and Gutenberg was compelled, on account of his court-service, to follow him thither. Thither Gutenberg also transferred his whole printing-office, and, as Eltville was not more than three hours distance from Mentz on the right bank of the Rhine, the transport of the printing apparatus could easily be effected and without any great cost. At Eltville there lived at that time two noble patricians, the brothers Heinrich and Niclas Bechtermüntze. There existed a close connexion between Gutenberg's relatives and the Bechtermüntzes; when the former came to Eltville, he was old and either could not or would not, on account of his court-service, occupy himself with printing. He, therefore, instructed the Bechtermüntzes in this art and gave them his printing-apparatus, but only for temporary use, as the materials did not belong to Gutenberg but to Dr. Humery.

Dr. Van der Linde (p. 68) tells us that

"About 1465 Gutenberg's typographical apparatus was transferred to Eltville, at that time the residence of the Archbishop of Mentz. Two brothers, Heinrich and Niklaus Bechtermünze, belonging to the Mentz

---

beträchtliche Verlassenschaft auf seines Bruders Kinder, wie die weitläuftige Theilungs-Urkunde vom Jahr 1476 (!) bewähret.—Nach Hansen Bechtermünz Tode verkauften die Erben das Druckerzeug an die zu Marienthal versammelte Kogelherrn, und, als diese zu drucken aufhörten, überliessen sie solches an "Friderich Hauman von Norembergk, dem Buchdrucker im Kirsgarten zu Menz." (Ungedr. Urk. 1508.) Dort war es wahrscheinlich, wo es ganz zu Grunde gieng.

nobility and related to Gutenberg, learned the new art from the inventor himself (!), who even handed his types over to them for temporary use. When Henry died, another patrician, Wigand Spyess von Ortenberg, took his place, and Nicl. Bechtermünze and he published in 1467 the *Vocabularium ex quo*, and a new edition on the 15th [read 5th] of June, 1469, both with the types of the Catholicon. The later editions of the same work of 12th March, 1472, and 19 [read 21] Dec. 1477, were printed with a quite similar [*sic*] type."

Dr. Van der Linde proceeds:

"After the death of Nicl. Bechtermünze, his heirs transferred their material to the Fraternity of the Common Life (Fratres vitæ communis) of Mariental in the Rheingau, near Eltville."

Dr. Van der Linde does not deem it necessary to remark that the Fratres are not known to have ever published a book in Gutenberg's or Bechtermünze's types; but, with that vagueness and want of research which pervades his whole book, proceeds (in Gothic type):

"they (*i. e.* the Fratres) printed *e. g.*, in 1474, Psalterium et Breviarium Moguntiense. In domo fratrum clericorum communis vite Vallis Sancti Marie in Ringkauia."

as if this book were printed with Bechtermünze's type.

He further tells us (p. 69), evidently quoting Schaab, that in 1508 the Fratres vitæ communis sold the Bechtermünze material [he could only mean the Gutenberg material] to Friedrich Hewmann, of Nuremberg, printer in the Kirschgarten at Mentz. But, unlike Schaab, Dr. Van der Linde thinks it quite superfluous to tell us that this double transfer of printing materials was an assertion of Bodmann, which he never substantiated by the publication of the document. Dr. Van der Linde, however, treats us (p. 69) to another particular, which it was Schaab's misfortune not to be acquainted with, and which would, if based on fact, enable us to dispense with Bodmann's *unpublished* deed of conveyance.

This particular is as follows: Friedr. Hewmann published on the 29th of August, 1509, Gabr. Biel, *Passionis dominice sermo historialis*. It is in this book of 1509 that Helbig made in 1855, what Dr. Van der Linde calls "a most important discovery for the history of typography," and in order not to deprive Helbig of the credit of this discovery he quoted Helbig's own words.

Helbig described his so-called discovery in these words: "To his astonishment, perhaps to his joy, he found in Biel's work, published in 1509, not the types of the Catholicon, which had been used in the books published at Eltville, but, indeed, the types used in the Letters of Indulgence of 1454 and 1455, in the Appeal against the Turks of 1455, the Calendar of 1457, the Bible of 36 lines—in a word, he recognized the oldest types of Gutenberg!" He describes six other works, seven in all, printed by the same printer in the same ancient types of Gutenberg (anciens caractères de Gutenberg).

These works are according to Helbig:

1. De fide concubinarum in sacerdotes, questio accessoria causa ioci et urbanitatis in Quodlibeto Heidelbergensi determinata . . . (with colophon): Impressum Maguntie per Fridericum Hewmann. (s. a.) 4° 10 leaves with a woodcut (a copy at Paris).

2. Diel (Florentius) Grammatica initialis valde resoluta . . . (with coloph.) Moguntiae, Frid. Hewmann, 17 Jul. 1509. Small 4°.

This book has also been seen by M. Deschamps; see his Dictionnaire de Géographie, art. *Mogontiacum*, col. 854, where he says that "the summaries and commencements of the chapters are incontestably (*sic*) printed with the types of the 36-line Bible."

3. Biel (Gabr.) Passionis dominice sermo historialis . . . (with col.) Moguntiae per Frid. Hewman A.D. 1509 d. 29 mens. Augusti. in 8°.

4. Zabern (Jac.) Ars bene cantandi coralem cantum in multitudine personarum laudem Dei resonantium . . . (with col.) Mogunt. per Frider. Hewman, 3 nov. (s. a.) in 12°.

5. Regimen Sanitatis. Wie man sich durch alle monath des ganzen jares mit essen und trinken halten soll . . . (with col.) Frid. Hewman imprimebat Moguntie A.D. 1509. in 4°.

6. Directorium missae de novo perspectum et emendatum. (with col.) Impressum Maguntie per Frid. Hewman Anno domini Millesimo quingentesimo nono. 1811. in 4°. A copy in the Darmstadt Library.

7. Brant (Sebast.) Liber Moreti docens mores Juvenum in supplementum illorum qui a Cathone erant omissi: in vulgare noviter translatus (with col.) Impressus Moguntie per Frid. Hewman, A. virginei partus, 1509. 10 leaves in 4°.

To this number I may add:

8. De Fide meretricum in suos amatores. Questio . . . determinata a magistro Jacobo Hartleib. (with colophon) Impressum Maguntie per Fridericum Hewmann. (s. a.) 10 ll. 4°. with a woodcut. (A copy at Paris).

9. Corvini (Laurentii) Latinum Idioma. Moguntiæ, per F. Hewmann (s. a.). A copy mentioned in the Sale-Catalogue (No. 109) of Sotheby, 7 Feb. 1870 (Culemann's Library).

10. Publii Virgilii Maronis Mantuani bucolicum decem æglogarum opus. Maguncie in ædibus Friderici Hewman. 4°. (s. a.). A copy in the Darmstadt Library. The title only is printed with the Missal-type in question.

11. Donati Romani editio minor reformata ex vetustissimis; with

the colophon: Donati Romani editio minor reformata ex vetustissimis. Impressa Moguntie, per Fridericum Hewman. Explicit. Anno Domini Millesimoquingentesimoduodecimo (*i. e.* 1512). 32 leaves small 4°.

I saw a copy of this work, on the 13th Oct. 1881, in the Library of Herr Frid. Culemann at Hanover. The book is entirely printed in the type in question, with the exception of the heading and colophon.

I think it necessary to translate a few pieces of Helbig's article on this discovery, which he published in the *Bulletin du Bibliophile Belge*, tom. xi, Bruxelles, 1855, p. 18.

"Some time ago I had the fortune to make a little discovery (une petite découverte) which is not without importance to clear up several obscure points relative to the history of typographical origines . . . . My little find (ma petite trouvaille) such as it is, presents, I dare to repeat it, an importance sufficiently great. You will be able to judge of it.—It is well known (Il est bien connu) that when Gutenberg, the illustrious inventor of typography, was appointed gentilhomme of the house of Adolf II. of Nassau, the archbishop and elector of Mentz, he ceded his printing-office to his relative Henri Bechtermünz, who commenced, at Eltville on the Rhine, near Mentz, his famous edition of the *Vocabularius ex quo*, finished in 1467. Henri Bechtermünz dying during the impression of this book, the printing-office was continued by his brother Nicholas, who was joined by Wigand Spies d'Ortenberg. When Nicholas Bechtermünz died, his heirs ceded the material of the printing-office to the Brothers of the Common Life, at Marienthal in Rheingau, near Eltvill.—The learned Bodmann in his Rheingauische Alterthümer (Mainz, 1819) tom. i. p. 136, quotes an extract from a deed of conveyance (*acte de vente*) of the year 1508, according to which this antique printing-office was sold the same year by the Brothers of the Common Life to Frederic Hewman or Hauman of Nuremberg, printer at Mentz in the Kirschgarten. Schaab (Annales de la Société d'Histoire du pays de Nassau, p. 64; and in his Erfind. der Buchdruckerk. i. 553) reminds us of this passage of Bodmann, but does not seem to believe in it [!].—Now, one day re-reading this interesting passage [of Bodmann], it occurred to me to examine with attention a certain book [namely, Gabr. Biel, Passionis dominicæ sermo historialis] printed by this Fred. Hauman, which was lying in a neglected corner of my library. I took it up without expecting to discover anything in it. I knew that the last productions of the presses of Nic. Bechtermünz are printed with other types than those of Gutenberg, and that among the known impressions of the Brothers of the Common Life there is not one [!] executed with these characters. Judge of my astonishment, of my joy perhaps, when I recognised in this old book, lately so scorned, *not** the types of the Catholicon of 1460, the only ones proceeding from Gutenberg which have been employed in the books issued from the presses at Eltville, *but indeed** the characters used in the Letters of Indulgence of 1454 and 1455, in the Appeal against the Turks of 1455, the Kalendar of 1457 described by Fischer, the 36-line Bible, and all the impressions of Albrecht Pfister—in one word, I discovered the oldest types of Gutenberg!"

* The italics are mine.—J. H. H.

I must give the last sentence in Helbig's own words: "Que l'on juge de mon étonnement, de ma joie peut-être, lorsque je reconnus dans le bouquin naguère si dédaigné, *non pas* les types du Catholicon de 1460, les seuls provenants de Gutenberg qui *aient été employés* dans les livres sortis des presses d'Eltvill, *mais bien* les caractères mis en usage dans les lettres d'indulgence de 1454 et 1455, dans l'appel contre les Turcs de 1455," &c.

It is quite natural that Helbig goes on to argue that his discovery would revolutionise the whole history of Gutenberg.

Let us now see what becomes of Helbig's discovery in the mouth of Theo. L. de Vinne, who published: *The Invention of Printing*, in 1877 (Lond. and New York).

On p. 443 he translates Helbig's last sentence thus:

> "But judge of my astonishment, of my joy, perhaps, when I recognized in the neglected book *not only** the types of the Catholicon of 1460, the only ones appertaining to Gutenberg that *could have been employed** in the books that proceeded from the presses of Eltvill, *but also** the types that had been used in the Letters of Indulgence of 1454 and 1455, in the Appeal against the Turks of 1455," &c.

Is this not a pretty translation from the French? Here Helbig is represented as having discovered *two* types of Gutenberg, even the types of the Catholicon, in a book printed in 1509.

It is not going out of my way to tell the reader that Mr. De Vinne is Dr. Van der Linde's pet author. The terrible Dr. Van der Linde, who roars like a lion against any one who does not share his opinions, and who has scarcely one kind word to say of anybody, becomes affectionate and meek and even humble when he mentions De Vinne. On p. 40 he says: "When I quote now and then the transatlantic author (*i.e.* De Vinne) then I am at the same time grateful and modest, for his book is really an elaborated, improved and illustrated edition of the English translation of my Costerlegend." It is only fair to add that Dr. Van der Linde is sometimes severe on De Vinne also. On p. 114 he points out a curious mistake in De Vinne's book (p. 91), where the latter deals with a German name, and addresses him thus: "You don't understand German, old boy." I think it

* The italics are mine, and correspond to the words which I have italicised in the French quotation from Helbig.—J. H. H.]

appears that this transatlantic old boy is somewhat (!) deficient in French too! When I add that this same De Vinne says on p. 441 of his work that "the Vocabularium ex quo was reprinted by Nicholas Bechtermüntz, in the same (!) types and in the same form, in the years 1469, 1472 (!), and 1477 (!)"—and that on p. 36 he makes the stoic Balbus in Cicero's *De Natura Deorum*, ii. 20, speak of "a number of solid and invisible [*sic!* should be indivisible] bodies," every one will be surprised at Dr. Van der Linde's humility in saying that De Vinne's book is an *improved* edition of his Haarlem Legend. I for one have a better opinion of Dr. Van der Linde's work on the Haarlem Costerlegend.

It will be seen from what has been said above that in the course of time *four* statements have been made which more or less bear on the document of Humery, dated 24 Febr. 1468.

The *first* (in point of time the last) statement is that of Helbig, that seven (eleven) books, printed by Fred. Heumann or Haumann, at Mentz, from 1506 till 1509 (should be 1512), contain the type of the 36-line Bible. As Helbig, in common with many others, ascribed this Bible to Gutenberg, his discovery, if founded on fact, would establish the existence of Gutenberg's type as late as 1512. Helbig made this statement after having read Bodmann's assertion referred to above (see p. 123), and after having examined *Gabr. Biel's Passionis dominice sermo*, printed by Heumann; and Dr. Van der Linde, on the strength of Helbig's discovery, established a Gutenberg-school as existing till 1509. Had he known the Donatus, which I saw at Hanover, he would, of course, have made the school last till 1512.

I have been able to examine the very book which Helbig had before him, namely Biel's *Passionis dominice sermo*, printed by Heumann in 1509, of which a copy is in the Brit. Museum (pressmark 845. h. 4). I have also examined five other books (preserved in the Paris, Darmstadt, and Culemann Libraries), printed by the same Heumann, in the same type; two mentioned by Helbig (*De fide concubinarum in sacerdotes questio*, and the *Directorium*), the others (*De fide meretricum in suos amatores questio, Virgil, Donatus*) not. At the first glance at the type, used for the *headings* or *rubrics* (in the case of the Donatus for the *whole* book) in these books, every one accustomed to a minute examination of type must see that it is a type indeed, in some respects, *very much like* that of the 36-line Bible, but yet *materially smaller*, and *consequently totally different.* Some of the capitals are entirely different; but even if Helbig had carefully examined the *form* of those capitals and some of the small letters, which resemble most those of the Bible, he would not have spoken of an *identity* between the two types. Nor does Fischer speak of any identity between Heumann's type and that of the 36-line Bible, though he minutely describes (*Typogr. Seltenh.* i. 66) the *Questio de fide concubinarum*, and mentions (ib. p. 86) the *Regimen Sanitatis*, and Biel's *Sermo.*

As Helbig's so-called discovery of the 36-line Bible type in Heumann's productions is disproved by the very book in which he imagined that he had made it, it is not likely to be verified by the five other works of Heumann mentioned by Helbig, which, indeed, I have not seen, but which Helbig does not appear to have seen either. It is true, Heumann *may* have produced other books, not yet divulged as works of his, but—neither Helbig nor Bodmann professes to know anything about such works. As far, therefore, as Helbig's discovery is concerned, I feel inclined to regard Bodmann's *unpublished* deed of sale of 1508—which, as far as I know, has never yet been found—as one of those fabrications with which he is known to have amused his bibliographical friends.

One thing is certain: the two types used by Heumann in the above enumerated books, are of the kind usual at the beginning of the XVI. century, and can have no connexion whatever with those usually ascribed to Gutenberg. In Heumann's time, and even much later, it seems to have been the fashion to *imitate* the types of the early Bibles. For instance, in a *Directorium Misse* secundum frequentiorem cursum diocesis Moguntinensis (Brit. Mus. 846. k. 16), which was evidently printed at Mentz about this period, the headings of the chapters are printed in a type just as closely resembling that of the 42-line Bible, as Heumann's type does that of the 36-line Bible. But yet the difference is as visible in the one case as in the other. At Mentz I saw a "Psalterium Spirense ad usum orandi" printed in 1515, with the same type as Heumann's. In Mr. Culemann's collection I saw a quire of a Missal, which had the colophon: "Impressum Moguntie per Petrum

Scheffer et finitum primo Idus Maij. Anno supra Millesimum Quingentesimo decimooctauo (*i.e.* 1518)." This Missal (at least the quire I saw) is printed in exactly the same type as Heumann's. Here is material for Dr. Van der Linde for a longer duration and much greater extension of the Gutenberg-school!

The *second* statement is that of Bodmann, that the types which the said Heumann used at Mentz were transferred to him by the *Fratres communis vitae* of Marienthal near Eltville (see above, p. 123). This statement, which, if proved, would establish the existence of Gutenberg's type from c. 1468–1508, was made by Bodmann on the strength of the deed of sale, as referred to above, which he said was *unpublished.*

I have taken the trouble to search for works published by the Fratres communis vitae of Marienthal. Their activity in printing is as yet but little known or even suspected. I give, therefore, a list of such of their works as were known or have been discovered by me. They employed two types, the one a little smaller than the other, and with these types published :—

I). Copia indulgentiarum de institutione festi presentationis beatae Mariae per . . . . Adolphum, archiepiscopum Moguntinum concessarum. Datum in civitate nostra Moguntina, die penultima mensis Augusti 1468.

Type I (large). It has no printer's name, no place, no date. The copy in the *Paris Library*, which is imperfect, has 12 leaves, in one quire of 6 sheets, small folio, with 40 lines on a full page. Cf. Fischer, Seltenheiten, vi. 126; Bernard, Orig. de l'impr. ii. 17. Not mentioned by Hain.

II). Gerson (Joh.) Opusculum tripartitum de praeceptis decalogi, de confessione et de arte moriendi.

36 leaves (a b c^{12}), 4°, with 25 uneven lines, no signatures, no place, no printer's name, no date. It is wholly printed in one (the large) type, and Bernard (*Orig. de l'imp.* ii. 18) is in error in saying that the Gerson is printed with the *two* types of the Psalter. The late Mr. Alfred J. Horwood, of the Middle Temple, possessed a copy, which I have been able to examine, and from which I append the description.

Leaf I blank; 2^a: [C]Ristianitati suus qualiscūq‖zelator. ꝓsperum ad virtutes‖; 35^a line 16: Explicit opusculū triꝑtitum de preceptis‖ decalogi De confessione ꝛ de arte moriē-‖di. ꝑ eximiū sacre theologie ꝓfessorē Ma-‖gistꝫ iohānem de Jersona alme vniuersi-‖tatis ꝑisiens' Cancellariū.‖; 35^b and 36 blank.

I saw another copy, agreeing with this, in the Darmstadt Library.

Cf. also Fischer, Seltenh., vi. 128; Hain, (7654 not seen) mentions an edition which differs from this.

III). Psalterium Breviariumque Maguntinense.

Hain (3862) and Brunet (I. col. 1237) mention this work, but in a vague way. Hain, who has not seen the book, speaks of 2 volumes: I. (341 leaves), II. (380 leaves); so does Brunet. They both speak of two varieties, and this is, as far as I know, the extent to which every writer has gone. I have examined all the volumes of this work, preserved at Darmstadt, Mentz, and Frankfurt a/M., which enables me to say that there are several editions, of certain portions at least, of the work. The following bibliographical description—the absolute accuracy of which I cannot guarantee, as I made the collation in the hurry of a journey, and without anticipating in the one place that I should find fresh varieties in the next place—will, I hope, be found useful towards a future, more complete and exhaustive, description.

It seems strange that both Hain and Brunet should think that the work was printed by Peter Schoefer.

At Mentz; Volume A* (Pars hiemalis):

1) *Kalendar;* a quire of 8 leaves:

Leaf 1ª:

[S]ubiectū volumen psalterij breuiarijq̧ ma-||gūtinens'. im-p̄ssorie artis īdustria p̱fectū. ᶜt'.'felicit̄ ɔsūmatū ē. in domo fratrū' clericoꝝ||coīs vite vallis scē marie eiusdē dioces' in Ringka-||uia. Anno dn̄i. M.cccc.lxxiiij. sabb'o post Remīscē. ||&c.; 1ᵇ line 1: Sequuntur bn̄dictiones in matutinis.||; 2ª–7ᵇ Kalendar; 8ª and 8ᵇ Litera dominicalis; Aureus numerus and Indictio. By the side of these on 8ª: Hee tres tabule Incipiūt. An-||no dn̄i Millesimo quadringē-||tesimo septuagesimo qr̄to. Et||&c.; 8ᵇ (by the side of the continuation of the Litera domin. &c.): Septuagesimā atq̧||interuallum alicuiꝰ ||&c.

The copy at Paris (Biblioth. nat. B 2442, reserve) agrees with this description, according to information received from Prof. Paul Meyer, who kindly collated it for me.

---

* There are four volumes at Mentz. As I did not notice that they bore any press-mark, I name them A, B, C, D for convenience of reference and identification.

2) *Psalterium*

Collation: a b c d e f g h i^{10}, 90 leaves; no signatures, with hyphens. Types: 1 (large) and 2 (small).

Leaf 1^{a} line 1 (in small type): Dñicis noctibȝ dū de tpe officiū d'r Inuiī. ab octaīs‖; line 20 (large type): [B]eat⁹ vir qui nō abijt in‖; leaf 89^{b} Greek text; 90 blank.

The copy at Paris agrees with this description.

3) *Temporale*

Collation: aa^{12} (registrum aduentus), leaves 1–12; a b c d e f g h i k l m^{10} n o^{8} p q^{10} r s^{8}(+9) 173 leaves; leaves 13–185 Temporale.

Leaf 1^{a} line 1: Incipit registrum aduentus.‖[S]i A fuerit lr̄a dn̄icalis. Aduētus dn̄i celebrat̄‖; 11^{b}, last line (28): dibȝ ij. ferie post dn̄icā iiij. Cetera vt in breuiario.‖; 12 blank; 13^{a} line 1: Dominica prima aduentus in primis vespis. An̄.‖[H]Ora est iam nos de somno sur-‖&c.; 185^{b} line 22: aucōnis de quo satis dictū est in loco suo.‖

The Paris copy agrees with this description.

4) *Commune Sanctorum*

Collation: a b^{10} c^{12} d^{4}, 36 leaves.

Leaf 1^{a} line 1: [I]ncipit ɔmune scōꝝ. Primo de apl'is. In vigi‖lia apl'oꝝ Ad ix An̄. In paciēcia vr̄a Cap̄ et‖; 33^{b} last line (24): dragesima. vt notat̄ dn̄ica prima post trinitatis.‖; 34–36 blank; (36 is cut away).

The Paris copy agrees with this description.

At Mentz; Volume B (Pars estivalis):

1) *Kalendar*, 8 leaves, same as in vol. A

2) *Psalterium*

Collation: a b c d e f g h i^{10}, 90 leaves.

Leaf 1^{a} line 1 (in small type): Dn̄icis noctibȝ dū de tpe officiū d'r. Inuitatoriū ab‖; line 21 (in large type): [B]eatus vir qui non abijt‖

3) *Temporale*

Collation: a b c d^{10} e^{6} f g h i k^{10} l^{8}, 106 leaves. No signatures.

Leaf 1^{a} li. 1: [I]N die scō pasce Ad matutinas. prius q̄ dicat̄‖; line 3: Lapidem exclusiue. Gl'a prī. Kyriel'. Xp̄eel'. Kyriel'. Pr̄‖

4) *Proprium Sanctorum*

Collation: a b c d e f g h^{10} i k^{12}, 104 leaves. No signatures.

This edition ends leaf 104^{b} line 20: ibidem. Cetera de festo dedicacōnis.

5) *Commune Sanctorum*

Collation : a b^{10} c^{12} (+12), 33 leaves.

Leaf 1 line 1 : [I]ncipit ɔmune sanctoꝝ. Primo de apl'is.|| ; 17ª line 1 : nō timuit. Fundatus enī erat supra firmā petrā. v̄||

At Mentz: Volume C (Pars hiemalis):

1) *Kalendar* = A^1.

2) *Psalterium* = A^2

3) *Temporale* = A^3

4) *Commune Sanctorum* = A^4

At Mentz: Volume D (Pars estivalis):

1) *Kalendar* (imperfect, only two last leaves) = Mentz A^1

2) *Psalterium*

Collation : a b c^{10} d e f g h^8 i k^{10}, 90 leaves.

Leaf 1 is wanting; I am therefore unable to identify the particular edition. It is, I believe, = Psalter of Darmst. 5610

3) *Temporale*

Collation : a b c d e f^8 g^{10} h i k l m n^8, 106 leaves. No signatures.

Leaf 1ª line 1 : [I]N die scō pasce Ad matutinas. prius q̄ dicat̄|| ; line 3 : v̄sū. lapidē exclusiue. Gl'a. Kyriel'. Xp̄eel'. Kyriel'. Pr̄||

4) *Proprium Sanctorum*

Collation : a^{10} b c d e f^8 g h i^{10} k l m n o p q^8 r^6, 142 leaves. No signatures.

Leaf 104^b line 20 : cantet̄ ibidem. Cetera de festo dedicacōnis||. After this the volume goes on, without any break, with the histories of some Saints : Boniface, Gregory, &c. This is explained on the recto of last leaf : Notandum quod huic breuiario sup*er*addite su*n*t ali||que historie speciales que no*n* sunt de registro. ser||uantur t*amen* in maiori ecclesia Maguntin*ensi*. Videlicet de||sanctis p*ro* parte estiuali, &c.

5) *Commune Sanctorum*

Collation : a b c^8 d^{10}, 34 leaves.

Leaf 1ª line 1 : [I]ncipit ɔmune sanctoꝝ. Primo de apl'is.|| ; 17ª line 1 : nō timuit. Fundatus enī erat supra firmā petrā. v̄||

¶ The Library at Mentz possesses two *vellum* fragments of some part of the Breviary, but my time did not allow me to ascertain which part they belonged to. (See also below, Darmstadt, W 5610).

At Darmstadt: pressmark W 5608 (Pars estivalis):

1) *Kalendar* (wanting?)

2) *Psalterium*

Collation: a b c d e f g h i^{10}, 90 leaves. No signatures; with hyphens. Leaf 1ª line 1 (in small type): Dñicis noctibꝫ dū de tpe officiū d'r. Inuit̄. ab octaīs||; line 20 (large type): [B]eatꝰ vir qui nō abijt in||; leaf 90 (blank) wanting.

3) *Temporale* = Mentz B^3

4) *Proprium Sanctorum* = Mentz B^4

5) *Commune Sanctorum*

Collation: a b^{10} c^{12} (+ c 12), 33 leaves. No signatures.

Leaf 1^a: [I]ncipit ɔmune scōꝝ. Primo de apl'is. In vig||

At Darmstadt: pressmark W 5609 (Pars estivalis):

1) *Kalendar* (wanting?)

2) *Psalterium*

Collation: a b c^{10} d e f g h^8 i k^{10}, 90 leaves. No signatures, but the quires are signed in writing b – l; the kalendar is, I believe, wanting in the volume.

Leaf 1ª line 1 (small type): Dñicis noctibꝰ dum de tpe officiū d'r. Inuitatoriū||; line 21 (large type): [B]Eatꝰ vir qui non abijt in ɔsi||

3) *Temporale*

Collation: a b c d e f^8 g^{10} h i k l m n^8, 106 leaves. No signatures.

Leaf 1ª line 3: v̄sū. lapidē exclusiue. Gl'a. Kyriel'. Xp̄eel', Kyriel'. Pr̄||

4) *Proprium Sanctorum*

As far as I was able to see, this part = Mentz D^5; but there may be some difference in some part of the volume.

5) *Commune Sanctorum*

Collation: a b c^8 d^{10}, 34 leaves. No signatures.

Leaf 1^a: [I]ncipit cōmune sanctoꝝ. Primo de apl'is||; 17^a line 1: nō timuit. Fundatus enī erat supra firmā petram. v̄||; leaf 34 blank.

At Darmstadt : pressmark W 5610 (Pars estivalis).

1) *Kalendar*, 8 leaves (perhaps = Frankfurt Kal.)

Leaf 1^a blank ; 1^b – 8^a Kalendar ; 8^b blank.

2) *Psalterium*

Collation : a b c^{10} d e f g h^8 i k^{10}, 90 leaves. No printed signatures, but the quires are signed in writing a — l, which includes the kalendar.

Leaf 1^a line 1 (in small type) : Dn̄icis noctib⁹ dū de tpe officiū d'r. Inuitatoriū‖ ; line 21 (large type) : [B]Eat⁹ vir qui nō abijt in cōsi‖

The Library at Mentz possesses of this edition the first quire only.

3) *Temporale* = Mentz D^3

4) *Proprium Sanctorum* = Mentz D^4

5) *Commune Sanctorum*

Collation : a b c^8 d^{10}, 34 leaves. No signatures.

Leaf 1^a : [I]ncipit cōmune sancto℞. Primo de apl'is‖ ; leaf 17 line 1 : nō timuit. Fundatus enī erat supra firmā petrā. v̄‖ ; leaf 34 blank.

At Frankfurt a/M : pressmark 315 (Pars estivalis) :

1) *Kalendar* = Mentz A^1

2) *Psalterium* = Darmstadt W 5608

3) *Temporale* = Mentz B^3

4) *Proprium Sanctorum* = Mentz B^4

5) *Commune Sanctorum* = Darmstadt W 5608

At Frankfurt a/M : pressmark 317 (Pars estivalis) :

1) *Kalendar*, 8 leaves.

Leaf 1^a blank ; 1^b line 1 : Secunt̄ bn̄dictiones in matutinis‖ ; 1^b line 31 : Ferijs tercijs. qn̄tis. et sabbato de scd'o nocturno‖ ; 2^a — 7^b Kalendar ; 8 (blank ?) wanting.

2) *Psalterium* = Darmstadt W 5610

3) *Temporale* = Mentz D^3

4) *Proprium Sanctorum* = Mentz D^4

5) *Commune Sanctorum* = Mentz D^5

As some of the parts are bound in the volumes in an order somewhat different from the above description I append a table showing their order in the volumes.

Mentz A . . .	1) Kalendar; (imprint 1474)	2) Psalterium;	3) Temporale, PH*;	4) Commune Sanctorum (Proprium Sanctorum wanting) ...
,, B . . .	1) Kalendar;	2) Psalterium;	3) Temporale, PE†;	4) Proprium Sanctorum and Commune Sanctorum
,, C . . .	1) Kalendar;	2) Psalterium;	3) Temporale, PH;	4) Commune Sanctorum (Proprium Sanctorum wanting) ...
,, D . . .	1) Kalendar;	2) Psalterium and Commune Sanctorum;	3) Temporale PE;	4) Proprium Sanctorum
Darmstadt W 5608	1) (Kal. wanting)	2) Psalterium and Commune Sanctorum;	3) Temporale PE;	4) Proprium Sanctorum
Darmstadt W 5609	1) (Kal. wanting)	2) Temporale PE;	3) Psalterium and Commune Sanctorum;	4) Proprium Sanctorum
Darmstadt W 5610	1) Kalendar;	2) Psalterium and Commune Sanctorum;	3) Temporale PE;	4) Proprium Sanctorum
Frankfurt 315 .	1) Kalendar;	2) Temporale PE;	3) Psalterium and Commune Sanctorum;	4) Proprium Sanctorum
Frankfurt 317 .	1) Kalendar;	2) Psalterium and Commune Sanctorum;	3) Temporale PE;	4) Proprium Sanctorum
Paris B 2442 .	1) Kalendar; (imprint 1474)	2) Psalterium;	3) Temporale, PH;	4) Commune Sanctorum (Proprium Sanctorum wanting)

* *i.e.* Pars hiemalis. † *i.e.* Pars estivalis.

T

This second table shows the number of different editions of each part.

Kalendar, with imprint.	*Temporale, PH*	*Psalterium.*	*Commune Sanctorum.*	*Proprium Sanctorum.*
Mentz A[1]	Mentz A[3]	Mentz A[2]	Mentz A[4]	Mentz B[4]
Kalendar, without imprint.	*Temporale, PE*	Mentz B[2]	Mentz B[5]	Mentz D[4]
Frankfurt 317	Mentz B[3]	Darmstadt W. 5608	Mentz D[5]	
	Mentz D[3]	,, W. 5609	Darmstadt W 5608	
	Darmstadt W 5609	,, W 5610	,, W 5609	
			,, W 5610	

iv) Letters of Indulgence with printed date 1484. Broadside folio sheet, 33 uneven lines in the large type, 15 lines in the small type.

See a notice of this Indulgence in *Archiv für Hess. Gesch.*, vol. x. p. 186, by H. Sahl, who discovered it in the binding of a work (*Newe Reformation der Stadt Nurenberg von* 1479) printed at Nürnberg (Koberger) 1484. It is printed with the two types of the Psalterium, and is preserved in the Darmstadt Hofbibliothek (see Ph. A. F. Walther, Hofbibliothek zu Darmstadt, p. 90), where I examined it on Oct. 3rd, 1881. The copy has not been issued, as the blanks for the name, month, and day of the month are not filled in.

v) Nic. de Lyra Postilla in 4 Evangelia, without date.

This *fifth* work is mentioned by Bodmann (Rheing. Alterth. i. 218) as having been printed by the Fratres, and he says that he saw a copy of it in the hands of Ritter v. Horn at Frankfurt a/M. I have seen a copy (perhaps the very one Bodmann had before him) in the Town Library of Frankfurt a/M. on the 10th Oct. 1881. It is a large folio of 300 leaves (collation: a b c(12+-)d e f g h i k l m n o p q r s t u x y z AB[12]), with 42 not always even lines; no printed signatures; no initial directors; with hyphens. Wholly printed in the large type (1).

Leaf 1 is wanting.

Leaf 2 li. 1: irascitur fratri suo. reus erit iudicio. et eodē modo dicit in alijs p̄— ||

Leaf 300ª li. 35: nrō ih'u cristo. Qui cūprē et spū scō viuit ꝛ regt ī secl'a secl'oꝝ. Amē ||

lines 36 and 37 blank.

li. 38: Explicit postilla super Johānem Nicolai de lyra.||

Leaf 300ᵇ blank.

This edition does not appear to be mentioned by Hain, nor in any other catalogue.

I can further describe as productions of the Marienthal press:

vi) Cerimoniae nigrorum monachorum ordinis S. Benedicti de obseruancia Bursfeldensi. The date of printing may perhaps be placed after 1474. See note below.

Collation: a b c d e f g h i k[10] l[12], 112 leaves, 26 uneven lines, with hyphens; no initials; no initial directors; no printed signatures; wholly printed in the large type (1).

Leaf 1ª: Prologus cerimoniarū nigrorū mona- || chorū ordinis sancti Bn̄dicti de obseruan- || cia Bursfeldensi. || [Q]uoniā apl'i pauli de solli- ||; 3ª: Tabula capl'oꝝ prime distinctōis. || De electione noui abbatis. C . . i. ||; 4ᵇ li. 13: Expliciūt tabule capl'oꝝ oīm distīctionū. || De electione noui abbatis. ||; 112ᵇ line 23: ageret. a' al's put sibi visū fue'it expedire. ||; line 24 blank; line 25: Expliciūt cerimonie nigroꝝ mōchoꝝ || ordīs scī bn̄dci de obs'uācia bursfeld'. ||

I found two copies of this work in the *Mentz* Library. It is mentioned by Hain 4883 (not from eyesight), who adds, between parentheses, *Forte Mogunt. Petrus Schöffer*, which I can say is not the fact. There is also a copy in the British Museum (pressmark 854. g. 3). In the Catalogue of that Institution the work is ascribed to the printer J. Veldener, of Cologne (!).

VII) Ordinarius Divinorum Monachorum Ord. S. Benedicti de obseruancia Bursfeldensi (After 1474?)

Collation: a b c d e f g h i^{10}, 90 leaves, 26 uneven lines, with hyphens; no initials; no initial directors; no printed signatures; wholly printed in the large type (1).

Leaf 1[a]: Prolog⁹ ordinarij d'inoꝝ nigroꝝ mōchoꝝ || ordīs scī bn̄dicti de obs'uācia Bursfeldēsi. || [Q]uia ꝓphetico oraculo dn̄m ī tȳ- ||; 2[a] li. 16: ꝓpellatur. Explicit ꝓlogus. || Sequitur tabula. ||; 90[a] li. 20: subsequi debent. Amen. ||; lines 21 and 22 blank; line 23: Explicit ordinarius diuinoꝝ nigroꝝ || monachoꝝ de obs'uācia Bursfeldensi. ||; lines 25 and 26 and 90[b] blank.

This work I found also in the Mentz Library. It is mentioned by Hain 12059 (not from eyesight), who remarks: (*Mogunt., P. Schöffer. Cohaeret fortasse c. n.* 4883). It is certainly printed in the Marienthal larger type (1)* There is a copy in the British Museum (pressmark 845. i. 1). In the *new* (printed) Catalogue of that Institution the book is ascribed to the printer, P. Schœffer, at Mentz (!).

VIII) Decor mariane vallis in Ringauia, 8vo. 32 pp. Bodmann (Rheing. Alterth. i. 217), speaks of this work as containing the history of Marienthal, and as having been printed in the XVth cent., probably in the Marienthal press. I have been unable to trace this book anywhere.

---

* Herr Culemann at Hannover has a leaf of this work which he told me he had found together with another blank leaf on which is *written:* "Anno Christi—1435—durante adhuc Sacro concilio Basiliensi ordinis S. Benedicti Reformatio ac Vnio Bursfeldina, per vtramque Germaniam inierit in monasterio Clusensi, Ducatus Brunsuicensis, ac Diocæsis Hildesheimensis. —— Anno — 1440 — Moguntiæ ab ingeniosissimo quodam Johanne Gutenbergo, fuit omnium primo inuenta, ac temporis progressu magis magisque aucta et illustrata, vtilissima illa Ars typographica sive impressoria.——Anno—1474—In Recessu annalis Capituli praefatae sacrae Vnionis Bursfeldensis decretum fuit a Patribus quod assumptarum et Apostolice confirmatarum Caerimoniarum ac diuinorum Liber, hucusque manuscriptus, debeat Moguntiae imprimi; Putoque inde prodisse hoc Exemplar primorum typorum.——Anno—1530—Iterum fuerunt Moguntiae typis pulchrioribus conjunctim excusæ, in folio quarto Martyrologium, Regula, Caerimoniae, ac Ordinarius diuinorum. Qui codex etiam habetur in Camera domini Abbatis in Marien Munster. Oretur pro beneuolo Scriptore fr. Jod. R."

Of the above eight works, printed from 1468 till 1484, Bodmann knew Nos. I, II, III, and V. He mentions them himself (Rheing. Alterth. i. 218) as having been printed at Marienthal by the Fratres communis vitae, and if he was acquainted with the works printed by Heumann, he must have seen that there is absolute difference between the types of the two offices. At any rate, we know now that there is no question of identity between them. We also know that hitherto no other types have been found which can be said to have belonged to the Fratres.

What then could the Fratres have transferred to Heumann by that *unpublished* deed of sale of which Bodmann speaks?

The *third* statement is again one of Bodmann (*Rheing. Alterth.* i. 136), that the *Fratres communis vitae*, of Marienthal, had bought [after Aug. 5, 1483?] type (namely Gutenberg's type) from the heirs of Hans Bechtermuncze (the son of Heinrich) of Eltville.

Now, it will be admitted on all hands that the Fratres of Marienthal used, till 1484 at least, two types in the works which are enumerated above, which in design and peculiarity stand separate from all other types used in the 15th century. Schaab (*Erfind. Buchdr.* i. 509) already said, "in their form they have something peculiar, characteristic, which we find neither in Gutenberg's nor in Schoeffer's office." Fischer (*Seltenh.* vi. 130) tells us: "manner, character, even the black (colour of the ink) indicate a particular printer." Consequently, it will be admitted on all hands that there is no identity of types either between those of the Fratres of Marienthal and the Bechtermunczes of Eltville on the one hand, or of the Fratres and Heumann on the other. Schaab (l. c.) speaks of "a close connexion (*Verbindung*) between the press of the Fratres of Marienthal and that of Gutenberg at Eltville," but he does not state what the nature of the connexion can have been, nor can I find that Bodmann gives any authority for his assertion that the Fratres had bought their type from the heirs of the Bechtermunczes. We know for *certain* that the Eltville press or presses produced, from 1467 till 1477, at least *four* works or rather *four editions* of one work, of which I shall speak when treating of the *fourth* statement. As I am equally certain that these are not printed in the types which we find in the books of the Fratres, it may be here said that *if* the types, which we at present *know* to have been used by the Eltville press or presses, by the Fratres of Marienthal, and by Fried. Heumann at Mentz, are the only ones they ever did use, then there can have been no connexion whatever between their several printing-offices, at least not in the way of a *transfer of types.* Consequently the theory of a continuance of a Gutenberg, or any other printing, school, through the Fratres or Heumann, cannot, under the present circumstances, be accepted.

It is worthy of remark that Bodmann, when treating of Marienthal, does not speak of any transfer of type whatever, and merely says (i. p. 212) that "the Fratres erected their own press in 1462, when Mentz was destroyed."

The *fourth* statement is that the Bechtermunczes were printing, in 1467, at Eltville, with the type of the Catholicon of 1460, and had obtained this type, in the first instance, from Johann Gutenberg, not as property, but by way of loan, when his dignity, as a member of the court of the Archbishop of Mentz, prevented him from printing himself; while, after 1468, they bought this very same type from the Syndic Homery, who was, according to the document of 26 Febr. 1468, the owner of Gutenberg's printing-office.

With regard to this *fourth* statement I can speak less decisively than with respect to the three others. But I will give what I have found.

On the 4th Nov. 1467, a Latin-German Vocabulary, known as the *Vocabularius Ex quo*, was published at Eltville (Altavilla) near Mentz, with the following colophon on leaf 166[b] (line 24):—

Presens hoc opusculū nō stili aut penne suf- || fragio s꞉ noua artificiosaq̧ inuencōne qua- || dam ad eusebiam dei industrie per henricum || bechtermuncꝫe pie memorie in altauilla est || inchoatum. et demū sub anno dn̄i M.cccc. || lxvij. ip̄o die leonardi confessoris qui fuit || quarta die mensis nouembris ꝑ nycolaum || bechtermūcꝫe fratrem dicti henrici et wy- || gandū spyesꝫ de orthenberg ē consummatū || Hinc tibi sancte pater nato cū flamīe sacro || Laus et honor dn̄o trino tribuatur et vno || Qui laudare piā semꝑ nō linque mariam.

Collation: a^{12} b c d e f g h i k l m n^{10} o p^{8} q^{10} r^{8}, 166 leaves, 4°, 35 uneven lines to a page; no printed signatures, with hyphens, no initials, no initial directors. Leaf 1 (blank?) wanting; leaf 2[a] (line 1): [E]xquo vocabularij varij autētici videlicʒ || hugwicō katholicō breuileg⁹ papyas || alij que codices sūt ĩ ꝯpacōne ꝑciosi in || collectōe ꝓlixi et ĩtellcōe obscuri et in || numēo multi ita paupes scholaēs eosdē de facili ꝛ | ; etc.

The unique copy of this edition in the Paris National Library wants the first leaf (probably blank), is otherwise in perfect condition, and has still at the foot of the leaves the signatures written in by hand.

The book was republished on the 5th June, 1469, with the following colophon on leaf 166^b (line 24):—

Presens hoc opusculū nō stili aut penne suf- || fragio sʒ noua artificiosaqȝ inuencōe qua- || dam ad eusebiam dei industrie per nicolaū || bechtermūtze In Eltuil est ꝯsūmatū Sub || anno domini M.cccc. lxix ipe (*sic*) die scī boni || facij quj fuit quinta die mens' Iunij || Hinc tibi sancte nato cū flamine sacro || Laus et honor dn̄o trino tribuatur et vno || Qui laudare piā semp nō linque mariam.

Collation: a^{12} b c d e f g h i k l m n^{10} o p^8 q^{10} r^8, 166 leaves, 4°, 35 uneven lines to a page, no printed signatures (the quires of the Paris copy are signed by the rubricator i-xvi, the last quire not signed), with hyphens, no printed initials, no initial directors.

Leaf 1 blank; 2^a: [E]xquo vocabularij varij autētici videlicz || hugwicō katholicō breuileg⁹ papyas || alij que codices sūt ĩ ꝯpacōne ꝑciosi in collectōe ꝓlixi et ĩ tellectōe obscuri ꝛ ĩ || numēo multi ita paupes scholaēs eosdē defacili ꝛ || etc.

Both editions are printed in one and the same type, which is said to be the identical type with which the Catholicon of 1460, and some other smaller works have been printed.

I have carefully compared these two Eltville editions of the Vocabulary, both preserved in the Paris National Library, with the Catholicon, and do not feel at liberty to deny that the types are identical. At one time I thought the Vocabulary type was thicker, but more closely placed, and therefore not taking more room than that of the Catholicon. But this idea I abandoned again. In fact the letters are so minute that I do not know how any difference, suppose it existed, could be detected. I found, however, certain *additions* in the type of the Vocabularies, which are not in the Catholicon, such as (1) a somewhat long sign for *us* (⁹) projecting above the line*; (2) a contraction for et (ꝛ),

* The Catholicon has such a contraction too, even two different ones; one small, for which see the words *Abestis*, *Accio*, *Adulatorculus*, *Alers*, *Anularis*, *Benignus*, *Berbex*, *Castellanus*, *penitus* (in vol. 2 leaf 1^{a2});

which, in the Catholicon, is always expressed in full (*et*). This sign for et (⁊) is the same as that which appears in the type of the Vocabularius Ex quo of 1472; see below (p. 148); (3) a contraction for tis (tꝭ). The edition of 1469 has all these additions, but here also a new s* makes its appearance by the side of the former s, which I find neither in the Catholicon nor in the Vocabularius of 1467, and which clearly belongs to the type of the edition of 1472, where I observed two kinds of s.

Authors, who ascribe the Catholicon of 1460 to Gutenberg, argue, not unreasonably, that Gutenberg must have granted the use of his types to the Eltville printers with the consent of Homery, whose property they were, when he himself became attached to the court of Archbishop Adolf (cf. Schaab, i. 473, sq.). As in the Vocabularius of 1469 Nicolaus Bechtermuntze alone is mentioned as printer, Schaab concludes that, his brother Henry having left heirs, Nicolaus must have obtained possession of the Catholicon type after Gutenberg's death, by a special agreement with Homery, who must have made him proprietor, with the exclusion of Henry's heirs and Wigand Spiess.

It may be observed that *a loan* of the Catholicon type by Gutenberg to Bechtermuncze before 1467, seems to accord ill with the fact that in 1468 the Archbishop of Mentz *handed* types, said to have been Gutenberg's, to Homery, its real proprietor. In fact, if we admit the Homery document to refer to the Catholicon type, and admit also that the Eltville Vocabularies are printed in this type, then the migrations of the Catholicon type have been rather strange: in 1460 (and perhaps in 1461) it is at Mentz; in 1467 at Eltville in the hands of Henr. and Nicol. Bechtermuncze; in 1468 in the hands of the Archbishop of Mentz

another larger, for which see *Athomus*, *Bachius*, *Biplex*, *Bito*, *Bitumen*, *Bovinus*, *Buris*, *Cachinnor*, *Caluo*, *Candela*, *Candidarius*, *Canopeum*, etc., etc. This larger one seems to have been occasionally used also for con-, see *Accio*, *Bobino*, *Matesis*. But in no instance do they resemble the long, thin sign which appears in the Vocabularies of 1467, 1469.

* There is no difficulty in distinguishing the new s from the old: see for an example the words *Abarim* (where the s of mons is the old, the s of moyses the new s), *Abdias* (where the new s occurs at the end of the words *legatus*, *missus*, and *gentes*, whereas *Abdias* and *seruus* have the old).

at Eltville, who in the same year handed it over to Homery at Mentz, the latter promising not to sell it outside the walls of Mentz; yet he must have transferred it very quickly again to Nic. Bechtermuncze at Eltville, as the latter already completed the new edition of the Vocabulary on the 5th of June, 1469.

It is possible that the Archbishop disposed of Gutenberg's type in his capacity of supreme ecclesiastical authority of the diocese, and would have acted in this capacity, even if Gutenberg had not been attached to his court, and need not necessarily have had Gutenberg's goods in his hands. It is also possible that the Homery document stands in connexion with Henry Bechtermuncze's death which had taken place before Nov. 4, 1467, and which may have necessitated some settlement in the Eltville printing-office. But if the transaction between the Archbishop and Homery has been a purely *administrative* one, and referred to the Catholicon type, it seems strange that it should have been expressed in such vague terms, that no mention should have been made of the Bechtermunczes, and that Homery should have made such a promise as is contained in the document of 1468, without stating the condition of affairs as we now presume it to have been.

Again, why should not Gutenberg have attempted to come to some arrangement with Homery regarding the latter's property when he himself ceased to make use of it, and transferred it to other persons? Above all, why should the two Bechtermunczes, and a third nobleman, have printed books, and published their name in them, with tools and type which were handed to them by a person who owed the money for them to another party? I confess I cannot myself suggest any satisfactory reply to these questions.

It is known that Bernard (Orig. de l'imprimerie, ii. 6 sqq.), seeing the difficulty involved in these extraordinary circumstances, contended that Henry Bechtermuncze (and not Gutenberg) was the printer of the Catholicon, and had established himself at least as early as 1458 at Mentz, whence he transferred his press afterwards to Eltville. Even Panzer had already some difficulty in explaining the use of the Catholicon type in 1467 by Bechtermuncze, if Homery had the type in his possession in 1468 (see his Annales, vol. ii. p. 119).

In the present state of our knowledge I do not pretend to decide one way or the other. The only thing I can say with certainty is that if the type of the Vocabularies of 1467 and 1469 is really identical with that of the Catholicon, and Gutenberg the printer of the latter work, the additions which we find in 1467, or perhaps as early as 1461, enable us to distinguish two, if not three, stages in this press.

My researches of the last few months, though not enabling me to decide any questions, yet enable me to advance our knowledge of the Eltville press or presses a little further.

It is known that the *Vocabularius Ex quo* was reprinted at Eltville, in 1472 and 1477. The 1472 edition has the following imprint on leaf 166b (li. 22):

> Presens hoc opusculū nō stili aut pēne suf= || fragio s; noua artificiosaq, inuencōne qua || dam ad eusebiam dei industrie. In Eltuil est || cōsūmatū. Sub āno dñj Mcccclxxij īpo die || Gregorij pape et doctoris || Sit bñdictus hō deus et de virgine natus || Nota ignota quj volt teutunica verba || Legatur (*) opus presens et retinre (sic) velit || Maxima de mīmis ex ptibus accipe totū || Inuenias quod amas si studiosus eris || Ecce Ihū xp̄e claudo pietate libellum || Leticie cupiens celestis habere locellum || Scā redēptoris genitrix q̄ virgo pudoris || Libri pressoris aīmā tege veste decoris ꝰtē ||

> Collation: a[12] b c d e f g h i k l m n[10] o p[8] q[10] r[8], 166 leaves, 4to, 35 uneven lines to a page, no printed signatures, with hyphens, no printed initials, no initial directors.
>
> Leaf 1 (blank) wanting; 2a: [E]xquo vocabularij varij autētici videlic3 || huguicio katholicō breuilegꝰ papyas || alij q, codices sūt in ɔpacōne p̄ciose in || collectōe ꝑlixi. et ītellectōe obscuri. et in || numēo multi ita q, paupes scholaēs eosdē de fa || &c.

I have seen copies of it 1) in the Paris National Library; 2) in Herr Culemann's Library, who has, besides, the single leaf which begins with *Amphorisma*, and the lower portion of the last leaf which contains the imprint; 3) in the Hamburg Town-Library.

Hitherto bibliographers have contented themselves with saying that this edition and that of 1477 are printed with a different type (cf. Schaab, i. 497); Dr. Van der Linde (p. 69) states they are printed with a similar (!) to that of the Catholicon. No facsimile has, as far as I know,

(*) In the Hamburg copy the "ur" have been scratched out.

ever been published of either edition. On my examining, a few months ago, the Paris copy of the edition of 1472, it seemed to me that its type was identical with the brief-type used for the text of the 31-line Letters of Indulgence of 1454.† It is known that this type has never yet been detected in any book; M. Didot even concludes (Nouv. Biogr. Gén. art. *Gutenberg*) that it must have been destroyed.

I now thought it had been my good fortune to discover it, and just in a place (Eltville) whither we might have expected it to be transferred.

On a closer inspection and comparison of the two types, however, I was compelled to abandon the idea of identity, as the new type is smaller than the old, though in design there is absolutely no difference between them. Mr. Blades (vol. 2, page xxxii.) has shown that some of Caxton's types have undergone a process of trimming; namely, a new *mould* was prepared, and in it was stamped, not the old original *patrix* or *punch*, but an old type (letter) trimmed, so that a new fount of type was produced, which was really the same as the old one, but not quite the same in body. But it is doubtful whether we could assume such a process to have been adopted with regard to the 31-line Indulgence type, and we must, therefore, treat the 1472 type as nothing more than a close imitation of the 31-line Indulgence type.

Another work was printed with the type of the 1472 Vocabularius, namely an undated edition of the Summa de articulis Fidei of Thomas de Aquino, of 35 lines, mentioned by Hain *1426. As Dr. Von Halm was so kind as to send this little work to Cambridge for my use, I have thought it better to have a page of it photographed and added to the present work. Its greatly irregular lines would justify us, I think, in ascribing to it a somewhat earlier date than 1472. On a measurement it will be seen that this type

† Though I made this observation independently, Mr. Bradshaw obliged me much by calling my attention to Dr. C. L. Grotefend's "Catalogue of Herr F. G. H. Culemann's Incunabeln-Sammlung" (Hannover, 1844), where on p. 10 the Vocabularius of 1472 is said to have "been printed with the small types of those Gutenberg Letters of Indulgence of 1454, which also contain the Missal-types of the 36-line Bible." This note was repeated in Sotheby's Sale Catalogue, Feb. 7, 1870, p. 73, (Culemann's Library); but here the note to the Vocabularius of 1477 is wrong, as it is said that this latter edition is printed with the same type, which is not the case.

prints about 23 lines in the same space where the Indulgence contains only 20, and yet in the latter document the down stroke of some of the letters of one line already nearly touches the up stroke of the line underneath.* It is true, in the 35-line Aquinas the lines appear in such close proximity that they would almost seem to overlap one another, but it may be doubted whether this result can have been obtained by a filing down of the Indulgence type.

As to the individual letters, in the 31-line Indulgence, which is not a lengthy document, we find only the capitals ABCDEIMNRST. Of these the CEIMS would seem to reappear almost unaltered in the Aquinas and 1472 Vocabulary type, but the ABDNRT are different, and represent more the form and size of the Catholicon type, of which the Aquinas type seems also to have taken the FGHOS.

These details, which I might give at even greater length, coupled with a mixture of types in the Vocabularies of 1467 and 1469, spoken of above (p. 143), point, in my opinion, to the fact that the office where the 31-line Indulgence of 1454 and 1455 was printed, and that where the Catholicon of 1460 was printed, and that where the Vocabularies of 1467, 1469, and 1472, and the 35-line Aquinas, were printed, were one and the same, and must have been in possession *not only of the types* with which these works are printed, *but also of the tools* for producing the types. Whether that office belonged, from 1454 to 1472, to one and the same *printer*, is a question which I cannot solve at present. Not before 1467 do we see the *name* of the printer mentioned. But it appears to me that in that year the Catholicon type (with its modifications), and the type of the 35-line Aquinas were already in one office at Eltville. I cannot deny that the circumstance of a type, resembling so closely that of the 31-line Indulgence, being found at Eltville in 1472, may favour the theory of a *transfer* of type, at some time or other, from the printer of that document (let us call him Gutenberg), to Eltville. It is exactly for this reason that I refrain from deciding

* It will be seen below that two other editions of this work have been printed in the Catholicon type, the one of 34, the other of 36 lines. Would the edition of 35 lines have to be placed between these two?

against such a transfer, however much I may distrust Bodmann's or any other person's unauthorised statements regarding this point. But, as I have said, I cannot decide against Bernard's theory that the Eltville press had first been established at Mentz. The additions to the Catholicon type appear already in 1461, but I cannot record a *mixture* of this type with that of the Aquinas and Vocabulary of 1472 earlier than 1467, though in this year it consists only of the sign for *et*, and is therefore subject to doubt; the *mixture* is more decided in 1469. The questions which remain to be solved are simply: 1) was the 31-line Indulgence printed at Mentz? 2) if so, by whom? 3) was the Catholicon printed at Mentz? As this last question is answered in the affirmative by the colophon of the Catholicon itself, the remaining questions are: 4) *who printed* the Catholicon? 5) is the type used in 1461 and in 1467 and 1469, which is usually regarded as the Catholicon-type, really identical with this type? and if so 6) *when, by whom* and under what circumstances was it transferred to Eltville?

In order to answer these questions we must, in my opinion, have more materials than we know of at present. We have actually no evidence which compels us to reject Bernard's theory that Henricus Bechtermuncze had first been established at Mentz and printed there the Catholicon. Nor is there at present any evidence to compel us to accept Gutenberg as the printer of the 31-line Indulgence. If we accept him as such, and also accept the theory that he used the church-type, employed in that document, for other works, it must again be asked: how could he have remained proprietor of this type after the law-suit of 1455—and if it did remain in his possession, what could have induced him to transfer this type before 1461 to another printer, and himself to call in assistance from Dr. Homery to cast another type?

I am not able to say in what books besides the Vocabularius of 1472 and the Summa of Thomas de Aquino, the small type imitated from the 31-line Indulgence type is found, nor during what period it continued to be used, nor again whether the larger or church type of the Indulgence is ever found associated with it in its later history.

There may be a good many other books in existence, printed with these types, but as yet unidentified or ascribed to some other printers. All I can say is that the Eltville Vocabularius of 1477 is printed again with a different type, and this time with a colophon in which *Nicolaus* Bechtermuncze is mentioned as the printer.*

A copy of this edition is preserved in the Royal Library at Munich, and was most kindly forwarded to me by the Librarian, Prof. Dr. Karl von Halm, for my inspection.

The imprint on leaf 172ª li. 25 runs as follows:

Presens hoc opusculum non stili aut penne || suffragio. Sed nova artificiosaq̧ inuencione || quadam ad Eusebiam dei industrie per Ny= || colaum Bechtermūcze in Eltuil est ɔsūatū || Sub Anno dñi. M.CCCC. lxxvij. Ipso die || sancti Thome apłi q̊d fuit Sabbato die mēs' || Decembris || Hinc tibi sancte nato cū flamine sacro || Laus et honor dño trino tribuat̄ et vno || Qui laudare piam semp non linq̄ Mariam || ; 172ᵇ blank.

Collation: A^{10} B C D E F G H I K L M N O P Q R S T V^{8} X^{10}, 172 leaves 4°. 34 mostly even lines on a page; with signatures, no printed initials, no initial directors, with double hyphens.

Leaf 1 blank; 2ª (with signature A^{2}): [E] X quo vocabularij varij autenti=||ci videlicet Hugwicio Katho=||

In order to show the results which, in my opinion, we have obtained, I subjoin an attempt at classifying the types and works attributed, in Dr. Van der Linde's book, to Gutenberg. This list is arranged chronologically under the several types, which again are placed in the order of their first appearance. Each work is described minutely whenever I think I may correct some errors or throw some light on the books mentioned. With respect to some of the books, however—which were beyond my reach, or the correct collation of which would require perhaps weeks or months; *e.g.* the 36- and 42-line Bible—I simply refer to the description of other bibliographers.

(*) Bodmann speaks of a *division of his goods* in 1476! Did Bodmann intend to represent him as dead in that year?

TYPES 1 AND 2,

used by the unknown printer of the 31-line Letters of Indulgence of 1454.

These types appear *together* in *four* issues of this Indulgence, which are really *one composition*, which has undergone successive modifications as regards the position of some of the words, which makes them appear different editions. The four issues may easily be distinguished by the lines 18–21 as printed on the accompanying folding plate.

a) Indulgence with printed date Mcccccliiii; 31 lines; Broadside folio. Types: **1** (large, church-type, used for the *rubrics*, and regarded as identical with that of the 36-line Bible); **2** (text or brief-type). Besides these two types we find a large initial V, and two large initials M, which differ from each other.

In this issue the blank space left between the word deuoti (the last in line 18) and the word Juxta (the last but six in line 19) is about 1½ line (for which see the folding plate).

As this issue also differs from issue *b*, by the setting up of the lines 25 and 26, I print these lines also on the folding plate.

Of this issue no *sold* copy has as yet been found. The following *unsold* copies, all printed on vellum, have come to my knowledge and been examined by me. **1**) in the Town-library at Brunswick, where I saw it on the 14th Oct. 1881.—**2**) in the Library at Wolfenbüttel, where I saw it on the 14th Oct. 1881, pasted on brown paste-board; it had formerly belonged to the Brunswick Library.—**3**) in the possession of Mr. F. Culemann, at Hannover, at whose house I saw it on the 13th Oct. 1881. The upper portion of this copy is complete as far as line 25; but it is combined with the lower part (lines 26–31) of a copy of one of the later issues (perhaps *d*), as is evident from line 26 which has ecctiasticis. Mr. Culemann told me that he possessed this piece before he obtained the upper portion, and he has written on the back, that this copy was originally in the Town Library at Brunswick, and was obtained by him in 1875.

Some of these copies (I believe two) were discovered, together with copies belonging to issue *b*, at Brunswick, in the binding of a copy of the Questiones theologice de incarnatione et sacramentis, said to have been printed by Mich. Wenszler at Basle, between 1470 and 1474, which was formerly preserved in the Ministerial (or Preachers') library, but is now in the town-library, at Brunswick. Cf. Pertz' account in the *Abhandlungen* of the Berlin Academy, 1856 (1857), who gives a facsimile of issue *b*, though he seems to imply that it is

31-line Letters of Indulgence. Only edition. First issue (a, 1454). Lines 17–21 :

presumant Alioquī dicta concessio quo ad plenariā remissionē in mortis articulo et remissio quo ad pcta ex ɔfidentia vt p̄mittiē ɔmissa nulli⁹ sint roboris uel momēti Et quia deuoti ———————————— Juxta dictū indultum de facultatibus suis pie eroga ——.merito huiusmodi indulgentiis gaudere debet In veritatis testimonium Sigillum ad hoc ordinatum presentib𝔷 litteris testimonialib𝔷 est appensum Datum———— Anno dn̄i Mcccclıııı die uero ———— Mensis ————

lines 25 and 26.

bus excessib𝔷 crim̄ib𝔷 atq̧ delictis quātūcūq̧ grauib𝔷 Sedi Aptice reseruatis Nec non a quibuscūq̧ excoīonū suspensioñ et interdicti Aliisq̧ sn̄ıs cēsuris ꝛ penis ecl̄iasticcis a Jure vel ab hoīe ꝓmulgatis si quas incurristi dando tibi plēissimā oīm pctoꝝ tuoꝝ indul-

---

31-line Letters of Indulgence. Only edition. Second issue (b, 1454). Lines 17–22 (including the blank line 19) :

presumant Alioquī dicta concessio quo ad plenariā remissionē in mortis articulo et remissio quo ad pcta ex ɔfidentia vt p̄mittiē ɔmissa nulli⁹ sint roboris uel momēti Et quia deuoti ————————————

Juxta dictū indultum de facultatibus suis pie eroga —— . merito huiusmodi indulgentiis gaudere debet In veritatis testimonium Sigillum ad hoc ordinatum presentib𝔷 litteris testimonialib𝔷 est appensum Datum ———— Anno dn̄i Mcccclıııı die uero ———— Mensis ————

lines 25 and 26 (or 26 and 27 including the blank line).

b⁹ excessib𝔷 crim̄ib𝔷 atq̧ delictis quātūcūq̧ grauib𝔷 Sedi Aptice reseruatis Necnon a quibuscūq̧ excoīcationū· suspensioñ et interdicti Aliisq̧ sn̄ıs cēsuris ꝛ penis eccl̄iasticis a Jure vel ab hoīe ꝓmulgatis si quas incurristi dando tibi plēissimā oīm pctoꝝ tuoꝝ indul-

---

31-line Letters of Indulgence. Only edition. Third issue (c, 1454). Lines 17–21 :

presumant Alioquī dicta concessio quo ad plenariā remissionē in mortis articulo et remissio quo ad pcta ex ɔfidentia vt p̄mittiē ɔmissa nulli⁹ sint roboris uel momēti Et quia deuoti ———————————— Juxta dictū indultum de facultatibus suis pie eroga —— . merito huiusmodi indulgentiis gaudere debet In veritatis testimonium Sigillum ad hoc ordinatum presentib𝔷 litteris testimonialib𝔷 est appensum Datum ———— Anno dn̄i Mcccclıııı die uero ———— Mensis ————

N.B. The lines 25 and 26 run as in issue *b*.

31-line Letters of Indulgence. Only edition. Fourth issue (d, 1455). Lines 17–21 :

presumant Alioquī dicta concessio quo ad plenariā remissionē in mortis articulo et remissio quo ad pcta ex ɔfidentia vt p̄mittiē ɔmissa nulli⁹ sint roboris uel momēti Et quia deuoti ———————————— Juxta dictū indultum de facultatibus suis pie eroga —— . merito huiusmodi indulgentiis gaudere debet In veritatis testimonium Sigillum ad hoc ordinatum presentib𝔷 litteris testimonialib𝔷 est appensum Datum ———— Anno dn̄i MccccIv die uero ———— Mensis ————

N.B. The lines 25 and 26 run as in issues *b* and *c*.

30-line Letters of Indulgence. First edition. Only issue (a, 1454). Lines 16–20 *(from Reiffenberg's facsimile)*:

opa q̄ ip̄i facere etiā teneantur Dūmodo tū ex ɔfidentia remissionis hmōi q̧ absit peccare nō p̄sumāt Alioquī dicta cōcessio quo ad plenariā remissionē in mortis articulo et remissio quo ad pcc̄a ex ɔfidentia ut p̄mittitur ɔmissa nullius sint roboris uel momenti Et quia deuoti ———————————— iuxta dictum indultū de facultatibus suis pie eroga —— merito huiusmodi indulgentijs gaudere debet. In veritatis testimoniū sigillū ad hoc ordinatū p̄ntib' lr̄is testimonialib' est appensum Datū ———— Anno dn̄i Mcccclıııı die vero ———— mensis ————

line 28.

Misereatvr tvi ꝛc̄ Dn̄s noster ut supra Ego te absoluo ab om̄ib' pcc̄is tuis ɔtritis ɔfessis et oblitis restituendo te vnitati

---

30-line Letters of Indulgence. Second edition. First issue (b, 1455). Lines 16–20 :

opa q̄ ip̄i facere etiā teneātur Dūmodo tū ex ɔfidentia remissionis hmōi quod absit pcc̄are nō p̄sumāt Alioquī dicta ɔcessio quo ad plenariā remissionē in mortis articulo et remissio quo ad pcc̄a ex ɔfidentia ut p̄mittitur ɔmissa nullius sint roboris uel momenti Et quia deuoti ———————————— Juxta dictum indultū de facultatibus suis pie eroga —— merito huiusmodi indulgentijs gaudere debet. In veritatis testimoniū sigillū ad hoc ordinatū p̄ntib' lr̄is testimonialib' est appensum Datū ———— Anno dn̄i Mccccl quīto die vero ———— mensis ————

line 28.

Misereatvr tui ꝛc̄ Dn̄s noster ut supra Ego te absoluo ab om̄ib' pcc̄is tuis cōtritis ɔfessis et oblitis restituendo te vnitati

---

30-line Letters of Indulgence. Second edition. Second issue (c, 1455). Lines 17–20 :

plenariā remissionē in mortis articulo et remissio quo ad pcc̄a ex ɔfidentia ut p̄mittitur ɔmissa nullius sint roboris uel momenti Et quia deuoti ———————————— iuxta dictum indultū de facultatibus suis pie eroga —— merito huiusmodi indulgentijs gaudere debet. In veritatis testimoniū sigillū ad hoc ordinatū p̄ntib' lr̄is testimonialib' est appensum Datum ———— Anno dn̄i Mccccl quīto die vero ———— mensis ————

N.B. The lines 16 and 28 run as in the preceding issue.

one of issue *a*; Sotzmann, in the *Serapeum* for 1843, p. 280, who prints lines 18–21 of the issues *a–c* of the 31-line Indulgence, and lines 18–20 of the 30-line Indulgence; De Laborde, Débuts de l'imprimerie à Mayence, p. 17 &c.

I have been unable to ascertain when and where the other unused copies, or fragments of copies, which I have seen, were found.*

b) Indulgence with printed date Mccccliiii; 32 lines, including a blank line 19. Broadside folio. Types 1 and 2, and the same initial V and two initials M as in issue *a*.

In this issue the blank space left between the word deuoti (the last in line 18) and the word Juxta (shifted on to the beginning of line 20) is a little more than 1½ line; the whole line 19 being here left blank; (see the folding plate). Of this issue also no sold copy has as yet been found. I have seen the following *unsold* copies, all printed on vellum, two of which seem to have been discovered with copies of issue *a*:—1) in the Town-Library at Brunswick, where I saw it on the 14th Oct., 1881.—2) in the Library at Wolfenbüttel, where I saw it on the 14th Oct., 1881, pasted on brown pasteboard. It is made up of three pieces, which, however, perfectly fit together, and clearly belong to one and the same copy. It had formerly belonged to the Brunswick Library.—3) in the possession of Herr F. Culemann, at Hannover, at whose house I saw it on the 13th Oct., 1881. He was unable to tell me whence he had obtained it.

A facsimile of this issue is given by Pertz (l.c.); and Sotzmann (l.c.) has printed the lines 18–22 (including the blank line 19). These will again be found on the accompanying folding plate, and I add the lines 25 and 26 (26 and 27), which differ from those in issue *a*.

It is not impossible that the issues *a* and *b* are experiments of the printer to accommodate the Pardoner or Seller of the Indulgence with the necessary blank space for filling in the names and dates. Issue *a*, with Juxta &c., commencing in the latter part of line 19, was probably found to be inconvenient to him, hence the word Juxta was shifted to the beginning of the next line, and all the following words accordingly, but line 19 was left entirely blank; this change produced issue *b*. The blank line being found unnecessary, the lower portion of the Indulgence was shifted up, and the third issue (*c*) was produced. This again was changed into issue *d*, by simply altering the date Mccccliiii into Mcccclv.

c) Indulgence with printed date Mccccliiii; 31 lines.

* If I could have described every separate fragment I have seen, I should have registered a still greater number of copies. But while on my travels I did not know all the points whereby to distinguish the different issues.

Broadside folio. Types 1 and 2, and the initial V, and two initials M.

Of this issue, which was ready at least before Nov. 15, 1454, *seven sold* copies have hitherto been discovered, and are preserved :—1) in the Meerman-Westreenen Museum at the Hague, issued at Erfurt, on the 15th Nov. 1454. This copy has been described by Schelhorn in his *Ergötzlichkeiten*, Ulm, 1763, p. 376–80. He presented it to Meerman. Cf. Dibdin, Bibl. Spenceriana, I. p. xliv.; Pertz, (l.c.)—2) in the Library at Wolfenbüttel, in a frame under glass. It is a fragment consisting of the left half as far as PAUL \|. The copy was issued in behalf of "Beseb'tol \|"; what was to follow must of course have been on the other half, which is wanting; that there were more persons than one appears from the word erogauerũt, which has remained in the following line. The date is intact, namely, "*die* uero *secunda* Mensis Decembris."—3) in the National Library at Paris, issued at Mentz, on the 31st Dec. 1454; cf. Pertz (l.c.). A facsimile of this copy in De Laborde, *Débuts* etc. p. 4.—4) in the Library at Cassel, issued at Eynbeck, on the 12th Jan. 1455 (the numerals iiii of the year having been altered with the pen to quinto, just as in the four following copies).—5) in the Library at Göttingen, issued at Lüneburg, on the 27th (not 26th) Jan. 1455.—6) in the Archives at Schwerin, issued at Lüneburg, on the 28th Jan. 1455.—7) in the Royal Museum at Copenhagen, issued at Copenhagen, on the 29th April, 1455.—8) in the Library at Göttingen, issued at Hildesheim, on the 30th April, 1455. (De Laborde says that the date of this copy was altered to 1455 by adding j to the numerals iiii; but this is not the fact, the date having been altered in precisely the same way as in the copies 3-6.)

I am able further to indicate the existence of the following *unused* copies :—9) an unused copy in the Town-Library at Brunswick, where I saw it on the 14th Oct. 1881. The date Mccccliiii has been altered, *by hand*, to Mccccly.—10) an unused copy in the possession of Herr F. Culemann, at Hannover, at whose house I saw it on the 13th Oct. 1881. He could not tell me whence he had obtained it.—11) another unused copy in the possession of Herr F. Culemann, at Hannover, at whose house I saw it on the 13th Oct. 1881. It consists of two pieces belonging to two different copies, namely, lines 1–9, which Herr Culemann informed me he had obtained from the Eschenburg Collection in Brunswick; and the lines 10–31, of which he could not tell me the origin.

All the copies are printed on vellum.

d) Indulgence with printed date Mcccclv; 31 lines. Broadside folio. Types 1 and 2, and the initial V, and two initials M.

This issue, which was ready before March 7, 1455, in all respects conforms to issue *c*, except that the date Mccccliiii has been altered to Mcccclv, and the last four lines from foot seem to have been a little shifted.

Copies of it, all on vellum, are preserved :—1) in Earl Spencer's Library at Althorp, issued at Würzburg, on the 7th March, 1455; cf. Dibdin, Bibl. Spenc. I. p. xliv. (*)—2) in the University Library at Leipzig, issued at Nuremberg on the 24th March, 1455.—3) the copy from which the transcript was taken which Laborde (p. 10) saw at Cassel, and which, according to Sotzmann's description (l. c.) may be still in the possession of the Baronial Family Zu Eyssenbach-Lauterbach, near Cassel. The original was issued at Erfurt on the 28th March, 1455.(†) 4) in the Library at Wolfenbüttel, issued at Goslar on the 10th April, 1455. I saw this copy on the 15th Oct. 1881, in a frame under glass.—5) in the Library of the late Sir Thomas Phillipps, at Cheltenham, issued at Würzburg, on the 13th April, 1455; see above No. 1 and note.—6) in the University Library at Heidelberg, issued "in Constancia" on the 21st of April, 1455, to "Judocus frümesser prespiter (sic) secularis Constanciensis dyocesis."—7) in the City-Archives at Augsburg, issued at [St. Gallen ?] on the 28th April, 1455; cf. Pertz (l. c.); Hassler, in Verhandl. des Vereins für Kunst in Ulm, &c., 1857, p. 34.—8) in the University Library at Leipzig, issued at Würzburg on the 29th April, 1455.—9) in the University Library at Göttingen, issued at Gottinghen on the 29th April, 1455. It was discovered in the City-Archives by Dr. G. Schmidt, see Serapeum, 1863, p. 81.—10) in the Library at Wolfenbüttel, in a frame under glass, a fragment consisting of the last 10 lines (therefore the two forms of absolution). Further, of line 11 (counting from foot) some strokes have remained, which, according to Prof. Dr. Von Heinemann, the Librarian of Wolfenbüttel, seem to indicate that the copy was sold "[die vero] xxx Mensis Aprilis." Of line 12 only so much has remained that the lower

(*) Dibdin speaks (in 1814) of *two* copies with the printed date Mcccclv, as being at Althorp. Pertz, who visited Althorp in 1856, pointed out (l.c.) that there were only two copies at Althorp, including the Indulgence of 30 lines. Consequently, Dr. Van der Linde (p. 525) speaks of Dibdin's second copy (of 1455) as *non existent*. But Dibdin could scarcely have spoken of such a second copy unless he actually had one before him. This was really the case; but the unsealed one of 1455, which he mentioned but did not describe, was some time after *exchanged* by Lord Spencer for the 30-line Indulgence, which had been purchased by Payne and Foss (see their Catal. of 1837, No. 6265, and Sotheby, Principia Typogr. ii. 210); the 1455 copy afterwards passed into the Library of Sir Thomas Phillipps (see my No. 5 of issue *d*).

(†) There is no evidence yet published to show to which of the several issues this copy belongs, so I leave it where I find it placed by others, until some one has an opportunity to examine it. It must be remembered that Laborde only saw a transcript of it in a volume of collectanea relating to the family above mentioned, in which, naturally, no difference would be made between the written and printed parts of the Indulgence.

portion of the v of the year is visible. At the foot, on the right-hand side, is written: "Johēs Droste ī p̄missȝ deputatꝯ"; on the left, "s' ad cistꝭ."

In 1876, Dr. Gustav Schmidt, Director of the Royal Dom-Gymnasium at Halberstadt, discovered four *unused* copies of this edition at Halberstadt, in the binding of a book preserved in the Library of the Dom-Gymnasium, the title of which Dr. Schmidt no longer remembers. One of the copies (which I shall call No. **11**) has remained in that Library. The *three* others (No. **12–14**) were sold to Mr. Albert Cohn, the bookseller at Berlin. In reply to my letter of Sept. 18th, 1881, this gentleman most kindly informed me that he sold: **12**) to the Duke d'Aumale; **13**) to M. Fillon (this copy was exhibited in the Paris Exhibition of 1879 on the Trocadero); **14**) to Herr Senator Fried. Culemann, at Hannover. This last copy I saw on the 13th Oct. 1881. The last two lines, and the latter portion of the 5th (from foot): In nomine &c., which had been cut away from this copy, have been added to it by Mr. Culemann, from *another* copy, of which he possessed at the time 5 or 6 lines. Another *unused* copy, **15**) in the British Museum (pressmark C. 18. e. 2, No. 125).

Before leaving the subject of the 31-line Indulgence I wish to make a few remarks. First, as to the presence of blank copies at Brunswick, which has been explained in a way which I think is not the right one.

In 1843 Holtrop, the late Librarian of the Hague, writing to Sotzmann (see "Serapeum" for 1843, p. 386) informed him that the book in which four blank copies of the 31-line Indulgence had been discovered at Brunswick was printed by Michael Wensler, in Basle, probably between 1470 and 1474. Holtrop further suggested that—as Wensler printed in that city in 1475, in conjunction with Bernh. Rihel, who, a year before (?), had printed a Latin Bible in conjunction with the same Berthold (Rodt, or Rüppel) of Hanau, who appeared in the Mentz Law-suit of 1455 as an assistant of Gutenberg—we might perhaps infer that, through him, the proof-sheets of the Indulgence had gone from Mentz to Basle and thence to Brunswick.

What was merely *suggested* by Holtrop in 1843, is told by Dr. Van der Linde in 1878 as an undoubted *fact* (see his Gutenberg, p. 45), without Holtrop's name being mentioned.

A more plausible explanation of so many blank copies (which I do not regard as *proof-sheets*, but as *unused* copies of *issues*, which either have been used, or were intended to be used) having been discovered at Brunswick (and

Halberstadt) may be attempted, by saying that the pardoners or persons sent out to sell the Indulgences, had most probably arrived with their wares at the two places mentioned, by the time that the Indulgence was no longer valid, *i.e.* May, 1455. When we observe the dates when, and the places where, the Indulgences which have come down to us, have been sold, we can follow the vendors on their journey from Mentz to Copenhagen, and see them in April, 1455, sell copies at Copenhagen, Hildesheim, Goslar, Göttingen. Brunswick and Halberstadt are on this route, and it may fairly be assumed that the pardoners, when the month of May had arrived, abandoned then and there the unsold copies, leaving them, most likely, in the first instance, in the hands of the local chief ecclesiastical dignitary, whence they came finally into the hands of the binders.

The idea of an assistant of Gutenberg, having been instrumental in bringing the copies, first from Mentz to Basle, and thence to Brunswick (and Halberstadt) may safely be dismissed from our minds.

There remains for me to notice an error into which, if appearances do not deceive me, De Laborde has fallen with regard to the issues of this Indulgence. In his work *Débuts de l'imprimerie à Mayence et à Bamberg*, Paris 1840, he speaks of an edition of this Indulgence of 32 lines, preserved at Brunswick. He arrives at this number of lines by printing Juxta as *the very last word* in line 19, and shifting all following words forward accordingly. To make the whole matter clear he prints, *in special type*, the end of the 20th and 21st line thus:

debet In veritatis testimonium
Anno dñi Mcccccliiii die uero

By this arrangement the word Mensis would fall on a separate line, and hence his edition of 32 lines.

De Laborde has been quoted by Brunet (s.v. Nicolaus V.)

From all that I have said on this document and from the lines which I print on the folding plate, it will be seen that no such edition has come to my knowledge.

I may add that Mr. Bensly, the Librarian of Caius College, Cambridge, examined for me, in September, 1881, all the copies preserved at Brunswick and Wolfenbüttel.

In his letter to me he made no mention of Laborde's edition of 32 lines. Within a few weeks afterwards I myself visited Mr. Culemann, at Hannover, and the Brunswick and Wolfenbüttel Libraries. I saw all the copies of the Indulgences in the possession of Mr. Culemann, and the two libraries, but no such edition as described by De Laborde came to light. Nor can I find that anyone else mentions this edition. There *is*, I may say, an issue of 32 lines (issue *b*) if we include in our calculation the line (19) which has been left blank, but De Laborde's notes do not refer to this point.

I cannot account for De Laborde's error unless I assume that in the notes he made at Brunswick he must have written that Juxta, which appears in the issues b, c, and d *at the beginning* of the line, occurred in one of the issues *at the end of the line.* Having returned from his journey he probably worked out his notes, and finding in them that Juxta was to come at the end of the line, he must by some measurement have fixed the word testimonium at the end of the next, and again the word uero at the end of the following line, and so on. De Laborde has done something similar with regard to the Strassburg lawsuit of 1439, where he gives in some places of his facsimiles something quite different from what he prints in his text. His indication of an edition of 32 lines of this Indulgence has caused me considerable trouble; but I believe I am justified in saying that it is a simple error on his part, and that no such issue exists.

Finally I have to take notice of a pamphlet entitled *The Signature of Gutenberg*, by Dr. P. De Villiers, London, 1878, in which the author professes to have "established the authenticity and *modus legendi* of the signature of Gutenberg." This gentleman imagines that he has discovered—in the strokes of the large capital R which is found, accompanied by a small ^{ta} and in some cases by some flourishes which look like S, on the back of almost all the *sold* copies of the Letters of Indulgence of 1454 and 1455—not only the letters which constitute the name of GUTENBERG, but also an S, which Dr. De Villiers explains to be the initial of the name of Sulgeloch.

In reply to this it may be said that it is now beyond doubt that Johann Gutenberg, though he seems to have been connected with the family who bore the name of Sulgeloch, never bore that name himself, and, therefore, could not have signed it on the back of any document whatever; and it is still more beyond doubt that the R, or R[ta], or R̄[ta] (which we find in some copies) on the back of the Indulgences, simply means Registrata.

It is written quite differently in the different copies, and the ink and penmanship of this endorsement, in the four copies which I have examined, correspond in each case exactly with that of the Pardoner who has entered the buyer's name and his own in the text. The Pardoners differ, as may be seen in De Laborde's or Dr. Van der Linde's book, according to the district in which they were *deputati* or *subdeputati* of Paulinus Chappe, and consequently the R or R[ta] differ. I have also seen several unsold copies, on which no endorsement is found at all. The R or R[ta] has therefore, beyond doubt, nothing whatever to do with Gutenberg's or any other printer's name.

TYPE 1 continued.

(For type 2 see above, p. 150, and for the imitation of it below, p. 180.)

It is generally assumed that this type continued to be used at Mentz for the printing of the following works:

2. Manung widder die Durke. For Jan. 1455. 4°, 5 printed leaves; the last page blank, 20 and 21 uneven lines to a page.

> I have had no opportunity of seeing this book, the unique copy of which is preserved in the Royal Library at Munich. I only know it from the description and facsimile published in 1808 by J. Christ. von Aretin (*Ueber die Folgen der Erfindung der Buchdruckerkunst*, 4° *München*). Aretin's facsimile is most likely not a faithful representation of the original, otherwise I should have some difficulty in believing that it could have been printed with the type of the 36-line Bible. As I am not prepared to say that the types differ, I class the "Manung" with those works with which it is usually placed. It was discovered in 1804 in the Convent of Jesuits at Augsburg. Cf. Bernard, *Orig. de l'impr.* i. 26.

3. Conjunctiones et Oppositiones solis et lunæ (usually

called Kalendar) for the year 1457. Broadside sheet, printed on one side only.

The upper half of a copy (the only one known) was discovered in 1804 in a file of accounts of the City of Mentz from 1420–1460, and presented by Gotthelf Fischer to the Paris Library. Cf. Bernard, II. 27. A facsimile of it may be seen in Fischer's *Notice du premier monument typogr.*, *Mayence*, 1804; Wetter's *Gesch.*, plate vi, etc.

4. Der Cisianus (*not* Cislanus) zu dutsche. Broadside sheet, printed on one side only; 36 lines, besides separate head-line.

The Tross copy, mentioned in the Supplement to Brunet's *Manuel* (1878, s. v. *Cislanus*) is now at Cambridge. It was bought in 1870, not in 1876. The size of the page is that of the 36-line Bible, but the type is in poor condition. The heading is: Dis ist der Cisianus zu dutsche vnd . . . (the rest lost).

5. Donatus. Edition (*a*) of 14 (?) leaves; 27 uneven lines on a page.

Of this edition the British Museum (pressmark: C. 18, e. 1 No. 2) possesses the following leaves or fragments of leaves. Leaf 2, lines 1 (?)—12; on the verso a portion of a 13th line is still visible; 4) intact, except that some letters are effaced by use; 6) lines 1 (?)—21; 7) lines 3 (or 4)—24 or 25; 8) 20 lines; 9) 21 lines and portions of a 22nd, they seem to be the lines 1–22; 10) intact; 11) intact; 13) the lower points of one line and 13 other lines intact.

As I have found it useful, for the identification of the different editions of Donatus, to have some idea of what text there is on the existing fragments, I have copied of each fragment a line or some words, which may help others whenever leaves or fragments should be found. Where I do not give the whole line, I give, as far as practicable, the first and last words of each line, representing by — that portion which is omitted.

Leaf 2ᵃ line 1 (?): hūc et hāc sacerdotē vto o sacerdos abl'to ab h' ꝛ ab hac ‖ sacerdote vl' sac'doti ꝛ pl'r nīo hij ꝛ hee sac'dotes gīo hoꝝ ‖ 3: et—sacer⸗ ‖ 4: dotes—sac'dotibꝰ ‖ 5: [F]Elix—singl'aris ‖ 12: [F]ructus—masculini licibꝰ ‖

Leaf 2ᵇ line 1 (?): vt̄s pl'es in ae dyptōgon desinūt ac̄es in am correptam ‖ 2: vts̄—correptā ‖ 3: dats̄—productam ‖ 4: [S] Ecūda—r s m ‖ 5: Quot—Da ex⸗ ‖ &c.

Leaf 4ᵃ line 1: qs̄ l' a quibꝰ Gnis neut' quod l' quid cuiꝰ cui qđ l' q̃d a ‖ 2: quo—a ‖ &c.

Leaf 4ᵇ line 1: ī masclīo ꝑductū in neut̄ vēo correptā vt quisqs̄ ‖ 2: [V] Erbū—cet̄ ‖ 17: amabo—indicat̄o

Leaf 6ᵇ line 4: [L]egens— ‖ 5: actīo— ‖

Leaf 7ᵃ line 1 (?): [L]egendus ꝑticipiū— ‖ 2: nuī — ‖

Leaf 8 contains the distinctive lines [I] Nteriectio— ‖; [A]mo verbū— ‖

Leaf 10[a] line 1: plsq̄ꝑfc̄o vt̄ doctū eēt l' fuiss; fut̄o vt̄ doceat̄ Cōiūctiuo || 9: [D]oceor—do || 10: cenī—do ||
Leaf 11[a] line 1: gissē legisses legiss; ꝛ plr̄ cū legissemꝰ legissetis legissēt Fu || 2: tūo— || etc.
Leaf 13[a] line 3 (or 4): [F]ero fers fert ptitū * vt auditꝰ futuꝫ vt audiendꝰ || ; 13[b] li. 8 (?) [F]eror— || 9 (?): ꝛ plr̄.— ||

On comparing the first line of this 13th leaf with that of edition b (No. 6) it will be seen that the setting up differs.

6. Donatus. Edition (*b*) of 14 (?) leaves, 27 lines on a page.

In the British Museum, in the same volume (No. 5), there is a fragment of a leaf of a Donatus, in this same type, on which 25 lines are visible; the text, which we find on leaf 13 of edition *a*, reads in this fragment: [F] Ero fers fert et plr̄ ferim[s] fertis ferunt Pretīto impfecto. I call this edition *b*.

After this follows a leaf, which is the last (14?) of an edition of 27 (?) lines, but, having nothing to compare it with, I am unable to say whether it belongs to edition *a* or *b*, or to some other edition.

7. Donatus of 30 lines. Edition composed of 12 (?) leaves, of which a fragment of the 8th (?) leaf printed on vellum is preserved in the Town Library at Mentz, where I examined it on the 6th Oct., 1881. Cf. Wetter, *Gesch. der Buchdruckerk.*, p. 433, with facs., pl. II.

The text of the fragment is not always legible; the first line of the recto reads: renī Pretīto pfc̄o ꝛ pl'qpfc̄o uī aāṫꝰ es...... || 2: ses— || 3: ul'— || 4: mem̄i— || 5: amē— || 6: maēris— || 7: pfecto— || 8: fueīmus— || 9: sem— || 10: fuissemus— || 11: ris— || 12: ritis (?)— || 13: ore (?)— || 14: tū— || 15: ......passiuo— || 16: [D]oceo— || 17: impfecto— || 18: docebāt— || 19: docuistis— || 20: ...... (?) docueras— || 21: Futuro— || 22: cebunt— || 23: nam— || 24: doceto— || 25: te Optaīo— || 26: īpfō (?)— || 27: docuissē— || 28: docuissēt— || 29: doceatis— || 30: ......[docea]s doceat ꝛ plr— ||

The verso is also much damaged; the commencing letters (one or two) have been cut away; I give, therefore, the last word in each line, though even here I had to guess in several instances.

1: [d]ocerē docēs docēt ꝛ plr̄ cū docēmꝰ doceretis || 2: —docu || 3:—docu= || 4:—cū || 5:—docuerīt || 6:—do || 7:—doc ||

* The rest of this line is the remainder of the preceding clause in the text.

8:—doce ‖ 9:—ēat ‖ 10:—Futūo ‖ 11—Pretiťo ‖ 12:—Cōiūc ‖ 13:—pſcọ ‖ 14:—Tuťo ‖ 15:—p̄ti (?) ‖ 16:—Fuťo ‖ 17:—docēdo ‖ 18:—verbo (?) ‖ 19:—docturus ‖ 20:—Pretiťo ĩ (?) ‖ 21:—docebam̄ (?) ‖ 22:—fuisti ē (?) ‖ 23:—fu ‖ 24:—eāt ‖ 25:—fue ‖ 26:—docebĩ ‖ 27:—scd'aȝ ꝛt (?) ‖ 28:—docean ‖ (?) 29:—doceminor ‖ 30:—do (?) ‖

The above works 4–7 are, of course, not placed in any *chronological* order, as I can assign no date to them.

8. 36-line Bible. 2 (sometimes misbound in 3) vols. Fol.

This Bible is known to some as Schelhorn's Bible, because he was the first to give an account of it (*De antiquissima Latinorum Bibliorum editione, Ulm*, 1760. 4°). Others call it the Pfister Bible, who assume that Alb. Pfister of Bamberg is the printer of it. I have not myself collated any copy, but the work has been described by Bernard (*Orig. de l'impr.* ii. 31) from the paper copy, in 3 vols., preserved in the Paris National Library. It is composed of 882 printed leaves, with 2 columns of 36 lines each on a page. The Paris Library possesses another copy of the last leaf which bears the date 1461 in rubric. Another detached leaf of the same Bible was found in the cover (consisting of different sheets of paper) of a Register of expenses of the Abbey of St. Michael at Bamberg, commencing the 21st March, 1460. From this discovery it has been inferred that this Bible must have been printed before this date. But it may be remarked that the cover may have been made for this Register any time after its commencement.

De Laborde (*Débuts de l'imprimerie à Mayence et à Bamberg*, p. 25) has pointed out that most of the copies of this Bible were preserved in Bavaria, and that a great number of fragments have been discovered in convents of that country. C. G. de Murr found in 1775, in the Library of the Monastery of Langheim, several ancient volumes, bound in vellum sheets of this Bible. Cf. Bernard, *Orig. de l'impr.* ii. 34 sqq., who, on p. 54 sqq., calls attention to the MS. Chronicle of Paulus Paulirinus (or Paulus de Praga), preserved at Cracow, who wrote in 1463 that when he was at Bamberg, a person engraved a whole Bible on small plates (*lamellae*), and finished the impression of it (*scriptura*) on vellum in four weeks.

Copies of it are preserved: 1) at Althorp (cf. Dibdin, Bibl. Spenceriana, i. 7); 2) in the National Library at Paris, 3 vols. on paper; 3) in the same Library, the last leaf of another copy with the date 1461; 4) in the British Museum; 5) at Jena; 6) at Leipzig; 7) at Antwerp, in the Musée Plantin, &c. &c. There are three leaves in the University Library at Cambridge. Mr. Bradshaw has observed that Lord Spencer's copy differs from that in the British Museum in the setting up of the first page.

Some bibliographers are of opinion that this type changed

hands after the printing of the above five works (namely Nos. 1, 2, 3, 7 and 8; the Cisianus and the Donatus, *a* and *b*, have never yet been noticed), and was acquired by Alb. Pfister of Bamberg. Bernard (*Orig. de l'impr.* ii. 53) shares this opinion with the exception that he ascribes the 36-line Bible to Pfister. The latter certainly published with this same type the following works:

I. Boner's Edelstein. Bamberg, 14 Febr. 1461. 88 leaves, folio, with wood-engravings, and 25 lines on a page.

A copy is preserved in the Library at Wolfenbüttel, which I saw on the 15th Oct. 1881, and from which I took the following description:

Leaf 1ª (after the woodcut): [S]Ins mals ein affe kam gerāt. Do er vil guter || nusse vant. Der hette er gessē gerne. Im was || gesagt &c. Colophon: zu bamberg disȝ puchleȳ geendet ist. Nach der ge- || purt vnsers herrē ihesu crist. Do man zalt tausent || vnde vierhundert iar. Vnd ym einundsechzigsten || das ist war. An sant valenteins tag. Got behut || vns vor seiner plag. Amen. ||

Another copy appears to be in the hands of Mr. Stöger at Munich; cf. Bernard, *Orig. de l'impr.*, ii. 36; Falkenstein, *Buchdruckerk.*, p. 134.

II. Boner's Edelstein (2nd ed.); no place, no date, no name of printer. 77 leaves, folio, with wood-engravings, and 28 lines on a page.

Cf. Brunet (Manuel, voce *Boner*), who saw a copy at Paris in 1835, which is now preserved in the Royal Library at Berlin. It has been described by Sotzmann (*Serapeum*, 1845, No. 21).

III. The four Histories (of Joseph, Daniel, Judith, and Esther) *in German*, 60 leaves, folio, with wood-cuts, 28 lines. Colophon: printed at Bambergk, by Albrecht Pfister, in 1462, not long after St. Walpurgentag.

Copies preserved: 1) in the Paris National Library; 2) at Althorp; the work has been described by Dibdin, Biblioth. Spenceriana i. 95; Bernard ii. 37; Falkenstein, Buchdruckerk p. 137.

IV. Belial, seu consolatio Peccatorum Jacobi de Theramo, *in German*, Bamberg; Albreht Pfister; no date, 95 leaves, folio, 28 lines to a page; no woodcuts.

The only copy known is in Lord Spencer's Library; cf. Dibdin, Bibl. Spenc. iii. 181; Brunet, Manuel, voce *Theramo;* Bernard, ii. 41.

v. Biblia Pauperum, *in German;* 18 (?) leaves (last leaf blank) in folio; with woodcuts.

Copies: 1) in the Paris National Library; 2) in Lord Spencer's Library; cf. Dibdin, Bibl. Spenc. i. 100; 3) in the Wolfenbüttel Library, where I saw it on the 15th Oct., 1881, and found only 14 leaves. Of each of these 14 leaves I give the first words, to enable others to ascertain, by a comparison with the other copies, the missing leaves. Leaf 1[aa] ysaias. Sich ein iūgfrau; 2[a] Dauid. Die kunig von; 3[a] Dauid. Sich ich hab mi —; 4[a] Dauid. Herē rich das pl=; 5[a] ysaias. Ir wert sepſē das; 6[a] Moises. Ich todt vnd ich; 7[a] Dauid. die lieb deines ha=; 8[a] Dauid. Schō ist er in seiñ; 9[a] Jacob. In irē rat ist nicht; 10[a] Dauid. Der mēsch mein[s]; 11[a] Dauid. Sein stat ist wor=; 12[a] Osee. An dē drittē tag w –; 13[a] Dauid. Herre du hast ni=; 14[a] ysaias. Ich hab in gesehē.

vi. Biblia Pauperum, *in German.*

This edition differs in many parts of the text and the arrangement of the woodcuts from the preceding. It is preserved in the Paris National Library. Cf. Notice des objets exposés, No. 49.

vii. Biblia Pauperum, *in Latin.* 17 (?) leaves, in folio; with woodcuts.

The only copy known is in Lord Spencer's Library; cf. Dibdin, Bibl. Spenc. i. 103.

viii. Quarrel of a widower (Ackermann von vogelwaid in Beham land), who had lost his wife, with Death; *in German. First* edition. 18 leaves; in folio; 28 very uneven* lines (especially on the first leaves); no initials; no initial directors; no woodcuts.

The only copy known is in the Wolfenbüttel Library, where I saw it on the 15th Oct., 1881.

Leaf 1[a]: Nn (*sic* for An) dem buchlein ist beschriben ein krig wañ einer || dem sein libes weib gestorben ist schildtet den todt || So verantwōt sich der todt also seczt der clager ein || capitel vnd der todt das ander bisz an das ende der || capitel sind. xxxiiij. dor iñ man hubsches sines ge= || tichtes behendikait wol vindet Der || clager hebt an || vber den todt zu clagen Das erst capitel ·:·:·:·:·:·:· · [G]Rīmiger abtilger aller leut schedlicher echter || &c.; 18[b] last line (28) rechter Richter erhor mich ·:·:· · ·

Cf. Falkenstein, *Buchdruckerkunst,* 139, who speaks of

* I am unable to arrange Pfister's books in a chronological order, as I had not sufficient time to study these books minutely. But it appears to me that some of the productions I describe ought to be placed, on account of their workmanship, before the Boner of 1461.

this copy as having 23 leaves; I have found only 18 leaves. Falkenstein further says that the first line commences An and he even adds (sic), but the line commences as I have given. Bernard (*Orig. de l'imprimerie*, ii. 44) copies Falkenstein. The Bamberg Library possesses, according to Falkenstein, 4 leaves of this edition.

IX. Quarrel of a Widower, &c.; *in German. Second* edition; 26 leaves; in folio; with woodcuts.

Copies: 1) in the Paris National Library; 2) in the possession of M. Nachler, at Berlin (see Bernard, ii. 44); 3) in the Wolfenbüttel Library; this copy I saw on the 15th Oct., 1881, and took from it the following description.

Leaf 1^a blank; 1^b woodcut; 2^a [G]rȳmiger abtilger aller leut. schedlicher echt vñ ‖ etc.; 4^a blank; 4^b, 10^a, 18^a, 23^b entirely occupied by a woodcut; 25^b last line (25): mit innkieit sprechen amen. 26 (blank) cut away.

The Library of Bamberg seems to possess four leaves of this edition also; another leaf is in Lord Spencer's Library.

Dibdin (Bibl. Spenceriana i. 121) speaks of a Latin Psalterium, 29 lines on a page, except the first, which has 27, as having apparently been printed by Pfister, which means, I suppose, in the 36-line Bible type, but I have not seen the book, and Dibdin's explanation of the look and size of the type is not decisive enough to ascribe it to this printer. Brunet speaks of the work as having been printed by Pfister, but evidently only follows Dibdin.

Another Psalterium was exhibited at the Caxton Celebration in 1877, lent by the Bodleian Library, composed of 126 leaves, with 20 lines on a page; the type of which *seemed* to *resemble* that of Pfister, which means, I suppose, the 36-line Bible type (see Catal. of the Caxton Exhibition, p. 93).

Bernard (who regarded type 1 as identical with that of the 36-line Bible) ascribes the Manung, the Conjunctiones and the Donatus of 27 lines (see below, p. 176) to another printer than Pfister, for three reasons:

1°) Pfister never used the small or brief-type which we find in the 31-line Indulgence; 2° Pfister lived at Bamberg, but the Donatus of 27 lines (edition C, see p. 176) and the Kalendar of 1457 were found at Mentz, the same place from which one of the earliest-issued Indulgences is dated; 3°) the typographical execution of the Indulgence is superior to that of Pfister's works.

As regards Bernard's first reason, it is of little weight, because the books we know as Pfister's productions, were not suitable for the use of this type. Bernard's second reason is of as little weight as his first, because a) the Donatus is most likely later than 1451, and not printed in the 36-line Bible type at all; b) the Kalendar of 1457 was, indeed, found at Mentz, but the "Manung" of 1455 was found at Augsburg, a place much nearer to Bamberg than to Mentz. Bernard's third reason is of still less weight than his first and second; the typographical execution of the Indulgence is certainly very good, but that of Pfister's books is by no means so bad as some people would have us believe, considering that all those enumerated above being more or less of a popular character, and must have been far more handled than a Bible; and considering also that the paper used for them was perhaps of an inferior kind, as they had to be much cheaper than a Bible.

I am far from certain that Nos. 2–8 (pages 157–160) are printed at Mentz; but having no evidence to prove that they were printed at Bamberg or any other place, I prefer to leave the controversy with regard to these books as it was. It even appears to me that the church-type of the 31-line Indulgence differs from the 36-line Bible type (cf. also Sotheby, Principia Typogr. ii. p. 191 sq.), but I do not know how to ascertain the identity of two types when they are so similar.

TYPES 3 and 4,

used by the printer (Peter Schoeffer de Gernssheim) of the 30-line Letters of Indulgence of 1454.

These types appear *together* in two editions (the second having two issues) of this Indulgence which may be distinguished by the way in which the lines 17–20 are printed, as given on the folding plate which faces p. 150 above.

1. (a) Indulgence of 30 lines, with printed date Mccccliiii. Broadside folio. Types: **3** (large, church-type, used for the rubrics); **4** (text–or brief-type). Besides these types we find a large initial U (which helps to distinguish this Indulgence from the 31-line Indulgence, which has an initial V), and two large initials M, which differ from each other.

Only one copy of this edition seems to have come to light, which was discovered in the binding of one of the books in the

Library at Louvain. Its description by De Reiffenberg in Vol. V of the *Nouv. Mém. de l'Acad. Roy. des Sciences de Bruxelles* (1829), and De Laborde, *Débuts de l'imprimerie à Mayence* (1840) p. 6 is, in each case, accompanied by a facsimile. It is now preserved in Lord Spencer's Library at Althorp, where it was seen by Pertz in 1857 (see his *Abhandlung* in the "*Abhandl. der kön. Akad. der Wissensch. zu Berlin,*" for the year 1856 (1857) p. 707). It was issued at Cologne, on the 27th Feb. 1455 (the printed date Mccccliiii having been altered with the pen to Mccccliiiij). In line 15 the misprint olia for alia occurs.

2. (b) Indulgence of 30 lines, with printed date Mcccclquīto. Broadside folio. Types 3 and 4, with the same initial U and two initials M, as in edition *a.*

This issue, which is the first of the second edition, and which was ready before the 11th April, is distinguished from the following issue, by its having in line 18 Juxta instead of iuxta. It is distinguished from edition *a* by having the misprint in line 15 corrected; and by lines 16 and 28 as given on the accompanying folding plate.

Two copies of it have been preserved: 1) in the Royal Library at Berlin, issued at Werla in Westphalia on the 11th April 1455. This copy has been copiously described by Pertz (l.c.) with a facsimile annexed.—2) in the British Museum, issued at Neuss near Düsseldorf, on the 29th April 1455. A photographic facsimile of this copy (which I have seen several times) may be seen to perfection in Humphreys' Hist. of the Art of Printing, pl. 12; and a misleading one in De Laborde's work, who seems to have taken a copy of the edition *a* as his model for this edition. This copy which when first known was in the possession of Neigebauer, passed successively into that of Dr. Kloss of Frankfurt, Mr. B. Heywood Bright, and the British Museum.

(c) Indulgence of 30 lines, with printed date Mcccclquīto. Broadside folio. Types 3 and 4, with the initials U and two M.

This issue, which is the second of the second edition, and which was ready before the 22nd February 1455, may be distinguished from the preceding by its having in line 18 iuxta instead of Iuxta.

Copies of it have been preserved: 1) in the possession of Herr F. Culemann, at Hannover. It was issued "in hildenshem Anno dñi Mcccclquīto die vero xxij mensis februarij" to "Religiosi illustri et nobili Dñi Magni episcopi Cathed in Ciui[te] Hildenshems."* I saw this copy, with the seal attached,

* Though Mr. Culemann's copy affords us *an earlier date* for *this* issue than for the issue *b*, yet I place it last, at the advice of

in Mr. Culemann's house at Hannover, on the 13th Oct. 1881; the Latin is written as I give it here. Mr. Culemann had appended a note to it that "Edwin Tross had obtained this copy at Hildesheim in 1850, together with other vellum documents, to be sold to gold beaters in France"; 2) in the Ducal Library at Wolfenbüttel, issued at Brunswick, on the 24th April 1455, with the seal attached to it. I saw this copy on the 15th Oct. 1881, in a frame under glass.—3) an *unissued* copy in the possession of Herr F. Culemann, at Hannover, at whose house I saw it on the 13th Oct. 1881. He was unable to tell me whence he had obtained this copy.*

No further trace of the Brief-type 4 has as yet been found. Some consider type 3 to be identical with that of the 42-line Bible, others see merely a resemblance between the two types (see Bernard, *Orig. de l'imprim.* i. 172), and it must be remarked that the capital P found in the Indulgence, does not seem to appear anywhere in the Bible. But I believe the question, as to who was the printer of this Indulgence, may now be regarded as settled for the following reasons:

In Mr. Culemann's house, at Hannover, I saw on the 13th Oct. 1881 an Indulgence of 33 lines issued in 1489 by the notorious "Raymundus Peyraudi archidiaconus Alnisiensis in ecclesia Xanton," at the order of Innocent VIII., "pro tuicione orthodoxe fidei contra Turchos." In this Indulgence, unquestionably printed by Peter Schoeffer, the initial M of the *second* absolution, is *identical* with the initial M of the *first* absolution of the 30-line Indulgence of 1454, and 1455; a circumstance which at once connects the printer of these two documents.

Bibliographers usually ascribe both the 31-line and the 30-line Indulgence to *one* printer (Gutenberg); but in dealing with anonymously printed books we must arrange them according to their type, and if two books are printed in different types, and we have no evidence to show that they are printed by one and the same printer, it becomes necessary to ascribe them to different printers. It is therefore not unreasonable that, if we ascribe the 31-line Indulgence to Gutenberg, we should attribute the other document, con-

Mr. Bradshaw who regards the small i of iuxta as a *correction* for Iuxta (in issue *b*) which was probably put by some one who regarded the word as the beginning of a new sentence.

* All the copies of this Indulgence are printed on vellum just as those of the 31-line Indulgence.

temporary with it, to some other printer. The connexion of the 1489 Indulgence with that of 1454, make it, in my opinion, clear that Schoeffer, who printed the 1489 Indulgence, also printed that edition of 1454 which we cannot reasonably ascribe to Gutenberg; that, therefore, in 1454 we have at least two rival printers at work in Mentz: 1) the printer of the 31-line Indulgence, whose name I cannot give, but who may have been Gutenberg, subsidized by Johann Fust;—2) the printer of the 30-line Indulgence, whom we may safely call Peter (Schoeffer) de Gernssheym.

Dr. Van der Linde (Gutenberg, p. 59) tells us that we meet Peter Schoeffer, "after his return from Paris, therefore, according to a document, before 1455, as a workman in Gutenberg's first office." But here Dr. Van der Linde goes beyond documentary evidence. In the notarial act of the Mentz Law-suit of 1455, the only document to which Dr. Van der Linde could refer, Peter Gernssheim is mentioned as a *witness* on the side of Johann Fust, but it is not said anywhere that this Peter was Gutenberg's *workman!*

I may remark that long before I had found the initial M in Schoeffer's Indulgence of 1489, Mr. Bradshaw held out to me that he regarded Peter Schoeffer as the printer of the 30-line Indulgence. For these reasons:

> 1457–1466 Schoeffer prints in partnership with Joh. Fust; 1467 he prints alone;
>
> 1457 and 1459 (August), he issues the Psalter with the capitals *printed* in colours;
>
> 1459 (Oct.) the Durandus, with the capitals *printed* (but in some copies only) in colours;
>
> 1460 the Clementinae without *printed* capitals;
>
> 1460–1489 no printed capitals in books;
>
> 1490 and 1502 the Psalter is reprinted, with the *printed* capitals (as an antiquarian reprint). After this date no books known with printed capitals.

Now, we have a folio Donatus (see p. 171 No. 8) printed in the 42-line Bible type, and according to the colophon: "per Petrum de gernssheym, in urbe Moguntina cum *suis capitalibus*."

It is usually said that as P. (Schoeffer) de Gernssheym does not here mention Johann Fust, this Donatus must have been printed after Fust's death. But as the *capitals*, of which Gernssheym speaks, occur only in the first two dated books and some copies of the third and in none whatever of the subsequent books except the merely antiquarian reprints of the Psalter in 1490 and 1502, and as it is altogether more consonant to method to place the Donatus in 1456 with the Bible printed in the same type, and so *before* 1457, we obtain a very natural chronology in Schoeffer's work as will be shown below by the numbers 3–8. A point which strongly corroborates this is that there seems to be no trace whatever of the *type* of the 42-line Bible after 1456. That which has very commonly been identified with it (the type which occurs in the Herbarius of 1484, and many subsequent books) is really larger and quite different, when the two are examined side by side. It would seem, therefore, that the Donatuses printed in this type, should be placed before, not after, this date.

TYPE 3 continued.*

Mentz.

Peter [Schoeffer] de Gernssheym.

before 15 Aug. 1456.

3. Donatus, of 24, 25 or 26 lines.

One leaf (which may be the 8th or 9th) of this edition (which probably consisted of 24 leaves) is preserved in the Library at Mentz, where I saw it on the 6th Oct. 1881. Some lines at the top or the foot have been cut off; I cannot say, therefore, with certainty, how many lines would go to a page.

Line 1 *recto* (of the fragment): lecturus uel legendus. Significationes partici || 2: piorū — ꝑti || 3: cipia — lecturus || 4: A — lectus || 5: legendus — actiuo. || 6: p̄sens — q̊t || 7: tria — locu || 8: tus — p̄sens || 9: et — crimīnatus || 10: criminaturus — ꝑtici= || 11: piorū — le || 12: gēs — sūt || 13: due — negligēs. || 14: [L]Egens — actiuo || 15: tꝑis — singularis || 16: figure — declina || 17: bitur — huius || 18: legentis — le= || 19: gentē — ab || 20: hoc — pl'r || 21: Nt̄o — et || 22: harū — legētibꝫ ||

* It is known that type 4 has never yet been found in any other book or document, except the 30-line Indulgence. It may be presumed that Schoeffer discarded it, and melted it down for his other types.

Line 1 *verso:* sus ntī qđ declinabitur sic. Ntō hic lecturus hec || 2: lectura — lecturi || 3: Dtō — lecturū || 4: hāc — lectu || 5: rū — hoc || 6: lecturo — gťo || 7: hoꝫ — le || 8: cturis — vtō || 9: o — lecturis. || 10: [L]Ectus — passiuo || 11: tpis — sim || 12: plicis — lectus || 13: hec — Dťo || 14: huic — hoc || 15: lectū — lecto || 16: ab — le= || 17: cte — lecto || 18: rum — lectas || 19: hec — hijs || 20: [L]Egendus — lectis. || 21: a — singula= || 22: ris — sic. ||

Mr. Culemann, at Hannover, possesses a leaf printed in this same type, which evidently belongs to an edition of 26 lines; but whether to this or another I cannot say.

Lines 1 and 2 cut away; 3: simplex ut nam cōposita ut namq₃. ordo cōiūcti= || 4: onū — cōiunctiones || 5: sunt — aut || 6: cōmunes — igitur. || 7: [P]Repositio — que || 8: p̄posito — signi= || 9: ficacionē — mi= || 10: nuit — quid. || 11: casus — accusatiuus || 12: et — accusatiui. || 13: ut — circa || 14: cōtra — pone || 15: per — supra || 16: circiter — pa= || 17: trē (?) — cis || 18: renū — ho || 19: stes — naues || 20: intra — augu- || 21: riū — ꝓpter || 22: disciplinā — ripā || 23: vltra — an || 24: nos — arbitros || 25: Da — cū || 26: coram — tenus. ||

Verso, line 3 (?) — le= || 4: gendā hoc legendū. Vtō o legende legenda legē= || 5: dum — legenda || 6: ab — legende || 7: hec — legendarū || 8: hoꝫ — legē- || 9: dos — le || 10: gende legenda — legendis. || 11: [C]Oniūctio — an- || 12: nectens — Cōiūctio || 13: in quot — figu || 14: ra — species || 15: habet — ex= || 16: pletiuas — copulati= || 17: uas — ut || 18: aut — qui || 19: dem — autem || 20: porro — aliter. || 21: Da — quādo || 22: quādoquidē — ne || 23: ue — quāob= || 24: rem — preterea || 25: Da — enimue || 26: ro — quidem ||

4. Donatus of 32 lines.

One leaf (which may be the 10th) of this edition (which probably consisted of 14 leaves) is preserved in the Library at Mentz, where I saw it on the 6th Oct., 1881. It is cut into 8 portions and is further mutilated at the left edge, whereby the first letters of the recto and the last letters of the verso have disappeared.

Line 1 recto: [ꝑf]ecto et plusq₃per . . . . . . m esse vel fuisse ^ Futuro || 4: [L]Ego verbum actiuū in indicatiuo modo dictū(?) tꝑis p̄= || 5: sentis — prime || 6: — et || 7: — le || 8: — Preteri || 9: — vel || 10: — et pl'r || 11: — ꝛ pl'r || 12: — secun= || 13: — legāt || 14: — legunto || 15: — impfecto || 16: — legere= || 17: — legissem || 18: — Fu || 19: — legāt || 20: — le || 21: — lege= || 22: — Preteri || 23: — legerimus || 24: — legissem || 25: — legissent ^ || 26: — lege= || 27: — tem= || 28: — et || 29: — esse || 30: — impfe= || 31: — P[reterit]o || 32: — legetur ^ ||

Line 1 verso: Imparatiuo modo tempore presenti legatur ^ Futur[o legi] || 2: tor — || 3: legeretur — || 4: vel — || 5: pn̄ti

— ‖ 6 : rito — ‖ 7 : cum — ‖ 8 : Infinitiuo — ‖ 9 : to — ‖ 10 : vel — ‖ 11 : sunt — ‖ 12 : Duo — ‖ 13 : Futurum — ‖ 14 : [L]Egor — ‖ 15 : legūtur — ‖ 16 : bare — ‖ 17 : terito — ‖ 18 : lecti — ‖ 19 : Preterito — ‖ 20 : ras — ‖ 21 : fueratis — ‖ 22 : getur — ‖ 23 : pore — ‖ 24 : legamur — ‖ 25 : et — ‖ 26 : senti — ‖ 27 : legeretur — ‖ 28 : terito — ‖ 29 : esses — ‖ 30 : vel — ‖ 31 : vtinā — ‖ 32 : mini (?) — ‖

5. Donatus, of 33 lines.

2 leaves, preserved in the Paris National Library; cf. *Notice des Objets exposés*, No. 38.

6. 42-line Bible, printed before 15 Aug., 1456. 2 vols. fol.

This Bible, usually called the Mazarine-Bible, was finished before the 15th Aug., 1456, according to the rubrication of the binder found in the paper copy preserved in the Paris National Library.

As I have had no opportunity to examine a sufficient number of copies to give an absolutely accurate bibliographical description of the work, I feel obliged to refer to the (not entirely accurate) descriptions of Bernard (*Orig. de l'impr.* i. 164, 177–192) and others. We gather from them that this Bible is composed of 641 printed leaves or 1282 pages in folio; each page having two columns, each of 42 lines, with this exception that, in some copies, the columns of pp. 1–9 contain only 40 lines, while the 10th page is composed of columns of 41 lines each, though this difference in the number of lines makes no difference in the space they occupy. Further, the first three rubrics of the first quire, and the first two of the first quire of the second portion of the volume are printed in the 40-line copies in red, whereas they are in MS. in the other copies. Bernard (i. 187 sqq.) has given his own view and that of Sotheby on this discrepancy in the number of lines; but there is still room for a more satisfactory explanation, which I hope will some day be attempted by Mr. Bradshaw, who has made a minute study of the early Bibles for many years.

7. 42-line Cantica ad matutinas.

The first leaf (the only one preserved) has recently been acquired by the Paris National Library. It is printed on vellum, and corresponds in every respect to the Mazarine Bible; double columns, number of lines, and MS. initials.

8. Donatus, of 35 lines.

Printed, according to the colophon: "per Petrum de gernss= heym, in urbe Moguntina cum suis capitalibus."

Four leaves and parts of a fifth and sixth are preserved in the Paris National Library; cf. *Notice des Objets exposés*, No. 66.

I have shown above, that one of the initials of the 30-line Indulgence is found in 1489 in Schoeffer's office. The Church-type of the same Indulgence links on (in spite of the different capital P) to the anonymous 42-line Bible of 1456. This Bible links on to the 35-line Donatus, which is in the same type and has Schoeffer's name and his coloured capitals. This again brings us to the Psalter which Joh. Fust and Peter Schoeffer published together on the 14th Aug., 1457, at Mentz, their first (dated) book, with their name and the capitals of the Donatus. As this work, and their other publications after this date do not come within the scope of my work, and have been more or less elaborately described by most bibliographers, I refer to their works for further information.

TYPE 5.

Mentz. 1460.

1. Joannis de Balbis, Catholicon. 1460. large folio. 373 leaves. 2 columns, 66 lines in a column, except the 3 columns for the table of contents, which have been *leaded* and contain only 56 lines; cf. Bernard, ii. 4. No printed signatures.

Collation: a b c d e f^{10} g^{4}, 64 leaves, 1–64, pt. 1 (grammar); a b c d e f g h i k l m^{10} n (n^{1} cancelled)^{6}, 125 leaves, 65–189, pt. 2 (Dictionary A–H); o p q r s t v x y z ɔ ꝯ aa bb cc dd ee ff^{10} gg^{4}, 184 leaves, 190–373, pt. 3 (Dictionary I–Z, colophon and table of contents).

Leaf 1^{aa} lines 1 and 2 left blank for the rubric, which, in the Cambridge and British Museum (No. 2) copy is filled in by hand; line 3: [P]Rosodia quedā ps || grāmatice nuncupa || tur. Partes siquidem || &c.; leaf 64^{bb} line 35: odus. Et cetera. ||; lines 36–66 blank; leaf 65^{aa} line 1: [J]Am diuina potencia auxiliante sup̄ deter || minauimus de quatuor pticulis pñcipalibꝫ || &c.; Leaf 189^{ab} line 54: tur festinans. uel consiliator. SEQVITVR.I ||;

lines 55-66 blank; leaf 189^b blank; leaf 190^aa line 1: [I] est impatiuus de eo is it. facit enī impatius || &c.; leaf 372^ab line 49: testas regnū et imperiuȝ in secula seculoꝝ Amen ||; lines 50-52 blank; lines 53-66: Altissimi presidio cuius nutu infantium lingue fi || unt diserte. Qui q̄ nūo sepe puulis reuelat quod || sapientibus celat. Hic liber egregius. catholicon. || dñice incarnacionis annis M cccc lx Alma in ur || be maguntina nacionis inclite germanice. Quam || dei clemencia tam alto ingenij lumine. dono q̄ g̃ || tuito. ceteris terraꝝ nacionibus preferre. illustrare || q̄ dignatus est Non calami. stili. aut penne suffra || gio. sȝ mira patronaꝝ formaꝝ q̄ concordia ꝑpor || cione et modulo. impressus atq̄ confectus est. || Hinc tibi sancte pater nato cū flamine sacro. Laus || et honor dño trino tribuatur et uno Ecclesie lau || de libro hoc catholice plaude Qui laudare piam || semper non linque mariam DEO. GRACIAS ||; Leaf 372^ba line 1: Sequitur tabula rubricaꝝ huius uoluminis. Et || &c.; leaf 373^aa line 7: Quinta ꝑs huius opis tractat de ethimologia || rectū litteraꝝ alphabeti ordinem tenens cxxxiiij ||; lines 9-56 blank; leaf 373^ab and 373^b blank.

The above collation has been taken from the copy preserved at Cambridge in one volume. I have further seen copies: (2) in the British Museum (2 volumes, pressmark C. 24. d. 7 and 8), in which the last line of the author's epilogue (testas, &c.) is separated from the colophon by *three* blank lines, as in the Cambridge copy—3) in the British Museum (press-mark C. 14. e. 1) with only *one* blank line between the epilogue and colophon.—4) and 5) in the Paris National Library (one blank line).—6) in the Wolfenbüttel Library (one blank line). There are a great many other copies (e.g. at Althorp, see Dibdin, Bibl. Spenc. iii. 37; and in the Library at Mentz), but these I have not seen. The British Museum has a copy on vellum (in 2 volumes, Grenville Collection, 11966 and 11967) in which the first two lines are printed in red thus: Ncipit summa que uocat̃ catholicon, edita a fra || tre iohanne de ianua. ordinis fratꝝ predicatoꝝ. ||. One blank line between epilogue and colophon. The British Museum (C. 18. e. 1 No. 28) has besides one vellum leaf. I saw another vellum leaf at Mr. Culemann's house.

2. Matth. de Cracovia, Tractatus racionis. 22 leaves (a^{10} b^{12}), with 30 uneven lines; no printed signatures; no printed initials; no hyphens; no initial directors; 4°: *

Leaf 1^a line 1: (M) ultoꝝ tam clericoꝝ q̄ laicoꝝ quere || la ē non modica. occupacio grauis || et questio dubiosa. quomodo quis ||; leaf 22^a line 27: secula. AMEN ||; line 28 blank; line 29: Tractatus racionis et consciencie de sumpcōne pa ||

* This work has been *interlined* or *leaded*, just like the table of contents in the Catholicon. A printer, who had made a study of incunabula, suggested to me that instead of the book having been leaded, the type had been cast on a different body (Germ. *Kegel*). I doubt whether this is correct.

buli salutiferi corpis dñi nostri ih'u xp̄i. Finit. ‖; leaf 22^b blank.

Several copies have been preserved of it: 1) in the British Museum (C. 37. d. 15†).—2) in the British Museum (C. 9. a. 27).—3) in the British Museum, Grenville collection, No. 11719.—4) in Lord Spencer's Library (cf. Dibdin, Bibl. Spenc. iii. 418).—5) in the Paris National Library.—6) in the Paris National Library, with the celebrated MS. note in a hand of the 15th century written on the verso of the last leaf at the foot of the page: [Ho]s duos sext*er*nos accomidauit m*ihi* hey*n*ric*us* Keppfer de mogu*n*cia ‖ [nu]*n*qua*m* reuenit ut reacciper*e*t*ur*. Quare ec*ia*m do.........meo p'.—Something after do has been erased, and the binder has cut away nearly the whole of the first word; also the n and first part of the u of nunquam, in the second line; and all that may have followed after the second line; some strokes of a third line are still visible. The portion of the last letter of the first word of the note which remains appears to me to be the remainder of an *s*; I read, therefore, Hos not Per, as has been hitherto read.—7) in the University Library at Cambridge.—8) in the Library at Mentz. I saw this copy on the 6th Oct., 1881; it is imperfect, as it wants the leaves 16 and 17.—9) in the Grand-ducal Library at Darmstadt (see Ph. A. F. Walther's Beiträge).—10) Herr Fried. Culemann, in Hannover.

3. Thom. de Aquino, Summa de articulis fidei. Edition a. 13 leaves (a^8 b^4 + 4*), 34 uneven lines; 4°. No printed signatures; no hyphens; no initials; no initial directors.

1^a line 1: [P] Ostulat a me uestra dileccio . ut'de ar ‖ ticulis fidei et ecclesie sacramentis ali ‖; leaf 13^a line 13: us. et spiritus sanctus AMEN ‖; lines 14 and 15 blank; line 16: Explicit summa de articulis fidei et ec ‖ clesie sacramentis . edita a fratre tho ‖ ma de aquino. ordinis fratrum predi ‖ catorum . Deo . Gracias ‖; lines 20–34 and 13^b blank.

Copies of it are preserved: 1) in the British Museum (C. 9. a . 24)—2) in the British Museum, Grenville collection, No. 11892.—3) in Lord Spencer's Library (see Dibdin, Bibl. Spenc. iii. 153).—4) in the Hague Library.—5) in the University Library, Cambridge.—6) in the Rev. John Fuller Russell's Library, 4 Ormonde Terrace, Regent's Park, London. —7) in the Darmstadt Hofbibliothek (V 3036/110).—8) in the University Library at Würtzburg. — 9) Herr F. Culemann, Hannover.—10) in the Wolfenbüttel Library. Herr Alb. Cohn in Berlin had a copy (Catal. 1877, No. 10) of this (?) edition, which differed in some respects.

† On the last (blank) leaf of this copy is written in a hand of the 15th century: *Sequitur Tractatus de expositione misse.* This tract may have been printed in the same type, but I have not been able to find out the tractatus indicated.

4. Thom. de Aquino, Summa de articulis fidei. Edition b. 12 leaves (a^{12}). 36 uneven lines; 4°. (*)

1^a line 1: [P] Ostulat a me uestra dileccio . ut de ar ‖ ticulis fidei et ecclesie sacramentis ali ‖ ; 12^b line 1: us . et spiritus sanctus AMEN ‖ ; lines 2 and 3 blank; line 4: Explicit summa de articulis fidei et ec ‖ clesie sacramentis . edita a fratre tho ‖ ma de aquino . ordinis fratrum p̄redi ‖ catorum . Deo . Gracias ‖ ; lines 8–36 blank.

Copies of it are preserved 1) in the British Museum, 671. b. 30).—2) in the Paris National Library.

TYPE 5*,

i.e. the Catholicon type with additions, 1461.
(at Mentz?)

1. Indulgence of 1461.

A formula of Indulgence (15 lines) granted by Pope Pius II. in 1461 for the restoration of a church at Nuhusen in Germany. The formula is signed by Reynhard, bishop, and Rudolph, dean, of Worms, and dated 1461. According to Bernard (*Orig. de l'imprimerie* II. 11), the fragment, a small piece of vellum, was discovered by Gotth. Fischer in the cover of a book at Mentz, and described by him in "*Notice des monuments typogr. qui se trouvent dans la Bibliothèque de S. E. M. le comte Razomowski, Moscou.* 1810. 8°, p. 11. Since the sale of this nobleman's library, the fragment has been lost sight of. Fischer published a facsimile of it in 1836 (*Einige Worte an die Mainzer bei der Feierlichkeit des dem Erfinder der Buchdruckerkunst Joh. Gutenberg zu errichtenden Denkmals. Moskwa,* 1836. 4°) (†) which was copied by Bernard, pl. X.

[Bulla anathematis edita a Pio II....adversus Dietherum ...archiepiscopum, Tiburi duodecim Kalendas Septembris 1461.]

(*) The difference between the twoe ditions *a* and *b* consists merely, I believe, in the number of lines on a page, for the text reads everywhere the same. The type appears to have been kept standing after the 34-line edition had been issued, and when a fresh issue became necessary, two more lines were put on each page, an arrangement whereby the odd leaf at the end was avoided, and the whole text brought into one quire of 6 sheets or 12 leaves. In the edition of 35 lines (see p. 180) the text of editions *a* and *b* has been closely followed, so as to make no difference in the entire number of lines.

(†) A copy of this facsimile is in the British Museum, (823. i. 7 No. 8).

Brunet (s.v. Aeneas Silvius) speaks of an edition of this Bull of 32 lines, said to be printed in the *Catholicon* type, as having been mentioned in a Catalogue, published in June, 1851, by the bookseller Fidelis Butsch, at Augsburg. It was, according to Brunet, afterwards acquired by the Mentz Library. In the summer of this year (1881) a notice went the round of the English daily and weekly newspapers to the effect that a Bull of 1461, printed in the Catholicon type, had been discovered by the Mentz Librarian.

On the 6th Oct. 1881, I visited the Library at Mentz, and asked for this Bull, and was shown a Bull of 1461, but —it was only the well-known Bull of 18 lines, printed in the Fust and Schoeffer type.

A few days afterwards I had an opportunity at Frankfurt to see Butsch's Catalogue, in the possession of Dr. Ernst Kelchner, and actually read the description of the Bull of 32 lines. I wrote at once to Butsch and inclosed postage-stamps for the reply, but I never received any answer to my letter.

Bernard (Orig. de l'imprim. i. 244) writes on this subject and says distinctly that there is no foundation for Butsch's statement, and that the whole matter turns upon the Bull of 18 lines.

As it seems incredible to me that a bookseller would announce for sale a Bull of 32 lines, when it has only 18, I cannot help mentioning this subject once more, in the hope that some further light may be thrown on this matter.

I have already pointed out above (p. 142) that if the type used by the Bechtermuntzes at Eltville in 1467 and 1469 is identical with that used for the Catholicon, it must yet be treated as in some respects a departure from the original type on account of certain *additions*. When I wrote this, I was under the impression that these additions did not occur before 1467, but when looking at Bernard's facsimile of the above Indulgence I saw that the contraction for us (^{9}) which distinguishes type 5* from type 5, occurs already in this Indulgence of 1461. I do not feel at liberty, however, as yet to place the type at Eltville.

Type 6,

used for the so-called *Donatus* of 1451.

Donatus minor; edition of 14 leaves, with 27 uneven lines on a page; with hyphens, no printed initials.

Only *two* leaves, the 5th and 10th * have been preserved to us, and are at present in the Paris National Library, bound in a cover like an ordinary book. On the recto of the 10th leaf, which is bound first in the cover, is written, in a hand of the end of the 15th century, if not later: *Vffgerichter Vertrag wegen der aigen guetter Zur Heydersshcim.* 1492. *A.* On the verso of the 5th leaf (the second in the cover) is written, on the top of the page, *Heydersshcym*, followed by a date partly cut away by the binder, but of which 14 is still distinctly visible, while the remaining strokes may indicate 51.

The fragments have been described by Gotth. Fischer (*Typogr. Seltenheiten*, i. 55, and *Essai sur les monum. typogr. de Jean Gutenberg*, p. 68) who regarded the types as moveable, but cut in wood, and thought that Albrecht Pfister modelled his types after them. Fischer had obtained the two leaves from the well-known Bodmann, who had discovered them in the Mentz Archives, where they served as cover for a register of accounts from 1451-1492. From this circumstance it is inferred that they must have existed as early as 1451. It cannot be denied that the type and the printing look decidedly primitive, when compared with the Letters of Indulgence of 1454. But yet it must be observed that the Register, when it was commenced, may have had another cover, and the leaves of the Donatus may have been taken for this Register any time between 1451 and 1492, if not later. It must not be forgotten that the leaves are not *printer's waste;* they have the initials rubricated in by the rubricator, and they bear traces of

* I have compared the two leaves with the Donatus minor printed at Cologne by Mart. de Werdena, which contains in every respect the same text. As this edition consists of 28 leaves, and the fragments show that each leaf contains the text of about two leaves of the Cologne edition, I think I cannot be far wrong in saying that the edition of which we treat was composed of 14 leaves, and that the Paris leaves are the 5th and 10th.

having been very much used. In the middle of the 15th century, when books were far more costly than at present, their leaves were not likely to be used as covers very soon after their manufacture. Therefore, if we were to believe that they had actually been taken for the Register at its commencement, the date 1451, which is usually assigned to this Donatus, would scarcely do justice to its printer, and to his place in history, as in that year the book must already have passed through several stages of its existence.

But the fact of their having been discovered by Bodmann, and by him communicated to Fischer, throws suspicion on the date claimed for this Donatus.

When I was in Paris last September, I took a tracing of the word *Heyderssheym*, and also of the numerals, found on the *verso* of the 5th leaf. This tracing I submitted to the Darmstadt Archivists, Dr. Schenk zu Schweinsberg and Dr. Wyss, who declared without hesitation that the name of the place was decidedly written in a hand of the end of the 18th or of the beginning of the present century. The question of the date is of course more difficult to decide. The Archivist of Würzburg gave me the same decided opinion as regards the word Heyderssheym.

As the circumstances in which the fragments were found are no evidence as to the date of printing, I place this type last in this List, and venture to add that I do not regard the type as identical with that of the 36-line Bible, though they resemble each other very much; nor do I think that the Donatus-type is the same as that used in the 31-line letters of Indulgence.

As I copied at Paris the first line of the recto and verso of each leaf, and also the first and last word of all the remaining lines, and this method has enabled me to ascertain that the fragments of an edition of 27 lines preserved in the British Museum belong to a different edition (see above, p. 150), I give what I copied, as this may help others in the identification of fragments.

Leaf 5[a] line 1: audiã audior audiar Vbi possũt hec discerni hec in ĩpa= ||; line 2: tiuo — lr̄am || 3: correptã — e || 4: cõuertit̃ — ɔiugacõ || 5: futuꝫ — sill'aꝫ || 6: — mittit — ꝓductã || 7: vt — verborũ || 8: quot — ꝛ || 9: cõmunia — lr̄a || 10: faciũt — in || 11: r — Neutra || 12: que — latina || 13: nõ — neut° || 14: passiua — sũ || 15: Deponentia — dẽpta || 16: latina — Cõ= || 17: munia — duas || 18: formas — di= || 19:

cim9 — te || 20: Numeri — Pl'is || 21: vt — lego || 22: Cōposita — p̄sēs || 23: vt — decli= || 24: nacione — le- || 25: gebā — legerā || 26: Futurum — Tres || 27: Que — legit ||

Leaf 5[b] line 1: [A] Duerbiū quid est ps orōis que adiecta v̄bo signi= || 2: ficacionē — quot || 3: accidūt — ad= || 4: uerbioꝝ — ā || 5: numeī — ā || 6: hortādi — quali= || 7: tatis — respō || 8: dendi — ꝓhibē || 9: di — illuc || 10: inde — cras || 11: aliqūdo — semel || 12: bis — affirmandi || 13: vt — optan || 14: di — de || 15: inde — Da || 16: sil'itudinis — vel || (*) 17: vti — male || 18: .Da — minime || 19: ualde — fortas || 20: se — re || 21: spondendi — seor || 22: sū — fi || 23: dius — si || 24: mul — forte || 25: fortuitu — maximū || 26: minimū — est || 27: In — ɔpatiuo ||

Leaf 10[a] line 1: plsq̄pf̄co vī doctū eēt l' fuissꝫ Fūo vī doceaī Cōiūctiuo m̄o || 2: tpe — doc || 3: tū — do || (†) 4: tū — p̄ti= || 5: to — fu || 6: tūo — docendi || 7: docendo — trahū || 8: tur — docturus || 9: [D]oceor — do || 10: cenī — do || 11: cebaī — doct9 || 12: sū — fuim9 || 13: estis — doctus || 14: erā — fuera= || 15: m9 — vl' || 16: docebē — Impatiuo || 17: mō — do || 18: ceam̄ — doce || 19: amur — īp || 20: f̄co — doceremī || 21: docerenī — fuissem || 22: eēs — eētis || 23: vl' — do || 24: ceare — doceātur || 25: Coniunctiuo — do || 26: ceare — doceantur || 27: P̄tēito — plī ||

Leaf 10[b] line 1: cū — fuerī || 2: sis — fueri= || 3: tis — vl' || 4: fuisses — fuis= || 5: setis — fu || 6: eīt — fuerīt || 7: Infinitō — doceī || 8: p̄tīto — Duo || 9: pticipia — docēd9 || 10: [L] Ego — īp || 11: f̄co — legeba || 12: tis — legis || 13: tis — lege || 14: rat — le || 15: get — tēpōe || 16: p̄senti — lega= || 17: mus — lega || 18: mus — tē || 19: pore — plī || 20: vī — p̄f̄co || 21: vī — legissetis || 22: legissent — le || 23: gatis — legas || 24: legat — le || 25: gerē — legerent || 26: Pretīto — legerim9 || 27: legeritis — legissem ||

Types 7 and 8.

Mentz.

Printer of the Darmstadt Prognostication for 1482.

After what I have said above (pp. 111–114) about the fraud committed in the Darmstadt copy of the Prognostication (said to be for 1460, its real date being 1482), these types can henceforth no longer figure as Gutenberg's types.

(*) Here the v alone is visible; there may be vl'.
(†) c (?) cut away?

visibilis forma·cuius et ymaginez gerat·et causa existat·sicut ablucō q̄ fit in aqua baptisma
tis repn̄tat interiorez mūdacōnez q̄ fit a pecc-
catis per virtutem baptismi

Vnt autez sacramēta noue legis septem
scʒ baptismus·confirmacō·eucaristia pe-
nitencia·extrema·vnctio·ordo·et matri-
moniuz·q̄ꝝ p̄ma qnq̄ ordinant̄ ad pfeccōnem
vnius hōinis in seipso Alia ūo duo ordinant̄ ad
pfcōnē et mlt̄iplicacōnē tocius eccl̄ie·vita eniʒ
sp̄ualis conformat̄ uite corpali In vita autem
corpali homo pficit̄ p̄mo quid̄ per generacōeʒ
qua nascit̄ in hoc mūdo Secūdo per augmētū
quo pducit̄ ad quātitatē et virtutem perfectā
Tercio p cibʒ·quo sustentat̄ vita hominis et
ūtus Et hec quid̄ sufficerent si nūq̄ʒ infirmari
contingeret sʒ quia frequēt̄ homo infirmat̄·q̄r
to indiget sanacōne Sic ē in uita sp̄uali Primo
quid̄ indiget homo regn̄acōne que fit per bap-
tismū s̄m illud Joh iij Nisi quis renatus fuerit ex aqua et sp̄u sancto non potest intrare ī
regnuʒ dei Secūdo oportet q̄ homo accipiat
perfectaʒ ūtutē q̄si per quoddā sp̄uale augmētū p sacramentū confirmacōnis ad sil̄itudinē
apl̄oꝝ·quos sp̄us sanctus in eos veniens cōfir-
mauit Vnde dn̄s eis dixit luce ult̄ Sedete in ci-
uitate donec induamini virtute ex alto Tercō
oportet q̄ homo sp̄ualiter nutriat̄ p eucaristie
sacramentū·s̄m illud Jo·vj Nisi manducaueri-
tis carnem filij homīs Quarto oportet q̄ hō
sp̄ualiter sanet̄ quid̄ per sacramentū peniten-
cie s̄m illud ps Sana animā meaʒ deus q̄r pec-
caui tibi Sp̄ualiter aūteʒ simul et corpaliter per
sacramentū extreme vnccōnis Juxta illud Jac
ult̄ Infirmat̄ in vobis et cet̄a Quantū autē

A CDEF HI . MNOPQRST V
O SS

A BCDEF G HIKL MNO P QR STV Z
A C I P R ST

[illegible] Page [illegible] of Thomas de Aquino, *Summa de Articulis Fidei*, printed at Eltville (circa [illegible])
Capitals extracted from the same.
Capitals extracted from the *Vocabularius Ex quo*, printed at Eltville, in 1472

ELTVILLE PRESS.

1467.

Type 1,

i.e. type 5*, or the Catholicon type, with an additional (long, thin) sign for us (ꝰ) and a sign for et (ꞇ), which latter belongs to the type of the Vocabularius of 1472.

(Printers): Henricus Bechtermuncze, Nycolaus Bechtermuncze frater Henrici, and Wigandus Spyes de Orthenberg.

1. Vocabularius Ex quo, commenced, according to the colophon, at Altavilla by Henricus Bechtermuncze, and finished 4th Nov. 1467, by Nycolaus Bechtermuncze, the brother of Heinricus, and Wigandus Spyes de Orthenberg.

The only copy known of it is preserved in the Paris National Library.

(For a description of the work see above p. 141).

1469.

Type 1,

i.e. type 5*, or the Catholicon type, with the additions of 1467, and a further additional s, belonging to the type of the Vocabularius of 1472.

(Printer): Nicolaus Bechtermuntze.

2) Vocabularius Ex quo, 165 leaves, in 4°, 35 lines on a page; finished, according to the colophon, on the 5th day of June, 1469, by Nicolaus Bechtermuntze.(*)

(For a description of the work see above p. 142.)

Copies of it are preserved: 1) in the Paris National Library; 2) in the Sunderland Collection, at Blenheim;

(*) In the spelling of the names I follow, as much as possible, the spelling of the documents.

3) in Lord Spencer's Library (see Dibdin, Biblioth. Spenceriana, iii. 129).

1472.

Type 2,

(an imitation of the Brief-type of the 31-line Indulgence. See above p. 146).

(Printer not named.)

1. Vocabularius Ex quo. Same colophon as in the editions of 1467 and 1469, but without the name of the printer. (For a description of the work, see above p. 145.)

2. Thomas de Aquino, Summa de articulis fidei et ecclesiae sacramentis, 12 leaves, small 4° (circa 1467–1472).

Collation: a[12], 12 leaves, with 35 very uneven lines to a page, no signatures; no initials printed in; no initial directors; no punctuation except the middle point (and even this sparingly used); with double hyphens. Described by Hain *1426.

Leaf 1ᵃ:

Ostulat a me uestra dilectio ut de ar=
ticulis fidei et ecclesie sacramentis ali=
qua vobis conpendiose ꝑ memoriali
transcriberem cuȝ dubitacōnibus que
circa hec moueri pn̄t Verū cū omne theologo=

12ᵇ line 23:

ale Ad quam gl'am nos perducat pater et fili=
us et spiritus sanctus AMEN

lines 26 and 27 blank.

Explicit summa de articulis fidei et ec=
clesie sacramentis edita a fratre tho=
ma de aquino ordinis fratrum predi=
catorum Deo Gracias

Bernard (*Orig. de l'imprimerie,* ii. 14 note) speaks of an edition of Matthaeus de Cracovia, Tractatus racionis, composed of 12 leaves, with 35 lines on a page, as printed in the type of the Vocabularius of 1472. He does not say where he saw the book. I inquired for it in the Paris National Library, but was informed that no such edition appeared to be there. I have made inquiries for it in several other Libraries, but with the same negative result.

As I observed by chance that Hain described an edition of Thomas de Aquino, Summa, of 12 leaves and 35 lines, I requested Dr. Karl von Halm, the Librarian of Munich, to send me the book for examination. He kindly complied with my request, and I am, therefore, able to say that there can be no doubt as to the identity of this type with that of the Vocabularius of 1472.

Nor have I any doubt but that Bernard's edition of Matt. de Cracovia is a slip of the pen for Thomas de Aquino. The Cracovia in the Catholicon type, described above, contains 1260 lines (42 pages, 30 lines on a page); the edition, as described by Bernard, could only have had 840 lines (24 pages, 35 lines on a page), and as the Vocabularius type of 1472 is rather larger than the Catholicon type, Bernard's edition would be an impossibility.

1477.

Type 3,

(Printer): Nicolaus Bechtermuncze.

1. Vocabularius ex quo. 4°, 21. Dec. 1477.

(For a description of this work see above p. 149.)

I may here observe that type 3 is exactly the same as that used by Peter Drach at Spire. When I received this Vocabulary from Munich, the only book I had seen of Drach was the Leonardi de Utino Sermones published in 1479, and it occurred to me that Bechtermuncze had probably ceased to print about this time and might have transferred his type to Drach. But this appears not to have been the case, as Drach published already on the 18th May, 1477, the Vocabularius Iuris utriusque, printed with the very same type, and must, therefore, have been in possession of his type simultaneously with Bechtermuncze. The question, therefore, arises, did Drach perhaps print the 1477 Vocabulary for Nicolaus Bechtermuncze? A careful examination of the books published with these types, would perhaps enable us to discover some features, which would mark out some works now usually ascribed to Drach, as productions of the Eltville press, suppose this to have been a separate one. But I cannot myself undertake, for the present, any such examination.

The above List, which commences on p. 150, enumerates the *eight* types on which the question of a Mentz Invention may be said to turn, and which recent Bibliographers (notably Dr. Van der Linde) ascribe, without hesitation, to Gutenberg.

From what I have said on pp. 111–114, it must be clear that types 7 and 8 (see p. 178) can have had *no connexion* with Gutenberg and must, therefore, be removed from the controversy; types 3 and 4 must, in my opinion, be ascribed to Schoeffer; of type 6 (which most Bibliographers consider to be identical with type 1) I can say nothing, except that I do not think it identical with type 1. This, therefore, and the remaining types 1, 2 and 5, are, if I am not mistaken, *the only ones which can be claimed for Gutenberg.*

One of the 14 works forming this group (the Catholicon of 1460) says that it was printed at *Mentz*, and there is nothing against our assuming that the 13 other works were also printed in that city.

But none of them reveal anything regarding the *printer.*

We are, therefore, to infer, if possible, from other circumstances who was the Inventor of printing.

It has been usual to refer us, for a final decision, to what we may call Gutenberg-*documents.* I have treated, at great length, of the 23 which are known to us. Let us now take a rapid review of them.

Documents 1 (p. 11), 13 (p. 63), and 17 (p. 105), are allowed, on all hands, to be forgeries of the well-known Prof. *Bodmann*, who had himself so well posted up in the handwriting and language of old documents that he was able to supply his credulous friends with anything they wished, and, of course, with much more than a genuine historian would desire.

Documents 2 (p. 12; now I believe in the Town-Library at Frankfurt), 4 (p. 18), 5 (p. 19), 8 (p. 58), 10 (p. 60), 11 (p. 61), 12 (p. 62), 15 (p. 103), 18 (p. 106), 19 (p. 106), and 21 (p. 114), need not concern us any more, as they merely establish the fact of Gutenberg's existence, which it is not my intention to deny. In the same category I place

Document 3 (p. 13). But here I have to correct an error. Of this document I say on p. 16 that the date of the Manuscript, in which it occurs, does not go further back than 1581. I wrote this from such information as I could gather at Cambridge and in the British Museum. No author had hitherto attempted to describe the Manuscript, and those who quoted it, called it a MS. of 1581 (see e.g. Dr. Van der Linde, p. 513). In September, 1880, I visited the Frankfurt Town-Library and asked for the volume, but it had been *lent out* to Erlangen, and I was unable to see it, though I remained for ten days at Frankfurt. An elaborate description of the MS. Chronicle has now appeared in "*Die Chroniken der deutschen Städte vom* 14. *bis ins* 16. *Jahrhundert*, Bd. xvii. (*Mainz*)," edited by C. Hegel, from which we learn that Johann Max. Zum Jungen, who died in 1649, bequeathed the volume, with other MSS. and books, to the Frankfurt Town-Library, in the Catalogue of which (Bibliotheca Jungiana), published in 1682, it is mentioned on p. 289. He (Zum Jungen) had bought it, in 1640, of Mattäus Merian, the Frankfurt engraver. Before Merian obtained it, the MS. had been in the possession of Wilhelm Fitzer, and in 1605 it was in the hands of the well-known Johann Friedrich Faust von Aschaffenburg. He, or some previous possessor, must have written the date 1581, which is now seen inside the binding under the title.

The contents of the volume embrace the period of 1332–1452, and its chief compiler was "*a witness of the events which he relates in the latter part of his work.*" Our document occupies the leaves 53–57[b] (pp. 73–78 of Hegel's edition), and is written, according to Hegel, by a different hand from that of the compiler, but a hand who wrote the three documents (dated 1341, 1430, which is ours, and 1437) found on the leaves 50[a]–66. The heading of our document: *die alte rachtunge, die erczbischof Cunradt selger gemacht hat*, occurs on 53[a]; under it is written by a later hand: *Anno dni* 1430; 53[b] is blank; 54[a]–57[b] the document; the name *Henchin zu Gudenberg* is found on 56[b].

Document 6 (p. 19) may safely be considered to be an *invention*, if not a forgery, either of Schoepflin or of Wencker.

Document 9 (p. 58), is a piece of oak, said to be a portion of Gutenberg's press, with an inscription bearing the initials J. G. and the date MCDXLI. It is regarded, I believe by most people, as a *falsification.* The thing was bought for a very large sum of money, by a Dresden gentleman, and is, if I am not mistaken, joined to other, new, pieces of wood, so as to form a press such as Gutenberg is *presumed* to have used. If the piece of oak could be considered to be a genuine relic of such a (printing) press, it would, of course, entirely alter the history of the Invention of printing. Even in the absence of any product of the Invention of such an early period, the relic alone would be evidence not only of a complete printing-office, but even of a Gutenberg who had been aware of having invented something important, and was bent on leaving his name to posterity; and we should have to adopt the date 1441, if not an earlier, as our starting point, and Strassburg as the place where the Invention had been accomplished. It is a pity that the circumstances under which the piece of oak was discovered (?) are not known, or at least have not been accurately described. If the locality where it was concealed and the history of this locality were known, it would perhaps enable us to form an opinion. Under the circumstances we are left face to face with the piece of oak itself and the inscription it bears. I have never seen it myself, and feel unable to pronounce for or against it. Dr. Van der Linde rejects the inscription because the year 1441 is expressed by MCDXLI, and not MCCCCXLI. It seems, indeed, that as a rule 400 was expressed in Germany and elsewhere by CCCC, instead of CD. The question remains, however, whether there were no exceptions to this rule. The CD was not unknown; we find it in dates (MCDLXXIV &c.) recorded by Panzer, ii. pp. 15, 16 (three times), 18, 23, 25, 26, 29, 45, 146. It is true these dates are found in books printed at Milan and Barcelona, and I cannot find an instance of CD in German books or documents; but to people who feel inclined to believe in the Invention of printing at Strassburg or at Mentz it would seem rather hazardous to reject the press on this ground.

Document 16 (p. 103) is a *forged imprint* by some person unknown.

Document 20 (p. 107) must be a forgery, if it ever has existed at all.

Document 22 (p. 116) is not a forgery, but simply an entry in an Anniversarium, which refers to a man who was dead before 1423, and who was perhaps Gutenberg's grand-uncle, but not Gutenberg himself.

When we set aside all these documents, which are either forgeries or documents which cannot help us in the controversy, there remain only three documents which can claim our further attention, namely, a) the Strassburg Law-suit of 1439 (document 7, p. 23); b) the Mentz Law-suit of 1455 (document 14, p. 63); c) Dr. Homery's Bond of 1468 (document 23, p. 119).

With regard to the several entries of which the Law-suit of 1439 consists I have first to add a few particulars which I learned at Strassburg last September. On p. 26 I say that "Vol. C may have shared the same fate (as Volumes A and B, which are said to have been burnt during the siege of Strassburg in 1870), but it is nowhere explicitly mentioned."

On my asking Dr. Brucker, the Strassburg Archivist, last September, whether he could tell me anything about this volume, I was shown a work written by J. F. Lobstein, entitled: *Manuel du Notariat en Alsace ou Notices sur la composition de toutes les études de cette ancienne Province*, 8° Strassburg, 1844, where on p. 159 the author says:

"the acts of the city-archives, which formed part of the chancery and of the Chamber of contracts and were deposited in the study of the oldest notary, commenced with the year 1500; those *anterior* to this period, had been delivered to the flames, at the celebration of the first *fête of the Supreme Being*, the 20th Brumaire of the year II (Nov. 20, 1793). A considerable number of protocols, of files containing documents of every kind, titles of nobility, ancient vellum charters, &c., all belonging to the archives of the town and of the province, loaded on fifteen wagons, were burned on this day, on the square of the Cathedral, in sight of the castle; we ourselves witnessed the event."

On p. 327 Lobstein relates:

"Among the protocols of the Chancery, those of the year 1439, which contained, among other things, the sentence of the Senate, between *Gutenberg* and *André Dritzehen*, have, unfortunately, been burned, but that of the Grand Senate of the same year, containing the depositions of the witnesses in this celebrated law-suit, have been preserved from destruction and deposited in the Town-Library."

I believe Lobstein is the only author who has recorded

the fate of the Sentence of the Senate, contained in Vol. C, which I had expected to find still at Strassburg.

All hope, therefore, of examining the volumes containing the entries of this Law-suit have vanished for ever, and under these circumstances it becomes difficult to express an opinion.

We know that the genuineness of the volumes has never been questioned by the Germans; Bernard examined volumes A and B and found them authentic (see above, p. 32); Dibdin saw one of them, and regarded it as a *copy* (see above, p. 28). Dibdin was not, I believe, an authority as regards manuscripts, and the only inference that could be drawn from his remark is that the manuscript he saw differed in style and character from 15th century writing which had come under Dibdin's notice, a kind of negative which appears to me insufficient for rejecting the document.

To me it always appeared suspicious that Schoepflin had just discovered documents which furnished him with evidence and a date which he had previously wished to find. It was his theory, and that of many of his friends, that the Invention of printing had taken place, in an incomplete form, and in secret, at Strassburg, *before* it had been perfected at Mentz. Everybody in his time, and long before him, talked of 1440 as the Mentz date, and by his documents, Schoepflin was, all at once, provided with a mechanical process, and that a most mysterious one, already in operation, at a most convenient time, namely in 1439 at Strassburg. Schoepflin was also distinctly under the impression that Gutenberg had printed books at Strassburg, and he even mentions some works as Gutenberg's products. But in his ignorance of incunabula, and misled by a date, he attributed books to Gutenberg which we now know could not have been printed by him. Such proceedings must arouse our suspicion.

It has been pointed out to me, 1) that if once we admit the *possibility* of the documents having been forged, we must not forget that Wencker, the Strassburg Archivist, discovered one portion of the Law-suit, and Schoepflin another; that, therefore, two dishonest men must have been concerned. 2) that even if we could surmount this difficulty, there would yet be another, namely that neither Wencker nor Schoepflin could, if they would, have forged such lengthy documents as those of the Strassburg Law-suit, because in their time people were too ignorant of the language and of palaeography to attempt such a thing.

With regard to this first objection I must remark 1) that no one ever saw, as far as I know, the Sentence of the Senate said to have been discovered by Wencker; and 2) that Schoepflin published it in 1760, therefore seventeen years after Wencker's death. As regards the second objection, Schoepflin had unrestrained access to the Strassburg Archives. If, therefore, he possessed the same faculties as Bodmann, and could imitate the handwriting of the 15th century, he had merely to take a document which contained sentences somewhat similar to those he wished to introduce into his document, to change the names and modify circumstances, and he had all he wanted.

I must not be understood to say that things have happened as I point out they *might* have happened; I merely want to say that I do not think a forgery *impossible*. I will even go further and say that the valuable bibliographical description, which De Laborde has given us of the two volumes which he has seen (see above, p. 24), must necessarily convey to us the idea that everything is genuine. But even here we must consider that Schoepflin may have found *blank* leaves in the volumes which enabled him to insert his documents. And when we deal with Schoepflin and Wencker, we must not forget what has been said above (p. 20 sqq.) where we see Schoepflin build a whole Romance upon fictitious documents, produced by himself or his friend Wencker.

I am allowed to publish a remark made to me by Dr. Brucker, the Strassburg Archivist, who pointed out to me, last September, that it had always appeared strange to him, that Schoepflin had *discovered* his volumes, which contained *legal* documents, in the *Pfennig-Thurm* of Strassburg, a place which was reserved, as the name indicates, for money-affairs, and not for acts of another nature.

But, though I may hesitate to pronounce against Schoepflin's documents of 1439, it seems that Dr. Van der Linde is anything but favourable to them. I must quote this author once more, in order that every one may judge for himself.

There is one remarkable passage in the Law-suit: namely the testimony of one of the witnesses, Hans Dünne, the goldsmith, who declares that "three years ago or thereabout he had earned from Gutenberg nearly 100 guilders, *merely for that which belonged to printing*" (see above, p. 49).

If this testimony be genuine, and the word "trucken" is to be taken in the present sense, it must be clear that *printing* had already been exercised some time before 1439 at Strassburg, and therefore long before we hear of it in Mentz.

Dr. Van der Linde seems to be aware of this difficulty. An invention of printing at Strassburg, and before 1450, appears inconvenient to him.

On pp. 327, 328 of his Gutenberg he speaks of Schoepflin's translation of "vier stücke" by "quatuor paginas," of "spiegel- and polier-arbeiten" by "artes mirabiles et secretae," as a translation to suit his own purpose, and he adds: "Schoepflin had the acts for an alarmingly long time under his keeping and Dünne's testimony appears at the end as if it had snowed into the document."

Dr. Van der Linde thinks it necessary to explain why he feels himself at liberty to hint at such a dishonourable act of Schoepflin's; he, therefore, adds in a note (p. 328):

"I object to any indignation which may be felt because I do not sufficiently respect the learned compiler of *Alsatia illustrata.* He, that could rob an abbey of its most precious books (psalterium 1457, 1459) under the pretence of wishing to send them, as an example of the ancient art of printing, to the royal Library at Paris, and afterwards sells them for his own private gain, has forfeited the right of being considered an honest man. The gaol holds people far more innocent."

Dr. Van der Linde's opinion, as to the honesty of the people he has to deal with, cannot always be implicitly relied upon (see above, p. 105). I am unacquainted with Schoepflin's offence of stealing books as related by Dr. Van der Linde, but I certainly feel bound to remark that if Dr. Van der Linde's suspicion with respect to Hans Dünne's testimony be well founded, he (Dr. Van der Linde) has pronounced in the most unmistakeable manner against the documents of the Law-suit of 1439. The clause containing Dünne's testimony happens to be among the facsimiles given by De Laborde; the writing and character of this clause differs in no wise from the other portions of the Law-suit as given by De Laborde; ergo: Dr. Van der Linde, who regards Dünne's clause as a forgery, is bound to regard the *whole* of the Law-suit of 1439 as a forgery.

Dr. Van der Linde can scarcely expect to be at liberty to set up systems, and manipulate documents as he pleases, eliminating from them whatever does not suit him.

Therefore, it appears to me that those who regard Dünne's testimony as a forgery of Schoepflin, have no choice but to reject the whole of the Strassburg Law-suit as a fabrication. On the other hand, those who accept it as genuine, can scarcely come to any other conclusion but that either *trucken* does not mean *printing books*, or that printing was going on as early as 1439 at Strassburg. I cannot find that any German Lexicon inserts the word *trucken*, as meaning *printing* books, from *this* source. Are we to assume that no one believes in it?

Document 14 (p. 63). Of the Mentz Law-suit of 1455 I have said already so much that I do not think it desirable to add more than that I should not feel justified in stating that I distrust the *transcripts* which are, for the present, our only guide. If we accept their text as genuine, Gutenberg may safely be regarded as a *Mentz printer*, who was established in that city at least as early as 1455. But—suppose we do this—I cannot find anything in the document which reveals Gutenberg to us as "the *Inventor* of Printing," and that is, after all, the question that concerns us. Nor can I find any such evidence in our last

Document No. 23 (p. 119): the Homery bond, which, if genuine (and I have already said that I have no grounds to suspect it), gives further confirmatory testimony as to Gutenberg having been a *printer*, but which leaves us in the dark as to whether he was "the Inventor," and as to what he did print, and what types had been in his possession.

To conclude: the question "was Gutenberg the Inventor of Printing" I must leave, to my great regret, unanswered, because all *data* for a decision are wanting. I believe, I may state the result of my inquiry to be as follows. As early as (Nov. 15) 1454 *two* printers were at work at Mentz; the name of one of them *may* have been Johann Gutenberg (perhaps subsidized by Johann Fust), but *it is not stated anywhere;* the name of the other is, in all probability, Peter (Schoeffer) de Gernssheym (see p. 166). That the *latter* did not consider himself to have been the *first*, or even the *chief*, printer (of Mentz), seems sufficiently clear from what we may call his own statement, in the imprint of the Justinianus of 24 May 1468, in which he speaks of two Johannes "Librorum insignes *prothocaragmatici* quos genuit ambos urbs maguntina." One of these Johannes must have been Johann Fust; who was the other? Everybody says Gutenberg, and I am in no position to contradict it. It is possible that Johann Mentelin, who printed at Strassburg already in 1460 (we may even say 1459), may have been meant, but we know nothing of his residence at Mentz.

Schoeffer repeated his statement in the reprint of the Justinianus in 1472, and in the Decretals of 1473, but omitted it in the reprint of the Justinianus in 1476.

The question: Where did Peter Schoeffer learn the art of printing, I cannot solve, for want of any distinct statement regarding this point.

That *prothocaragmatici* does not necessarily mean the *first* (primi) typographers on earth, we know from the way in which *protho-* was used in the later Middle Ages, it simply signifying chief, principal.

In the Grammatica, published in 1468 by Schoeffer, appeared the well-known lines:

> "At Moguntina sum fusus in urbe libellus,
> Meque *domus* genuit *unde caragma venit.*"

These verses are said to originate with Joh. Brunnen (otherwise called Johannes Fons) the chief corrector in Schoeffer's office and the author of the work. But here we are confronted with the difficulty that the book in question was printed in Schoeffer's office, which we know to be not the office in which Gutenberg is said to have started. Therefore, as early as 1468, a distinct statement is made by a Printer *at Mentz*, as to *where* the Invention of Printing had taken place. And yet we are now continually pressed to believe that it has taken place, not in *the* locality named, but in another, namely in the house which Gutenberg occupied from the moment he came to Mentz till his law-suit with Johann Fust, which was *not* the house where Schoeffer printed in 1468, and whence he tells us that the *caragma* had come. Dr. Van der Linde explains this difficulty with his usual facility (see his p. 285).

The first distinct mention of the name of Gutenberg is found, as far as we know, in a Chronicle published, on the 14th July 1474, at Rome, by Joh. Philippus de Lignamine. The publisher, whose name appears in the imprint, was House-physician to Pope Sixtus IV, and had established a printing office at Rome. I cannot say who was the compiler of this work, but Eckhard and Muratori ascribe it to "Ricobaldus Ferrariensis, or another anonymous author of the same period." It is preceded by a letter of the Publisher to Sixtus IV, occupying the first seven leaves. Leaf 8 commences: Incipit Crononica (*sic*) summoru*m* || Pontificu*m* Imperatoru*m*q*ue*: Ac || de septe*m* ętatibus mu*n*di ex. s. || Hyeronimo: Eusebio aliisque ui||ris eruditis excerpta. & primo ||.

The first portion of the Chronicle (that ascribed to Ricobaldus) goes down to 1312. After this comes a continuation, beginning with the year 1316, which is said to be the work of Joh. Ph. de Lignamine. In this continuation—which is, like the whole of the Chronicle, a series of insulated paragraphs, sorted, as far as possible, into strict chronological sequence—comes, between two entries, relating one to 14 July 1459 and the other to 1 October 1459, the following undated paragraph:

> Jacobus cognome*n*to Gutenbergo: ſpatria || Argentinus & quidam alter cui nomen || Fustus imprimenda*rum* littera*rum* in mem- || branis cum metallicis formis periti tre- || centas cartas quisq*ue* eo*rum* p*er* diem facere || innotescu*n*t apud Maguntia*m* Germanię || ciuitatem. Johannes quoq*ue* Mentelinus || nuncupatus apud Argentinam eiusdem || p*ro*uincię ciuitatem: ac in eodem artificio || peritus totidem cartas p*er* diem i*m*primere || agnoscitur. ||

Here therefore, is a plain statement that in the summer of 1459 two presses were at work at Mentz and one at Strassburg in the hands of Gutenberg, Fust, and Mentelin respectively; but not a single word is to be found which even touches upon the *Invention* of the art.

It is to be remarked that the same Chronicle says, under the year 1464:

> "Conradus Suueynem: ac Arnoldus panarcz Vdalricus Gallus parte ex alia Teuthones librarii insignes Roma*m* uenie*n*tes primi imprimendorum librorum artem in Italiam introduxere trece*n*tas cartas per diem imprementes."

The Chronicle was reprinted at Rome on the 10th February 1476 by Johannes Schurener de Bopardia, without De Lignamine's Letter to Sixtus IV. It contains the two passages quoted above without any alteration, except that instead of *Gutenbergo*, we find *Cutenbergo*, and for *panarcz* there is *Pannartz*.

The Chronicle was republished by J. G. Eccard (Corpus historicum Medii Aevi, vol. 1 (1723), col. 1299), and L. A. Muratori (Rer. Ital. Scriptt., vol. 9 (1726), col. 263). Both print *Gutenberger*, and both print *Justus* instead of *Fustus*.

To quote later documents or writers than those of 1468 and 1474, just mentioned, would be unsafe for my purpose, as after these dates we unavoidably plunge more and more into the dark region of *tradition*. Dr. Van der Linde has (p. 151) drawn up a List of what he calls "Witnesses," which may be consulted.

Beyond 1454 (the date when printing makes its appearance in a *perfect* state) I *cannot* go, simply because there is nothing to rest myself upon. The diary of Jean Le Robert, the abbot of Cambray, speaking of books "jeté en molle," in Jan. 1445, (cf. Bernard, *Orig. de l'impr.* i. 97) affords a point to look back upon, but for the present it would only encourage me to indulge in speculation, which it is the whole object of my book to discourage to the utmost of my power.

INDEX.

www.ingramcontent.com/pod-product-compliance
Lightning Source LLC
Chambersburg PA
CBHW021823230426
43669CB00008B/846

* 9 7 8 3 3 3 7 0 4 1 7 3 1 *